THE CULMINATION

The Culmination

HEIDEGGER, GERMAN IDEALISM, AND
THE FATE OF PHILOSOPHY

Robert B. Pippin

THE UNIVERSITY OF CHICAGO PRESS

CHICAGO AND LONDON

The University of Chicago Press, Chicago 60637
The University of Chicago Press, Ltd., London
© 2024 by The University of Chicago
Published 2024
Printed in the United States of America

33 32 31 30 29 28 27 26 25 24   2 3 4 5

ISBN-13: 978-0-226-83000-1 (cloth)
ISBN-13: 978-0-226-83001-8 (e-book)
DOI: https://doi.org/10.7208/chicago/9780226830018.001.0001

Library of Congress Cataloging-in-Publication Data

Names: Pippin, Robert B., 1948– author.
Title: The culmination : Heidegger, German idealism, and the fate of
philosophy / Robert B. Pippin.
Other titles: Heidegger, German idealism, and the fate of philosophy
Description: Chicago ; London : The University of Chicago Press,
2024. | Includes bibliographical references and index.
Identifiers: LCCN 2023021463 | ISBN 9780226830001 (cloth) |
ISBN 9780226830018 (ebook)
Subjects: LCSH: Heidegger, Martin, 1889–1976. | Kant, Immanuel,
1724–1804. | Hegel, Georg Wilhelm Friedrich, 1770–1831. |
Philosophy, German. | Idealism, German. | Metaphysics.
Classification: LCC B3279.H49 P526 2024 | DDC 193.092/2—dc23/
eng/20230513
LC record available at https://lccn.loc.gov/2023021463

♾ This paper meets the requirements of ANSI/NISO Z39.48-1992
(Permanence of Paper).

For Lauren and Kent and Joe, Drew and Morgan and Margot,
with boundless love and gratitude.

Contents

Preface

In the course of writing a recent book about Hegel's *Science of Logic* (2019) and so about Hegel's metaphysics, I recalled that the only other commentator known to me to take as seriously as I did (in the way that I did) that at the heart of Hegel's enterprise was the identification of logic (a theory of pure thinking) with metaphysics (an account of being) was Martin Heidegger.[1] But Heidegger did not mean to offer a mere interpretation. He was also trying to say that all metaphysics up to and including Hegel had been working under the same assumption, starting with Plato's claim that reality was Idea and on through scholastic and early modern metaphysics. Moreover, Heidegger claimed that this assumption about the primary availability of being to discursive thinking, in all the developing variations in later philosophy and especially in modernity, had set in place by its implications various notions of primacy, significance, orders of importance, social relations and relations with the natural world that had led to a disastrous self-estrangement in the modern West, and a forgetfulness and lostness that ensured a permanent and ultimately desperate homelessness.[2] For Heidegger, Hegel had taken that mostly implicit assumption as far as it could be taken, and so was its "culmination" in the claim that the Absolute had been achieved, that all dualisms had been reconciled and that a complete account of the intelligibility of being and thereby an account of any possible being had been realized. But for Heidegger, this culmination allowed us to see, in

1. Schelling might count as another example, but it is important to Heidegger that Schelling's rejection of the very idea of a science of logic as a science of being is much too hasty and so does not appreciate Hegel's culmination of metaphysics.

2. And, in its ultimate late-modern consequences, the technological en-framing (*Gestell*) of all possible meaningfulness.

its very radicality and ambition, the disclosure of the inner dynamic of all Western philosophy, and thereby that the most fundamental question of metaphysics, the meaning of being qua being, had not yet even been posed or acknowledged as such since the pre-Socratics. This primary identification of Being with knowability had become so fixed in place that it was not even noticed anymore, ensuring that it was also not questioned and that its implications for what by contrast was taken to be merely subjective, psychological, and insignificant had simply been accepted.

This raised a pointed question that arises for anyone who, like me, still thinks of Hegel as a powerful philosophical thinker from whom we still have much to learn: is Heidegger right about what remained unasked, *and*, more importantly, is it true that its remaining unasked *counts* as a serious objection to Hegel's culmination, an objection that was existential as well as theoretical? This question turned on an issue that can seem quite extravagant outside of the world of Hegel scholars: is there, *could* there be, such an Absolute, and if not, what implications follow for the underlying assumption identified by Heidegger as the basis for such an absolute claim: that logic is metaphysics (as the inner dynamic of all metaphysical thought)—that, in other words, being qua being should be understood as intelligibility and ultimately, in principle, knowability, that the domain of the knowable exhausted the domain of all possibly meaningful being? That came to seem to me an unacceptable claim and even a chimerical goal for pure thinking or first philosophy to aim at. To many philosophers after Kant, this might seem far too obvious to mention, but that now seems to me a simplification of the problem. There is no such absolute congruence of thinking and being, but that then means that the philosophical desideratum, the identification of the meaning of being with intelligibility and ultimately knowability, cannot claim to comprehend all that there meaningfully is and could be. If the conceptual in Hegel's sense is not unbounded but bounded with respect to the meaning of Being, Heidegger's only topic, how should philosophy respond to this revealing culmination?

Heidegger realizes that the issue of Hegel's culmination could not be addressed except within the context of German Idealism. The major figures for Heidegger were Kant and Hegel, so I address mostly his work on those two. His lectures discuss Fichte, but he essentially treats him as a Kantian, at least during the phase of Heidegger's career when he considered Kant a righteous champion of the finitude of thought in the first edition of *The Critique of Pure Reason*. (Heidegger later changed his mind and rejected that view.) And Heidegger's interest in Schelling requires its own category.[3]

---

3. MGI, 58–87. That category concerns the problem of freedom. Heidegger's focus is often on Schelling's 1809 freedom essay. See note 1 in chapter 1. I hope to address his Schelling

As I will try to show in what follows, the issue will come down to the very broad problem of the sources of meaningfulness for human life, the status of the horizon of possible meaningfulness in a historical world.[4] For Hegel, as the culmination of the philosophical tradition, the answer to that question is (and has always been, from Plato on[5]) reason, that the exfoliation of all possible intelligibility is the way in which human beings reconcile themselves to their world and so find themselves at home in it. This is true from the heights of speculative thinking to the self-legislated authority of moral law, to the claim for the rationality of modern ethical life, to the sweeping claim about our possible reconciliation with the course of history itself. For Heidegger this is ultimately dogmatic; it can be shown to be inadequate and that there must be sources of meaningfulness other than this, which, by being ignored, send the fate of reason so understood into misleading, obscuring, and ultimately unacceptable directions. The question of just what Heidegger thinks has been forgotten, obscured by this dogmatic insistence, poses the greatest difficulty in any overall interpretation of Heidegger, but on the main issue, as I just stated, I think Heidegger is right.[6] Neither Kant nor Hegel is in a position to give a defensible, nondogmatic, non-question-

---

interpretation in a later work. (Heidegger's idea seems to be that while Schelling is the peak or *Gipfel* of German Idealism, Hegel is its culmination, *Vollendung*.)

4. I first defended this interpretation of the meaning of Being problem (as the role of meaningfulness in the availability of beings) in Pippin (2007) and then developed it further in Pippin (2013a). A somewhat similar view has more recently been used as the basis of a convincing case for the unity of Heidegger's thought by Sheehan (2015).

5. My concentration in what follows is the critique of German Idealism, not the overall accuracy of Heidegger's history of Being. I take no stand on that, but I should note that I do not agree with the way Heidegger consistently characterizes Plato, especially since, for the most part, he ignores the zetetic character of the Socratic enterprise and the Platonic doctrine of eros. "For the most part" because in WT, he is aware that "not a single one of Plato's dialogues arrives at a palpable, unequivocal result," but he means only that "which sound common sense could, as the saying goes, hold on to" (71). (Not that Heidegger would mind the charge of misinterpretation. He also remarks in WT that Kant would get an F for his interpretation of Plato, but "only Kant has creatively transformed Plato's doctrine of ideas" [77].)

6. I know from experience that even posing the matter in this general way immediately raises the fear of "irrationalism." This is particularly the case in those who invoke the Davos encounter between Cassirer and Heidegger in 1929, as if a staged battle between Enlightenment rationalism and the supposedly romantic dark irrationalism of interwar German thought. That this is not so, that it is a gross simplification, has been well established by Gordon (2010), with implications for the whole range of pseudo-oppositions used to characterize Heidegger. The same is true of Truwant's very fine recent book (2022). See especially chapter 10 and his conclusion. The deeper contrast is between rational explicability and the complexities of interpretative struggles with meaningfulness. The latter is no more "irrational" than invoking an insight about the sources or failures of meaningfulness from poetry and film (even though there are those who would do so).

begging answer to the question of the *Sinn des Seins*, the meaning of being. Again, to many this will seem so obvious as not to be worth mentioning any longer, but I think Heidegger is also right in charging that *all* enterprises in philosophy as such, including those in the twenty-first century, whether the metaphysics of modality, new metaphysical realism, or resting content with the analytic clarification of our concepts, still subscribe to the basic premise Heidegger has identified: that the primary availability of the beings to human being is as material for cognition, possible contents for assertoric judgment, in whatever subfield of philosophy undertaken, or else they content themselves with isolated intellectual exercises without much sense of why any of it should matter.[7] If pressed on the question of mattering, something like the assumption Heidegger has identified will emerge.

7. Mattering is clearly a mode of what Heidegger calls the meaning of the being of Dasein–Care (*Sorge*). While our practical engagement with the work world is the primary example Heidegger uses in BT, his interest in the possibility of "world disclosure" in our engagements with nature, with other human beings, with objects of concern that are not tools, and so forth, all call for a broader term for the nature of this Care-driven engagement, and I will often use "mattering." It surfaces in Heidegger in this way at BT 141: "a Being towards the world that 'matters' to one [*Sein zu der einen 'angehenden' Welt*]." The general notion of the world's availability presupposing this regime of mattering should lessen any opposition between strictly pragmatist and hermeneutical readings of BT.

Acknowledgments

I would like to express my gratitude to the John Simon Guggenheim Memorial Foundation for a fellowship granted to me for the academic year 2019–2020 and to the Division of the Social Sciences at the University of Chicago for a research leave that allowed me to accept the fellowship that year, during which portions of this book were written. I am grateful as well to participants in several discussions of various chapters given as lectures in the last few years, especially at the Society for Philosophy and Phenomenological Research, the Heidegger Circle, the University of Potsdam, and the Society for German Idealism and Romanticism. I am especially indebted to Terry Pinkard for many invaluable comments on the manuscript and likewise for comments from an anonymous reader for the University of Chicago Press. An early version of chapter 7 was published in the *Journal of Speculative Philosophy* 33, no. 3 (2019), https://doi.org/10.5325/jspecphil.33.3.0349, and I am grateful for permission to reprint it here. My thanks, too, to my philosophy editor at the University of Chicago Press, Kyle Wagner, for his thoughtful support of this project and several previous ones, and to Karl von der Luft for his generous editorial assistance.

Sigla

MARTIN HEIDEGGER

AS   "Anaximander's Saying," in OBT, 242–281.

BCA   *Basic Concepts of Aristotelian Philosophy*. Transl. Robert D. Metcalf and Mark B. Tanzer. Bloomington: Indiana University Press, 2009. (GA, Bd. 18)

BN1   *Ponderings II-VI, Black Notebooks 1931–1938*. Transl. Richard Rojcewicz. Bloomington: Indiana University Press, 2017. (GA, Bd. 94)

BN2   *Ponderings VII-IX, Black Notebooks 1938–1939*. Transl. Richard Rojcewicz. Bloomington: Indiana University Press, 2017. (GA, Bd. 95)

BN3   *Ponderings XII-XV, Black Notebooks 1939–41*. Transl. Richard Rojcewicz. Bloomington: Indiana University Press, 2017. (GA, Bd. 96)

BP   *The Basic Problems of Phenomenology*. Transl. Albert Hofstadter. Bloomington: Indiana University Press, 1988. (GA, Bd. 24)

BT   *Being and Time*. Transl. John Macquarrie and Edward Robinson. New York: HarperCollins, 2008. (GA, Bd. 24)

CP   *Contributions to Philosophy. From Enowning*. First translated by Parvis Emad and Kenneth Maly (Bloomington: Indiana University Press, 1999); re-translated as *Contributions to Philosophy (Of the Event)*, trans. Richard Rojcewicz and Daniela Vallega-Neu (Bloomington: Indiana University Press, 2012). I use and much prefer the latter translation. (GA, Bd. 65)

CUD   *Colloquium Über Dialektik*, Heidegger et al., in *Hegel Studien*, Bd. 25, 1990.

DT   *Discourse on Thinking*. Trans. John Anderson and E. Hans Freund. New York: Harper, 1966.

EF   *The Essence of Human Freedom: An Introduction to Philosophy.* Trans.
      Ted Stadler. New York: Continuum, 2002. (GA, Bd. 31)

EG   "On the Essence of Ground," in P, 97–135.

EH   *Erläuterung zu Hölderlins Dichtung.* Frankfurt: Klostermann, 1981.
      (GA, Bd. 4)

ENP   *Einleitung in die Philosophie.* Frankfurt: Klostermann, 1996.
      (GA, Bd. 27)

EP   "The End of Philosophy and the Task of Thinking," in M. Heidegger,
      The End of Philosophy, transl. Joan Stambaugh, 427–449. Chicago:
      University of Chicago Press, 2003. (GA, Bd. 14)

FCM   *The Fundamental Concepts of Metaphysics: World, Finitude, Solitude.*
      Transl. William McNeill and Nicholas Walker. Bloomington: Indiana
      University Press, 1995. (GA, Bd. 29–30)

GA   *Gesamtausgabe.* (Frankfurt: Klostermann, 1978–).

GI   *Der deutsche Idealismus. Fichte, Schelling, Hegel und die philosophische
      Problemlage der Gegenwart.* Frankfurt: Klostermann, 1997. (GA, Bd. 28)

HCE   *Hegel's Concept of Experience.* New York: Harper and Row, 1970.
      (GA, Bd. 5)

HG   "Hegel and the Greeks," in *Pathmarks,* 323–336.

HM   "Hegel und das Problem der Metaphysik," in GA, Bd. 80.1, Teil 1: 1915–
      1932, Vorträge, 281–326.

HPS   *Hegel's "Phenomenology of Spirit."* Transl. Parvis Emad and Kenneth
      Maly. Bloomington: Indiana University Press, 1988. (GA, Bd. 32)

HS   *Seminare: Hegel—Schelling.* Frankfurt: Klostermann, 2011.
      (GA, Bd. 86)

ID   *Identity and Difference.* Transl. Joan Stambaugh. Chicago: University of
      Chicago Press, 1969. (GA, Bd. 11)

IM   *Introduction to Metaphysics.* Transl. Gregory Fried and Richard Polt.
      New Haven, CT: Yale University Press, 2000. (GA, Bd. 40)

KPM   *Kant and the Problem of Metaphysics.* Transl. Richard Taft. Blooming-
      ton: Indiana University Press, 1997. (GA, Bd. 3)

KT   "Kant's Thesis about Being," in *Pathmarks,* 337–364.

L   *Logik. Die Frage nach der Wahrheit.* Frankfurt: Klostermann, 1976.
      (GA, Bd. 21)

LH   "Letter on Humanism," in P, 277–290.

LO   *Logic: The Question of Truth.* Transl. Thomas Sheehan. Bloomington:
      Indiana University Press, 2010. (GA, Bd. 21)

LP   "Language in the Poem. A Discussion of Georg Trakl's Poetic Work,"
      in OL, 159–198.

MGI   *The Metaphysics of German Idealism.* Transl. Ian Alexander Moore and
      Rodrigo Therezo. Cambridge: Polity Press, 2021. (GA, Bd. 49)

ML   *The Metaphysical Foundations of Logic*. Transl. Michael Heim. Blooming-
      ton: Indiana University Press, 1984. (GA, Bd. 26)

N   *Nietzsche*. Volumes I-IV. Transl. David Farrell Krell. New York: Harper
      and Row, 1984. (GA, Bd. 69 and 94)

OBT   *Off the Beaten Track*. Transl. Julian Young and Kenneth Haynes. Cam-
      bridge: Cambridge University Press, 2002. (GA, Bd. 5)

OL   *On the Way to Language*. Transl. Peter Hertz. New York: Harper
      and Row, 1971. *Unterwegs zur Sprache*. Pfüllingen: Neske, 1959.

OWA   "On the Origin of the Work of Art," in OBT, 1–56. (GA, Bd. 9)

P   *Pathmarks*. Transl. William McNeill. Cambridge: Cambridge Univer-
      sity Press, 1998. (GA, Bd. 9)

PHK   *Phenomenological Interpretation of Kant's Critique of Pure Reason*.
      Transl. Parvis Emad and Kenneth Maly. Bloomington: Indiana Univer-
      sity Press, 1997.

PIA   *Philosophische Interpretationen zu Aristotles*. Frankfurt: Klostermann,
      1985. (GA, Bd. 61)

PIK   *Phänomenologische Interpretation von Kants Kritik der reinen Vernunft*.
      Frankfurt: Klostermann, 1977. (GA, Bd. 25)

PLT   *Poetry, Language, and Thought*. Transl. Albert Hofstadter. New York:
      Harper and Row, 1971.

PR   "Preface," in Richardson 2003, viii-xvii.

POR   *The Principle of Reason*. Transl. Reginald Lilly. Bloomington: Indiana
      University Press, 1991. (GA, Bd. 10)

PS   *Plato's Sophist*. Transl. Richard Rojcewicz and André Shuwer. Bloom-
      ington: Indiana University Press, 2003. (GA, Bd. 19)

QT   *The Question Concerning the Thing: On Kant's Doctrine of the Tran-
      scendental Principles*. Transl. James D. Reid and Benjamin D. Crowe.
      London: Rowman and Littlefield, 2018. (GA, Bd. 41); and *Die Frage
      nach dem Ding. Zu Kants Lehre von den transzendentalen Grundsätzen*.
      Dritte, durchgesehene Auflage. Tübingen: Max Niemeyer, 1987; origi-
      nally 1962.

ST   *Schelling's Treatise on the Essence of Human Freedom*. Transl. Joan
      Stambaugh. Athens: Ohio University Press, 1985. (GA, Bd. 42)

TB   *On Time and Being*. Transl. Joan Stambaugh. New York: Harper
      and Row, 1972.

VA   *Vorträge und Aufsätze*, Bd. 3. Pfüllingen: Neske, 1967.

W   "Fortgeschrittene: Phänomenologische Übungen" (*Hegel, Logik,
      I. Buch*). Seminar 1925–1926 WS. Student notes complied by Helene
      Weiss. Stanford Special Collection, M0632, Box 3, Folder 7. All cita-
      tions are from Gonzalez 2021.

WP   "Why Poets," in PLT, 89–139. OBT, 200–241. (GA, Bd. 6)

WT   *What Is Called Thinking?* New York: Harper and Row, 1968.
(GA, Bd. 8)

G. W. F. HEGEL

A, I   *Aesthetics: Lectures on Fine Art.* Transl. T. M. Knox. 2 vols. Oxford:
AND II   Clarendon Press, 1975.

EL   *The Encyclopedia Logic.* Transl. by T. F. Geraets, W. A. Suchting,
H. S. Harris. Indianapolis: Hackett, 1991.

PHG   *The Phenomenology of Spirit.* Transl. by T. Pinkard. Cambridge: Cambridge University Press, 2018.

PN   *The Philosophy of Nature.* Ed. and transl. M. J. Petry. London: Humanities Press, 1970.

PSS   *Hegels Philosophie des subjektiven Geistes/Hegel's Philosophy of Subjective Spirit,* 3 vols. Ed. and transl. M. Petry. Dordrecht: Reidel, 1978.

SL   *The Science of Logic.* Transl. George di Giovanni. Cambridge: Cambridge University Press, 2010. (Page numbers are to the German edition, cited in the margins of di Giovanni's translation.)

IMMANUEL KANT

AK   *Gesammelte Schriften.* Berlin: Preussische Akademie der Wissen-
schaften, 1910–.

MF   *The Metaphysical Foundations of Natural Science,* in *Immanuel Kant:
Theoretical Philosophy after 1781.* Ed. Henry Allison and Peter Heath;
transl. Gary Hatfield, Michael Friedman, Henry Allison, Peter Heath.
Cambridge: Cambridge University Press, 2002.

FRIEDRICH NIETZSCHE

TI   *Twilight of the Idols,* in *The Anti-Christ, Ecce Homo, Twilight of the Idols,
and Other Writings.* Ed. Aaron Ridley and Judith Norman. Cambridge:
Cambridge University Press, 2005.

F. W. J. SCHELLING

PR   *Philosophy of Revelation* (1841–42). Transl. Klaus Ottmann. Thompson,
CT: Spring Publications, 2020.

SECTION ONE
Preliminaries

1

The Issues

This overcoming of Hegel is the intrinsically necessary step in the development of Western philosophy, which must be made for it to remain at all alive. Whether logic can successfully be made into philosophy again we do not know; philosophy should not prophesy, but then again it should not remain asleep. (BP, 178)

In Hegel, philosophy—that is, ancient philosophy—is in a certain sense thought through to its end. He was completely in the right when he himself expressed this consciousness. But there exists just as much the legitimate demand to start anew, to understand the finiteness of the Hegelian system, and to see that Hegel himself has come to an end with philosophy because he moves in the circle of philosophical problems. (BP, 282)

The philosophy of the Greeks attains dominance in the West not on the basis of its originary inception but on the basis of the inceptive end, which in Hegel is brought to fulfillment in a great and final manner. Where history is genuine, it does not perish merely by ending and expiring like an animal; it perishes only historically. (IM, 202)

The completion [*Vollendung*] of philosophy is neither its end, nor does it consist in the isolated system of speculative idealism. The completion is only as the whole course of the history of philosophy, in whose course the beginning remains as essential as the completion: Hegel and the Greeks. (HG, 327)[1]

1. These formulations about Hegel can be found throughout Heidegger's career, but there are other formulations—not necessarily inconsistent, but complicating formulations. For example, at the beginning of his 1941 lecture course on "The Metaphysics of German Idealism," he calls out not Hegel's *Logic* but Schelling's 1809 essay, "Philosophische Unter-

My questions in the following are (i) whether Heidegger, mostly but not exclusively in the first two decades of his career, correctly estimated the significance of Kant and German Idealism as the culmination of the Western philosophical tradition and of Hegel as the philosopher we most need to "overcome"; (ii) whether he was justified in claiming that this tradition, culminating in Hegel, had failed or "perished historically" (that philosophy had exhausted its possibilities, and all that was left was for it to recount its own moments in either some triumphalist mode or some deflationary irony [Hegel vs. Derrida, say]); and (iii) whether this failure tells us something crucial for the very possibility of a renewal of philosophy. These questions do not concern so much the scholarly accuracy of Heidegger's account (although I believe and will try to show that he understood the Idealist tradition and its significance better than anyone had hitherto) but whether he was justified in his claim that the source of this failure lies in the fact that metaphysical tradition has ignored or "forgotten" a fundamental question, one it assumes everywhere but does not address. Consider the larger context for that issue in the following way.

One of the "areas of specialization" treated as a subfield for hiring purposes in anglophone academic philosophy is "nineteenth- and twentieth-century European philosophy." It would not be unreasonable to be somewhat skeptical that such a broad category is actually a single historical specialty, since it encompasses so many different approaches, raises so many different issues, and uses such different vocabularies, and its philosophers are as much at war with themselves as in any other historical period. But from a sufficiently high altitude, there is an issue that surfaces with remarkable frequency and intensity after the collapse of the Hegelian system into warring camps and a growing fatigue with the aridity of neo-Kantianism, one that is at the heart of Heidegger's critique: *human finitude*, and in particular the finite capacity of what Hegel called "pure thinking," or empirically unaided reflection, the very activity that philosophy consists in.

This is not just an issue between Heidegger and Hegel. "Hegel" emerges as much more than that when we note that much of the most important European philosophy in the twentieth century also has a complicated and unusually deep connection to Hegel.[2] Foucault's famous remark about Hegel is typical: "But to make a real escape from Hegel presupposes an exact

---

suchungen über das Wesen der menschlichen Freiheit und die damit zusammenhängenden Gegenstände," the "peak" (*Gipfel*) of the metaphysics of German Idealism and therewith an articulation of "all the essential determinations of metaphysics" (MDI, 1).

2. A case could also be made, and often has been, that the origins of the anglophone analytic movement are essentially animated by an anti-Hegelianism, Russell's broad swipes at Hegel being the best known.

appreciation of what it costs to detach ourselves from him. It presupposes a knowledge of how close Hegel has come to us, perhaps insidiously, it presupposes a knowledge of what is still Hegelian in that which allows us to think against Hegel and an ability to gauge how much our resources against him are perhaps still a ruse which he is using against us, and at the end of which he is waiting for us, immobile and elsewhere."[3]

The same prominent pride of place can be found in Derrida's extraordinary claim, "We will never be finished with the reading or rereading of Hegel, and, in a certain way, I do nothing other than attempt to explain myself on this point."[4] Levinas tells us that anyone who sets out to write something philosophically ambitious should begin by "setting his positions on Hegel."[5] Deleuze probably expresses the most negative attitude: "What I detested most was Hegelianism and the dialectic."[6] Similar passages, with varying degrees of frustration, admiration, or contempt (accompanied by an unusually consistent theme of being somehow "trapped" by Hegel or unwittingly caught up in his game with his rules), can be found in Adorno, Lyotard, Deleuze, Bataille, and others,[7] and they all echo similar critiques from the nineteenth century—Schelling's, Marx's, Kierkegaard's, Schopenhauer's. Aside from a few issues in Frankfurt School critical theory, "Hegel" mostly exists as that obscure object of rejection. Different issues are involved in each thinker's disaffection, but what is of interest to me in the following is that general theme just noted—an emphasis on the finitude of philosophical thinking as the issue Hegel (and indeed the entire post-Platonic philosophical tradition) most misunderstood. As Heidegger put it, Kant, the origin of "German Idealism," originally realized that all cognition should be understood as *human* and therefore finite cognition (QT, 93); this is meant as a limitation far deeper than psychological or anthropological, an expression of fundamental human finitude, the proper recognition of which should

3. Foucault 1981, 74.

4. Derrida and Houdebine 1973, 39.

5. Levinas 2003, 95.

6. Deleuze 1995, 6. See this summary of relevant remarks in Houle and Vernon (2013), xii: "Hegel and Hegelianism are routinely name-called: the 'long perversion,' 'the long history of the distortion,' the 'dead end,' a philosophy that 'betrays and distorts the immediate,' animating 'no more than ghostly puppets.' Hegelians are singled out as those 'lacking the wit to laugh.' The arc of Deleuze's anti-Hegelian rhetoric perhaps reaches its apex in *Difference and Repetition*: 'It is only in relation to the identical, as a function of the identical, that contradiction is the greatest difference. The intoxications and giddinesses are feigned, the obscure is already clarified from the outset. Nothing shows this more clearly than the insipid monocentricity of the circles in the Hegelian dialectic.'"

7. This is another way of characterizing that post-Heideggerian tradition as antirationalist without being empiricist (except for the unusual hybrid position of Deleuze and his "transcendental empiricism").

occasion a revolutionary turn in our understanding of philosophy. But even Kant could not appreciate the radicality of his insight and, according to Heidegger, in the second edition deduction in *The Critique of Pure Reason* largely abandoned his insight.[8] He at least kept faith with the assumption common in the Christian era that any successful claim to knowledge, no matter how apparently successful, must still be understood as in some way limited because it's always comparable, unfavorably, with divine cognition. By contrast, with Hegel, philosophical cognition, if it is to be cognition at all, must be "absolute," and it is this rejection of finitude that so dramatically sets off Hegel's position in particular. Hegel called the most important book in his project, his *Science of Logic*, a "science of pure thinking" and meant thereby to emphasize an insistence on the absolute autonomy, or the self-determining and self-grounding character of such pure thinking. He also wasn't hesitant in characterizing such thought, when properly understood, as "infinite." In this context, infinity means that empirically unaided or pure thinking is answerable only to itself, not to ideal or noetic and certainly not empirical objects, and that it can answer the questions it cannot but put to itself. Its image is a circle; pure thinking begins and ends with itself. This language and approach are distinctly Hegelian, but they are a radicalization of (and so take us beyond) Kant's notion of reason's general autarky. Kant's claim about reason's *self-legislative* power and a new characterization of thinking as exclusively a spontaneity were introduced into the idealist tradition and became a common element in the celebration of freedom in that era. Pure thinking could be self-grounding and self-articulating, as well as (for Kant) self-limiting, but also substantively productive in a category theory. In this sense, it is a culmination. Pure thinking in the classical and modern traditions was autonomous in the sense that it was indebted only to its own objects—objects available only to pure thinking. The culmination of that thought is that pure thinking is indebted only to, answerable only to, itself, (pure spontaneity). Hegel thought he had shown that Kant was wrong about the human limitations of these results and that reason was successful in such attempts, that philosophy had achieved that "absolute" status just noted. It had achieved what had always been its inner aspiration.

(A qualification is needed here on Heidegger's claim that Hegel repre-

---

8. "But Hegel's step from Kant to absolute idealism is the sole consequence of the development of Western philosophy. It became possible and necessary through Kant because the problem of human Dasein, the problem of finitude, did not properly become a problem for Kant himself. That is to say, this did not become a central problem of philosophy because Kant himself, as the second edition of the *Critique of Pure Reason* reveals, helped to prepare the turn away from an uncomprehended finitude toward a comforting infinitude" (FCM 208–209).

sents the culmination, the completion, and also the end, the exhaustion, of the metaphysical tradition. It is needed because in his Nietzsche lectures of the 1930s and '40s, and in later texts like *Wozu Dichter?*, he also claims that *Nietzsche* represents the failure of that tradition. In the latter case, though, I think [without being able to demonstrate here] that he is making a separate point about the post-Hegelian philosophical world. Nietzsche represents himself as, and is often widely believed to be, the *beginning* of the postmetaphysical fate of philosophy and as standing on the other side of that divide, the other side of the "culmination."[9] Heidegger wants to show that *even* in this case, Nietzsche is still trapped within traditional metaphysical thinking and, accordingly, reenacts its dead-end and ultimately nihilistic fate.[10] At any rate, Heidegger continues to characterize Hegel and the end of German Idealism as the manifestation of the culmination of metaphysics, and that is what I will concentrate on in what follows.)[11]

These sweeping claims about German Idealism and Hegel require us to understand (i) what in the Western philosophical tradition are the continuous commitments that Hegel has brought to a culmination; (ii) what Heidegger means when he claims that by such a culmination Hegel has made finally clear what those commitments are and what it must mean to ground them absolutely and finally; (iii) why, in doing so, that completion has revealed that the basic question of metaphysics, the *Grundfrage*, has been left out, omitted (*ausgeblieben*); and (iv) finally that this is all not a matter of an omission that can simply be supplied, something missing that can be filled

9. "Neither Kierkegaard nor Nietzsche had the courage and above all the power—if anything—to break off from philosophy" (BN1, 57).

10. For example, "*Nietzsche*—in what single sense is Nietzsche a transition, i.e., a preparation for another beginning of the history of beyng? (Transition does not mean here the conveyance out of one state of beings into another state of the *same* beings; such a transition—of something that is not destroyed or disturbed in its being—is an object of historiological calculation and determination.) Nietzsche is a transition *only* in the sense that he metaphysically anticipates the consummation of modernity and thereby posits the end appropriate to the history of being, and *with* this end (which he himself was *not* able to recognize and know as such, because he still thinks metaphysically, as the ultimate and definitive proponent of metaphysics) the *possibility* of a preparation of the decision in favor of the other beginning is made ready" (BN, 10). And, "*Nietzsche*, thinking in advance, entered the desert of that devastation which sets in with the unconditionality of machination and brings forth its first 'results' in the exclusively subjective character of the human animal as predatory animal" (BN, 12).

11. As we will see many times in what follows, Heidegger mostly characterizes the true task of metaphysics as the interrogation of the meaning of Being (into the "truth of Being and the grounding of that truth" [BN, 8]), but he uses conventional characterizations as well: that metaphysics relies on the distinction between sensible and nonsensible, that it is an attempt to think unconditionally, or that it represents an absolute commitment to the principle of sufficient reason.

in[12] or supplemented, but that requires a complete transformation (*Verwandlung*) in the self-understanding of philosophy itself. These are the basic themes that will appear in different contexts and in different ways throughout what follows, but we can get oriented by summarizing Heidegger's own high-altitude view of the issues in a lecture from 1930 that has only recently (2016) been published in his collected works, *Hegel und das Problem der Metaphysik* (Hegel and the problem of metaphysics), a deliberate echo of his book published the year before, *Kant und das problem der Metaphysik*. The summary is somewhat breathless, but it will give us some orientation.

Heidegger begins by noting that Hegel, "the culminator," had correctly seen that the underlying commitment of the Western tradition is that metaphysics, first philosophy, the exploration of the questions that all other philosophical, empirical, and practical issues must presuppose, is "logic." He does not, of course, mean formal logic, the rules for well-formed formulae and truth-preserving inference, the rules of thinking that abstract from all content,[13] but what Heidegger calls *begreifendes Denken* (HM, 288), conceptualizing thinking. He means a commitment to the view that what he calls the actuality of the actual, or the real essence of anything, is what can be grasped conceptually (concepts traditionally known as categories), a determination of what must be the case for anything to be a determinate thing at all. This is an enterprise of pure, or empirically unaided, thinking. It must be if it is to determine what *must* be the case in response to the basic question "what is it for a being to be able to be this or that being?" This is formulated more traditionally (in the terms of ancient metaphysics) by the claim that the reality of things is *logos*, or reason (HM, 288) What is, then, he asks, the "essence" of *logos*, *Vernunft*, reason? In Hegel's account (here as the culmination of modern or post-Cartesian metaphysics), the claim is that this essence is "spirit" (*Geist*), understood as "self-knowing" (*Sichwissen*) or reflection, the quest by self-conscious subjectivity to assure itself of the objectivity of the categoriality it requires. Here the bearing of Kant on these issues will be crucial, as we shall see in section 2. This, then, suggests a possible duality between self-knowing subjectivity and independent objects, and so the culmination requires an overcoming of any such possibility, a foreclosing of any skeptical objection. The overcoming of such a possible opposition is the achievement of the Absolute, and in that sense the culmi-

---

12. See BN1, §218, where Heidegger insists that this is not a matter of mere "errancy" (*Irrtum*). His discussion here about the inevitable imbrication of disclosure with concealing is posed in different terms, empowerment (*Ermächtigung*) and dis-empowerment (*Entmächtigung*). 69.

13. Which content is nevertheless assumed to be one sort of content, the *Seiende*, the beings, the present at hand substances, already a metaphysical commitment, as we shall see.

nation of the ancient and modern traditions. (At one point, Heidegger summarizes the topic of the Absolute as the goal of all metaphysics with a string of appositives: God, Spirit, the self-knowing of the essence of reason, logos [HM, 294]). For Hegel, this is all achieved *historically*, not as a Spinoza-like deductive system. But once this is achieved, we will have understood that the truth of anything at all *is* the becoming of the self-knowing of spirit (remembering again that for Heidegger the central commitment or at least goal of German Idealism is the identity of thinking and being, what he means here by saying the "the truth" *is* "the becoming of the self-knowing of spirit"). This is said to count as the eventual achievement of a form of freedom, the reconciliation of spirit with itself as not mere subjectivity but as that subject-object speculative identity, and so a reconciliation with its world. In a language I hope we can become accustomed to, Heidegger's formulation is that the logic of the tripartite structure of Hegel's *Science of Logic*—Being, Essence, and Concept—where "the logic of" means a reflection on the possible thinking of any possible being (*Seiende*), is "the making possible [*Ermöglichung*] of the thinking of the thinking of beings, and thereby the making possible of the being [*Sein*] of beings" (HM, 291).

We say, with Heidegger, "once achieved historically" and other such formulations meant to gloss the notion of a culmination, but obviously a controversial issue lies behind the summary phrases. What is a *historical* culmination? Heidegger discusses this in several contexts. One of the clearest is in his 1957 essay *The Principle of Reason* (*Der Satz vom Grund*), in which he discusses what is mostly called the principle of sufficient reason, first formulated as such by Leibniz. "There is nothing without a ground/ reason." "All beings have a ground." "Sufficient reasons must be given for anything being what it is." Heidegger does not claim that the principle was unknown prior to Leibniz, but it had not been explicitly formulated until him, or not for twenty-three hundred years. He points out that the principle is not primarily about propositions and their justification but is ontological. There can be no being or event without a reason for it being and being as it is, and he then leads the audience he is addressing to appreciate that the principle really asserts that the principle about all the beings (*Seiende*) is also a determination of being qua being, Being (*Sein*), *as* sufficient reason, or discursive intelligibility. *That* is taken to be the meaning of Being (though unacknowledged), and it is this fundamental ontological claim that was "hidden" until Leibniz made it explicit. Hidden until made explicit is the *nervus probandi* of the culmination claim, and while it does not presume any detailed account of it necessarily emerging, there is some claim involved about the fate of reason itself, what Heidegger calls here and elsewhere a *Geschick,* or destiny of Being. Heidegger indulges in his later highly metaphorical agentive language by invoking Being as itself taking a turn, that Being has "awakened and taken a turn" (POR, 55). The fact that presuppositions about various ontic claims, about beings and their ground, should at some point become initially apparent and then further pursued is not in itself mysterious, and Heidegger has no stake in showing exactly why that took twenty-three hundred and not twelve hundred years. He is dealing with the history of Western thought as it is and is suggesting only that what he is pointing to has been implicit ("hidden," "concealed") until a thinker formulated it. Moreover, this explicitation is only minimally and initially on view in Leibniz. It is only the beginning of the realization of the meaningfulness of Being as cognizability, the objectness of objects, and so the assumption eventually of modem science and technology: "The sovereignty of the principle of reason begins only now in the obvious sense that all cognition thoroughly responds to the demand that sufficient reason be unconditionally rendered for every being" (POR, 55).

And so eventually, "Being as the objectness of objects gets distended [*eingespannt*] into the relation between cognition and the subject. From then on, this relation between subject and object counts as the sole realm wherein a decision about being is solely made about beings regarding their being, the realm wherein a decision about being is always made solely in terms of the objectness of the object but never about being as such" (POR, 55).

That the full implications of Plato's understanding of the meaning of Being as Idea or of Leibniz's principle require gradual exfoliation over time until, finally, Hegel, is all we need to get minimally in view this notion of destiny, *Geschick*. And, as the last quotation indicates, this dynamic of hiddenness and disclosure can be said to culminate in the disclosure of what had always remained hidden, even if decisive in the tradition: the disclosure of the complete hiddenness from us of the meaning of Being at issue in our dealing with beings. That is what Hegel "accomplishes." And there is little doubt that Hegel thinks of himself as signing on to the principle of cognizability as the meaning of Being. Consider the remark opening his lecture course in Berlin in 1818: "One cannot think highly enough of the greatness and power of spirit; the sequestered nature of the universe harbors no power which can oppose the courage of cognition; it is necessary that it open itself before one and lay its riches and its profundities before one's eyes and bring joy to them."[14]

---

14. Hegel 1956, 101–2. Quoted by Heidegger in POR, 85.

And so it is finally the systematization, noted above, of what is claimed to represent the underlying continuity of Western metaphysics (if not explicit until German Idealism) that can reveal *finally* what is missing or left out, or what remains unasked. For the *Grundfrage* in this tradition, both ancient and modern,[15] is the question of the Being of beings, *Seiende*, but that is understood in the way sketched above, as what is categorially necessary, or necessarily presupposed for any being to be the determinate being it is. This means that being is already understood as what Heidegger will call throughout his career "standing presence" (*ständige* or *beständige Anwesenheit*) (HM, 299).[16] By this he means a being that is determinate, discriminable from other beings, and so potentially available to a subject in the present and able to endure through a temporal phase. The comprehensive concept for such an understanding is *ousia*, substance. (This establishes already the crucial inseparability of any understanding of the meaning of being and time, something Heidegger frequently reminds his listeners in this lecture.) This then raises the question that is the heart of the matter for Heidegger: *Why* have we not asked whether *this* (let us say as shorthand, determinately standing being as thinkability) should be *assumed* to be the orientation for *any* inquiry about the meaning of being qua being? What grounds justify such an orientation? Is it possible that a finite, mortal being can understand itself as an in-principle, completely self-knowing being with respect to the fundamental issues of first philosophy?[17] If the question is the meaning of Being as such, it must mean the meaning available for the one being open to that question, and that being is not rightly understood as exclusively self-consciousness, a pure thinking being, but as a living, finite being—what Heidegger calls Dasein—and the task of first philosophy must be reformulated in the light of the analysis of that being, a *Daseinsanalytic*. So, instead of a *Phenomenology of Spirit*, culminating in the self-knowing of a *Science of Logic*, we need a "metaphysics" of Dasein (HM, 315).

The idea that the task of first philosophy should have always been the Absolute in this way can at first sound mystifying. But it should not be. Philosophy is not an empirical enterprise. Its stock in trade are claims for an a priori status, and the modality of the a priori is necessity. In that context, every philosophical judgment, from Aquinas on substance to Quine

---

15. We shall deal with Heidegger's unusual claims about historical "epochality" in later discussions.

16. See also HM 308. Heidegger is offering an interpretation of the implications of Aristotle's question, *ti to on*, what is being, as a question about the "beingness" of a being, any determinate being, a *tode ti* or this-such (HM, 296).

17. "... *daß* Sein ousia sei, *bleibt außer Frage*, gefragt wird nur noch, was jeweils die ousia sei und wie sie näher zu bestimmen sei" (HM, 299).

on ontological relativity, claims an absolute status. That *The Critique of Pure Reason* proposes both necessary conditions for the possibility of experience (not what probably or empirically are such conditions) forever and with necessity also forever forecloses the possibility of knowing the nature of things in themselves, including such knowledge as whether we are free beings or not. It is not that we have simply not yet figured out how to know such things. To be sure, Hegel occupies a particular position in philosophy because of the scope of what he claims that philosophy *is* able to establish. And we will be investigating that status throughout. But when Heidegger argues against any absolute status for philosophical judgments, he is not merely arguing against Hegel or an old-fashioned self-understanding but *against all traditional philosophy itself*, including logicism, conceptual analysis, ordinary language philosophy, formal semantics, and so on.[18] In Hegel's case, there is a specific meaning to the claim for an Absolute, which is that the full determination of all beings in their knowability (the meaning of Being for Hegel), and therewith the full determination of what beings must be, has been systematically provided. This is essentially the same *kind* of claim that, say, Quine or Carnap made, just not systematically, but it is Hegel's greater ambition that Heidegger is after.[19]

The contrary "finitist" position denies this, and does so for a variety of reasons, involving different commitments in each thinker. But it would not be an exaggeration to say that the most influential (indeed, for many of the philosophers just cited) and most radical insistence on such finitude is the philosophy of Martin Heidegger.[20] Moreover, increasingly after *Being*

18. It no doubt does not need to be noted that Heidegger's position shares very little with attempts like logical positivism to argue as well against metaphysics. What Heidegger wants to do is renew metaphysics on a proper footing.

19. I don't pretend that this all exhaustively characterizes all the paths pursued in contemporary philosophy. Indeed, the most widespread assumption in contemporary academic philosophy is that philosophy must content itself with the task of conceptual analysis, the attempt to get clearer about just what the conceptual content is when we use a concept. Greater clarity, or the avoidance of confusion and misleading implications, is all we can hope to achieve. I can say here only that it seems to me that this task already assumes a number of issues that are deeply metaphysical, including the nature of concepts, their relation to language, the problem of thick concepts that do not lend themselves to analytic clarification or Socratic definitions, the inter-relation of concepts, the status of empirically nonderived but substantive concepts, and many other such questions that inevitably lead us back to "first philosophy." In this context, admittedly, such can only be a suggestion.

20. One scholar aware of the importance of the confrontation with Hegel in Heidegger's work is Otto Pöggeler throughout his life work, and not so much in his best-known work (1987), although he does say there, "If Heidegger differentiated his hermeneutical phenomenology from Husserl's transcendental phenomenology and finally dissociated himself from Husserl, then this differentiation and dissociation refer back to the creative protest against Hegel" (xi).

and Time, Heidegger came to characterize what he was about as an attempt to "overcome" Hegel, whom he consistently characterized as the "culmination" of the entire Western philosophical tradition as well as German Idealism, and as we have just seen and need to explore, his main target was just this claim about pure thinking and its infinity or unboundedness. "Culmination" (*Vollendung*) is an appropriate characterization, at least in that Hegel thought of himself that way, although he of course regarded the culmination as successful, not the exposure of the permanent inadequacy of what had culminated. (Heidegger notes this negative sense, that a culmination or completion can reveal a fundamental failure and that "with German Idealism, it seemed as if philosophy as such had reached an end and had entrusted the administration of knowledge exclusively to the sciences" [QT, 39]. Even the "return to Kant" in neo-Kantianism was merely a way to insist on this fact, a positivism that insisted that only the sciences could count as "demonstrable truth" [QT, 40].)

Now, when this topic is introduced—the finitude of thinking—one thinks first of the claim that what philosophers take to be pure thinking is actually "impure," even an epiphenomenon, that what might appear to be the results of philosophical argumentation—liberal political theory, for example—is actually "bourgeois" philosophy, unwittingly a reflection of the way of thinking supporting the self-interests of a governing social class; or that what might appear to be independent ratiocination is actually responsive to repressed desires unconsciously determining the paths and destination of conscious thinking; or that such putatively pure thinking is actually in the service of some basic psychological drive—the will to power, for example.

Heidegger's critique of idealism is not like this. He will also want to show that philosophical thinking is actually "dependent thinking," but the dependence is on historically contingent manifestations of the meaning of Being,[21] and he does not challenge the power of thinking to exfoliate the general nature of this dependence and the implications of denying it. Heidegger's enterprise is itself an exercise in a kind of pure—in the sense of not empirically guided—thinking, hermeneutic rather than analytic, but not in any service to material interests. Rather, for Heidegger the tradition is unknowing about itself *as thinking*, about what philosophical thinking is and requires, not unknowing about the supposed fact that there is no pure thinking. And this blindness is never treated as a simple mistake, a philosophical error that can be corrected by some clarification. He implies that

---

21. I will follow the convention, born out of respect for what Heidegger calls the "ontological difference" (the difference between questions about beings or a being and the question of the meaning of Being), of capitalizing Being when it occurs in the latter sense.

this "forgetting" is motivated. There is some sort of anxious realization of contingency, or a groundlessness, and so an experience of estrangement from the world that prompts an anxious forgetting of our original experience of the meaningfulness of being. (This calls to mind Nietzsche's claim that forgetting is an "active power.")

This is not to say that the very language of forgetting is not paradoxical. ("We all understand being and yet we do not grasp it" [EF, 31]). The active power of forgetting, or the fact that forgetting in this context is motivated, or even that it involves what Heidegger calls "willfulness" in such attempts, is not, as Heidegger uses it, itself something willed ("up to us") in the conventional sense. As is often pointed out in philosophy, when we attribute to someone a "strong will power" or a failure of will power, what accounts for why and how some have what appears to be such strength, and who does not? It can't be "the will to have will power." As an analogy in the early Heidegger, we can say that when anxiety, *Angst*, or even the foreboding sense of possible anxiety, prompts a "retreat," a "fleeing" into inauthenticity or bad faith, a turning away from what we are "called" on to face (the "call of conscience"), the subject in question does not "do" this or "will" it. We cannot live without the tranquilizing state of the ordinary, but we don't recognize that or decide anything on the basis of it.[22]

The tricky complications here are like the paradox of bad faith; in order to hide something from ourselves, we also have to hide from ourselves that we are doing so. The bottom line is: we do not know, are not aware of forgetting or of what we have forgotten (that is the point), and rely on the metaphysics of presence, with its profoundly comforting and so tempting implication that the way human beings can come to be at home in the world is by understanding it, making it ours by doing so, and by realizing our nature by exercising our rational capacity.[23] That *reason* saves us from such homelessness has become far more comforting than all of the implications of abandoning that metaphysics and that comfort—none of which we can be said to be "in charge of."

This is all tied to Heidegger's view that true metaphysical thinking is not to be understood as a strictly cognitive exercise of pure reason, and this is linked with the hermeneutic rather than analytic character of thinking. For him this means that such interpretive or "meaning-seeking" thinking is inseparable from how such thinking should matter to any thinker and so

22. There are parallels here with Freud, as one of the earliest "importers" of his thought to America, the psychoanalyst Leo Loewald, noticed; also with Sartre on the inevitability of bad faith. But these are analogies meant to make the general point.

23. In EF, Heidegger even notes that "we begin our existence with this *forgottenness of our understanding of being*" (30, emphasis in the original).

with what we expect any such thinking to do for us. And this mattering is complicated by the fact that such thinking is burdened by a dependence on a ground we constantly experience as beyond our ability to grasp conceptually. This is a situation that is no mere philosophical puzzle but an existential burden. Here is a typical formulation: "The concept is thus something like a determinative representation. The fundamental concepts of metaphysics and the concepts of philosophy, however, will evidently not be like this at all, if we recall that they themselves are anchored in our being gripped [*in einer Ergriffenheit gegründet*], in which we do not represent before us that which we conceptually comprehend, but maintain ourselves in a quite different comportment, one which is originarily and fundamentally different from any scientific kind" (FCM, 9).

"Anchored in being gripped" is an indication of the different sort of dependence or finitude that Heidegger wants to insist on. (In HM, he says that we should ask after the unasked and unknown *Grundfrage* in a new way, which he describes as *lebendig*, where that means "out of an actual inner need of Dasein" [313].)

This is so, even though he will occasionally formulate the task of philosophy in other ways. For example, in the 1935 *Introduction to Metaphysics*, he notes that "philosophy is one of the few *autonomous* creative possibilities, and occasional necessities, of human-historical Dasein" (IM, 10, my emphasis). Philosophy might be in some sense autonomous (it is in the service of no other mode of thinking), but its creative possibilities are still available only for a human-historical Dasein. As he goes on to say, in explaining that "metaphysical" questions are "historical through and through," "Our asking of the fundamental metaphysical question is historical because it opens up the happening of human Dasein in its essential relations—that is, its relations to beings as such and as a whole—opens it up to possibilities not yet asked about, futures to come [*Zu-künften*], and thereby also binds it back to its inception that has been, and thus sharpens and burdens it in its present. In this questioning, our Dasein is summoned to its history in the full sense of the word" (IM, 47).[24]

The "fundamental metaphysical question" Heidegger refers to here is his famous question about the meaning of Being, the *Sinn des Seins*, and we will need to understand in what sense Heidegger thinks that this is not at bottom a cognitive question, that addressing it requires a different sort of understanding before his critique of Hegel can be made clear. This all

---

24. He also writes that "philosophy has no object at all. Philosophy is a happening that must at all times work out Being for itself anew [that is, Being in its openness that belongs to it]" (IM, 90).

also means that Heidegger's confrontation with Hegel and Idealism is much more than an episode in the history of philosophy. It is the most serious challenge to the self-understanding of the rationalist tradition that begins with ancient Greek philosophy and, in some sense or other, does indeed culminate in Hegel, and he means to offer that challenge from within that tradition, claiming to reanimate the (forgotten) highest aspirations of metaphysics.[25] So, while the details of the critique are often very hard to get into proper focus, the stakes for philosophy could not be higher.[26] Heidegger's sense of this importance is revealed in quite an unusual passage about the "failure" of German Idealism. It is worth quoting in full since it also expresses the perfervid atmosphere of crisis in the mid-'30s.

> Among us at that time something happened that is all too readily and swiftly characterized as the "collapse of German idealism." This formula is like a shield behind which the already dawning spiritlessness, the dissolution of spiritual powers, the deflection of all originary questioning about grounds and the bonding to such grounds, are hidden and obscured. For it was not German idealism that collapsed, but it was the age that was no longer strong enough to stand up to the greatness, breadth, and originality of that spiritual world—that is, truly to realize it, which always means something other than merely applying propositions and insights. Dasein began to slide into a world that lacked that depth from which the essential always comes and returns to human beings, thereby forcing them to superiority and allowing them to act on the basis of rank. (IM 48)

He is no doubt referring here to the rise of a scientistic neo-Kantianism as a response to this collapse, a response he obviously believes was not up to

---

25. "Philosophy is the theoretical conceptual interpretation of being, of being's structure and its possibilities" (BP, 11). And, "The a priori character of being and of all the structures of being accordingly calls for a specific kind of approach and way of apprehending being—a priori cognition" (BP, 20). This thesis also covers any philosophical empiricism. The claim that all knowledge is derived from sense experience, and that there can be no other knowledge, is not itself an empirical claim but a claim by pure thinking, and it asserts its own form of absoluteness.

26. This goes well beyond the culmination of the metaphysical tradition as traditionally understood, since the broad assumptions about possible determinateness extend well into such developments as the Tractarian Wittgenstein, conceptual analysis, linguistic analysis and dominant assumptions in the philosophy of science, the justifiability of state authority, the theory of communicative action, and other contemporary domains. To be is to be determinate; to be is to be thinkable, knowable. This is a common assumption in all of them.

the magnitude and importance of what he treats as the glorious but doomed ambitions of German Idealism.

Finally, there is an interpretive problem of some complexity that should be very briefly addressed at the outset. It concerns the reception of Heidegger in the anglophone context and the vexed, contested question of the unity (or not) of Heidegger's thought. Two facts are relevant. The first is that Heidegger's most influential book, by a massive margin in anglophone philosophy, was and remains *Being and Time* (1927), along with texts written before and just after. (I am limiting myself mostly here to anglophone academic philosophy. The role of Heidegger in the public discussion of existentialism, literary hermeneutics, and his early and continuing influence on theology are different issues.)[27] There are a number of themes in that book—especially the question of intentionality, the role of concepts in experience, realism vs. idealism, issues in the philosophy of mind and language, and the famous authenticity issue—that connect with recognizable issues in that tradition, and the originality, freshness, and boldness of Heidegger's position understandably inspired a postwar interpretive tradition that had a major impact at a number of American universities.

This affinity with recognizable philosophical problems was not the only reason for this emphasis. Starting in the 1930s, Heidegger began writing in quite a different way, so different that many philosophers had the impression that he had abandoned the enterprise that so inspired them: a *Daseinsanalytic* from BT, with its themes of being-in-the-world, a practical sense of intentionality and thrownness, a temporalizing subject, anxiety, and being-towards-death. (One frequently hears from philosophers who admire the "phenomenological Heidegger" that they "cannot make any sense" out of the "later Heidegger.") Instead Heidegger started to make comments that were taken as critical of BT and phenomenology,[28] and (the second relevant fact) in his 1946 *Letter on Humanism*, he stated much more explicitly than he had before that there had indeed been a turning or a "reversal" (*Kehre*) in his thought, that BT had always been intended as preliminary and that that work could not be properly understood without fitting it into the greater project of thinking about the meaning of Being. In the *Letter*, he writes,

27. See the helpful narrative by Woessner 2011.

28. Some are mildly self-critical, as when he writes in the Nietzsche lectures that his own fundamental ontology had "run the risk of reinforcing subjectivity." N, vol. iv, 141. Others are harsh, as in a letter where he wrote that the publication of BT was a disaster, and there is his remark to Gadamer that what happened to fundamental ontology was that "Nietzsche destroyed me." The passages are quoted in Taminiaux 1991, xxii.

The lecture "On the Essence of Truth," thought out and delivered in 1930 but not printed until 1943, provides a certain insight into the thinking of the turning from "Being and Time" to "Time and Being." *This turning is not a change of standpoint from Being and Time,* but in it the thinking that was sought first arrives at the locality of that dimension out of which *Being and Time* is experienced, that is to say, experienced in the fundamental experience of the oblivion of being. (LH, 250, my emphasis)

Crudely stated, Heidegger is distinguishing the question of the *meaning of Dasein's being* from the problem of *the meaning of Being as such* (and so requires consideration of the oblivion or forgetting of such a question, even in Dasein's interrogation of its own being), and he is saying that he now needs to make much clearer the "locality of the dimension out of which *Being and Time* is first experienced." "Clearer" here is probably the wrong word, because this language already is straining to express something Heidegger feels cannot be expressed otherwise, and his views on the necessity for such unusual formulations expand dramatically from the 1930s and beyond. (This is sometimes categorized as Heidegger's shift from a phenomenological approach to an interrogation of "the history of Being.")[29] By the mid- to late '30s, in his *Beiträge,* his *Contributions to Philosophy (Of the Event),* his formulations are ever more puzzling. Even one of his most sympathetic interpreters, especially of the later Heidegger, William J. Richardson, is wary of entering the *Beiträge* thicket, calling it, in an understatement, "hardly the most lucid of his writings," noting that Heidegger had good reasons to choose not to publish it and that it is marked by "dark ravines and valleys that may wisely be left for subsequent explorations."[30] By 1962, when Heidegger wrote a preface to Richardson's work, this new linguistic style had reached such a difficult level that even warnings about dark ravines and

29. Taminiaux 1991 gives us a good summary of this view of the change in Heidegger's thinking. "Between the first text (BT) and the second (OWA), the meditation on the *aletheia* of *physis* has shifted the site of truth: it is no longer authentic existence as Dasein's coming to self-concerning with its ownmost possibility, but the unconcealment of Being, inasmuch as it provides clearing and lighting to beings, while exempting itself from them" (109). This seems to me too strict a contrast; the latter is what the former was always intended to provide a path towards. For another thing, Heidegger had already proposed his history of Being project, even using the terms "destruction" and "deconstruction," in his Winter Semester seminar of 1919–20. See Kiesel 1995, 60–61. One of the most persuasive summaries of both the continuity and the different emphases in Heidegger's work is given by Pöggeler 1972, 145. He sketches a three-phase view with differing emphases on (i) the question of the meaning of Being, (ii) the question of the truth of Being, and (iii) the question of the event or *Ereignis* of being. For another, equally compelling account, see Sheehan 2015.

30. Richardson 2003, xxxviii.

valleys seemed inadequate metaphors. It certainly required quite creative translations. "[The process of] presenc-ing (Being) is inherent in the lighting-up of self-concealment (Time). [The] lighting-up of self-concealment (Time) brings forth the process of presenc-ing (Being)." (Anwesen [Sein] gehört in die Lichtung des Sichverbergens [Zeit]. Lichtung des Sichverbergens [Zeit] erbringt Anwesen [Sein].)[31]

There is no problem or set of problems in the anglophone or any tradition that this calls to mind and addresses in a novel way, and anyone happening on it for the first time as a statement of Heidegger's position would be understandably baffled. Even in the history of philosophy, while there are very difficult passages, as difficult as this, in the later Platonic dialogues, in Aristotle, and in Hegel and Schelling—and in Wilfrid Sellars, for that matter—there are no claims like this one. That is, to be sure, just what one would expect in Heidegger's attempt to begin philosophy anew, to recover a question that has been lost, forgotten, since the pre-Socratics, but it does not offer any clear way into this new problematic, and Heidegger's later work has mostly become the research area of Heidegger scholars and some literature departments and does not have the wide resonance in recognizable areas of philosophy that BT and the lectures from the '20s did.[32]

But the later work, or at least some elements of it, is not avoidable for anyone who, like me, thinks that Heidegger's interpretations and critique of German Idealism (which extend well into his later work) do raise important and recognizable issues for philosophy itself, and who believe, like me, that Heidegger is right that BT is finally misinterpreted if it is not read in the light of the larger "meaning of Being" question pursued in the later work.[33] In this, the latter dependence, one simply takes Heidegger at his word. In his preface to Richardson, he says what he will repeatedly say in many other contexts: "The distinction you make between Heidegger I and Heidegger II is justified only on the condition that this is kept constantly in mind: only by way of what [Heidegger] I has thought does one gain access to what is to-be-thought by [Heidegger] II. But the thought of [Heidegger I] becomes possible only if it is contained in [Heidegger] II" (PR, xxii).

31. Ibid., xx–xxi.
32. There are other exceptions to this generalization. The work of Mark Wrathall, Iain Thompson, Julian Young, Jeff Malpas, and others might all be cited as working on the later Heidegger from, let's say, still within and engaged with the general anglophone framework.
33. Again, this is not to say that there is not a great deal of tremendous value in the BT-centric approach. My question concerns Heidegger's claims about the finitude of human thinking and the implications of this for the possibility of philosophy as traditionally understood. That question requires that a much broader range of texts be considered.

Admittedly, it is easy to lose track of what I am claiming is a core continuity in Heidegger's thought once he begins to focus on the history of Being
and his attention shifts to language with a corresponding shift in his own
language. (Although already, the very notion of a "history of being" has to
be read in a Heideggerian way. He certainly does not mean that reality, beings, changes in time. What has a history is the kind of availability of beings
"destined" by a horizon of possibility availability, the meaning of Being as
such.) The later works compress a great deal of Heidegger's basic approach,
and his references to beings and Being are often intensely elliptical. Consider briefly an example. Here are some passages from his 1958 essay *The
Principle of Reason*. "Seen in terms of being, this means that being lasts as
the withdrawing-proffering of the temporal play-space for the appearing
of what, in response to the *Geschick* and its bidding, is called 'beings.' . . .
For beings are always individually occurring beings and thus multifarious;
contrary to this, being is unique, the absolute singular in unconditioned
singularity" (POR, 84).

All we need to recall to avoid misunderstanding here is that Heidegger
has rejected understanding beings as mere objects standing over against a
subject as a derivative and misleading assumption, and his references to Being are not to a being. So "being lasts as the withdrawing-proffering" must
refer to an ultimate source of meaningfulness that emerges historically,
contingently, in a way that orients Dasein but cannot be determinately dis-
criminated. Or, simply said, it emerges at a time ("proffers") but elusively,
not as the subject of judgment ("withdraws"), and amounts to the temporal play-space, the horizon of possible sense, within which and in terms of
which beings in their significance (in tune with that overarching possible
significance) show up, become salient, "appear." This salience and so availability is possible only "in response to the *Geschick*"—an availability only in
terms of an orientability set by what has emerged as such a possible source
of meaningfulness. "Destined" in this sense functions like thrownness in
the phenomenological register. Any other reading makes a hash of all of
Heidegger's restrictions on what he could mean. And he is even clearer elsewhere that he has not abandoned the mutual implicability of the meaning of
Being and the meaningfulness of Dasein's being. "The *Geschick* of Being is
not only not a self-contained ongoing process, but it is also not something
lying over against us. Rather it is more likely that the *Geschick* itself is as the
conjunction being and human nature" (POR, 94).

Heidegger's 1929 *Kant and the Problem of Metaphysics* is still recognizably
from the BT period, but even from 1929 his approach in posing the problem
of German Idealism is set out more in terms of the Being problematic and

the history of philosophy as a whole, rather than in terms of the analytic of Dasein.[34] In the Kant book, he insists that

> Immediately prior to the integral interpretation of transcendence as "Care," the fundamental-ontological analytic of Dasein intentionally seeks to work out 'anxiety' as a "decisive basic disposition," in order in this way to give a concrete reference to the fact that the existential analytic was constantly guided by the question of the possibility of the understanding of Being from which it arises. It is not with the intention of [offering] some world-view-derived proclamation of a concrete ideal of existence that anxiety is supposed to be the decisive basic state of attunement. Rather, it derives its decisive character solely on the basis of the consideration of the problem of Being as such. (KPM, 166)

He is right about this. *Being and Time* itself does emphasize its "stalking horse" quality, a preliminary way to introduce the question of the meaning of Being problem (e.g., §5), although its incomplete nature (a Division One and Two, but not the planned third) can make that hard to see. In BP, he describes his version of the phenomenological reduction this way:

> Being is always being of beings and accordingly it becomes accessible at first only by starting with some being. Here the phenomenological vision which does the apprehending must indeed direct itself toward a being, but it has to do so in such a way that the being of this being is thereby brought out so that it may be possible to thematize it. Apprehension of being, ontological investigation, always turns, at first and necessarily, to some being; but then, in a precise way, it is led away from that being and led back to its being. We call this basic component of phenomenological method—the leading back or re-duction. (BP, 21)

The being we are led back to in BT is Dasein, and this can be confusing. For there is no other being like Dasein, whose own being is what Heidegger calls "existence," a being of pure possibility that flees its call to itself to interrogate the meaning of its being, until wrenched out of its daily thoughtlessness (if it ever is) by anxiety. At the end of the day, Dasein cannot articulate any such meaning because Dasein cannot bring itself into any stable view;

---

34. That 1929 lecture series (GI) begins (§4a) with a discussion of the "metaphysics of Dasein," but from §4b on, he wants to pose the issues in terms of "Die Seinsfrage als Grundfrage des eigentlichen Philosophierens," and then launches into a discussion of the finitude of thought in Fichte.

its radical temporality and ever impending death render that impossible.[35] But how, then, does the phenomenological reduction work, given that Dasein's condition is so distinctive that its being would not seem to open up any space for considering the being of history, of art, of nature, and especially of Being just as such? The incompleteness and uniqueness of this region of being is obvious.

Of course, the pioneering and extraordinarily influential work of Hubert Dreyfus and his many students has rightly noted the significance of the *Daseinsanalytic* and thrown being-in-the-world for opening up the question of the possible availability of Being as such as an original attunement to a kind of meaningfulness. In BT this is shown to be the case within, for example, an equipmental context, with beings salient because of a practical project, and with intentionality understood as much more than intentional consciousness of objects. Any disclosure of being, its original availability, is a matter of circumspective concern and so an appropriate comportment, and not as the object of mere perceptual attending. But as Heidegger keeps insisting, he means this as an initial illumination of a much larger point. The crisis of Western metaphysics is not the result of a forgetting of such equipmental contexts, and the existential crisis of Dasein, and its lostness, homelessness, and inauthenticity, must be understood within that larger context—that is, within the history of Being.[36]

And it is certainly true that it is Dasein's finitude that shows us how to begin thinking about our finitude with respect to the problem of Being. For Dasein is described as always already "thrown" into its world, inheriting a structure of significance, mattering, salience, and importance that forms a horizon of possible meaningfulness for any Dasein's self-interrogation. (As we shall see in the next chapter, everything depends on what Heidegger means in such claims by the notion of "world.") Crudely put, this contingent ground, contingent because no account of why there is one such inheritance rather than another is possible, has, in Heidegger's word, come to "prevail" (*walten*) and cannot itself be the object of any sense-making interrogation because it is presupposed by any mode of comportment or understanding at a time. Reflecting on it, "turning around" to grasp it, simply, as it were, brings it along

35. A problem that is addressed in BT by "being-towards-death," a way of being that is not a consciousness of or contemplation of one's death, but a way of being oriented from, attuned to, one's mortality.

36. Heidegger notes that his "sole intent," in taking his "departure from what lies to hand in the everyday realm, from those things that we use and pursue" was "to provide a preliminary characterization of the phenomenon of world " (GA 9: 155 n. 55/370 n. 59, GA 29/30: 262). And, "It never occurred to me, however, to try and claim or prove with this interpretation that the essence of man consists in the fact that he knows how to handle knives and forks or uses the tram" (GA 29/30: 263). Translation by McManus 2013, 248.

as, again, always already assumed.[37] So, however Dasein comes to understand itself, authentically or inauthentically, it reflects this dependence on a prior ground of possible meaningfulness. "Dasein is itself by virtue of its essential relation to Being in general. This is what the oft-repeated sentence in *Being and Time* means: the understanding of Being belongs to Dasein" (IM, 31).

The inseparable interconnection of topics—the meaning of Dasein's Being and the meaning of Being qua Being, available as the history of Being—is central to BT, but the incomplete and the preliminary character of that work (as well as the drama of the existential themes of anxiety, death and being "the null basis of a nullity") can make one lose sight of it. In §65, the meaning (*Sinn*) in question in the question of the meaning of Dasein's being is said to be the "'upon-which' [das *Woraufhin*] of a primary projection in terms of which something can be conceived in its possibility as that which it is" (371). The meaning of my laptop is what I understand when I understand it, and what I understand is knowing how to use it, to project its possibilities. But those are my possibilities (*my very own* possibilities in authenticity) and will involve the existential-temporal dimensions of care. I understand it, project its possibilities, in terms of my distinctive being-towards-the future, and ultimately in the way I am my being-towards-death. This path back to the question of authenticity is the path back linking the understanding of the meaningfulness of beings to my being at issue for myself, as Heidegger notes in the first paragraph of 372. But clearly those possibilities for the laptop for me—e.g., showing a PowerPoint as part of a lecture as a professor in a philosophy class—is itself only possible, only possibly something that makes sense, in a historical world at a time, a horizon of possible meaningfulness that "happens" and can be disclosed as an issue unto itself; or, in other words, as the issue of the meaningfulness of Being qua Being.[38]

37. Heidegger is well aware that this can all sound like a version of Jaspers's "world view" (*Weltanschauung*) philosophy, a kind of historical anthropology, and he works hard to disabuse the reader of any such notion. He believes that any such account must presuppose an account of human nature or human capacities that relies on the metaphysics of presence. See also: "Phenomenology is the investigation of life itself. Despite the appearance of a philosophy of life, it is really the opposite of a world view. A world view is an objectification and immobilizing at a certain point in the life of a culture. In contrast, phenomenology is never closed off, it is always provisional in its absolute immersion in life as such. In it no theories are in dispute, but only genuine insights versus the ungenuine." This is from Heidegger's 1919 *Kriegsnotsemester* seminar, "The Idea of Philosophy and the Problem of Worldviews," from Franz Joesef Brecht's transcript, distilled by Oskar Becker. Quoted in Kiesel 1995, 17.

38. I agree with Withy 2022 in her discussion of the "upon which" passages that Heidegger does not mean to "identify" being and "meaning" (78). Hammers and tables are surely not meanings. But that just seems to me to make Heidegger's point: that while there is no

So in the following, I will rely on some important continuity between Heidegger I and Heidegger II on the central question of the meaning of Being, that BT is misunderstood if it is not seen in the context of the problem of the consequences Heidegger constantly points to as the implication of the "forgetting"—nihilism, meaninglessness, thoughtlessness. It is true that Heidegger will eventually start talking simply about Being and the question of Being, without this journey through the analysis of Dasein, but there is no way he wants to turn the question into one about something substantive, with strange agentive powers. In my view, this is often what happens in some so-called Continental and theological approaches to the late Heidegger. So, one can read in commentaries formulations like this: "poeticizing is basically, as it were, a function of the malfunction of being. Being is both differentiated by the fourfold and in motion through presence."[39] Shorthand or elliptical expressions almost always confuse the issue in Heidegger. To say that Heidegger's view of history consists of various ways of "forgetting Being"[40] sounds far too much like abandoning God than what it refers to: forgetting the source of possible meaningfulness and so courting meaninglessness, or forgetting the worldliness of the world. Even expressions like "Dasein is dependent on Being" promote the same confusion.[41] That would be exactly the "errancy" he wants to avoid: conflation of the question of the meaning of Being with the question of the meaning of a being, or what we mean when we say that something exists. He continues to think of Dasein's world as the condition of our accessibility to beings other than ourselves; he treats the question of the worldhood of the world as the question of the possible meaningfulness of Being and so continues to hold that beings are accessible originally, in-a-world, in their meaningfulness for Dasein, in their

existential dependence of entities on Dasein and its attunement to meaningfulness, he is still insisting that even so, any sort of appeal to entities as such in this sense is empty. See Carman 2003 on how Heidegger might work out the difficulties this "ontic realism" raises. The situation is somewhat similar to Kant's claim that things-in-themselves are not in space and time. He does not mean they are "somewhere else," but that they are neither in space and time, not "not in space or time." The way Withy makes this point, though, leads her to claims like "What 'makes' something be a student essay is that cases of Dasein comport towards it in the light of that involvement, *taking* it to be an essay" [*sic*] (79). Perhaps I misunderstand the import of the scare quotes, but in Heidegger a sheaf of papers cannot become an essay by being *taken* to be one by Dasein.

39. White 1978, 156. Likewise, with such shorthand expressions, quite common in the literature, the question of being as "the question is what it is to be an entity" (Witherspoon 2002, 91) sends us off on a false trail. The question is "what does it mean to be," or "how is it that being is meaningful at all"—that is, how meaningful in the context of Dasein's world of interrelated significances. For a criticism of the "agentive" approach, see Sheehan 2015, 225.

40. McCumber 1999, 12.

41. This is not to say that Heidegger himself is not guilty of such misleading ellipses.

significance. The continuity of his emphasis on meaningfulness as the crux of the issue of Being's availability is the interpretation I want to defend in the next chapter, and if that is only roughly correct, formulations like those above, both in the BT interpreters and in the "mystery of Being" interpreters, are far removed from Heidegger's basic project. We can call this a resolute reading of Heidegger.[42] It extends throughout his career and I want to argue it is crucial for understanding his account of the limitations of German Idealism. (Put another way, we understand any being "projectively," in terms of its possibilities in a world in the context of Dasein's practical comportments. But it is, while not wrong, too elliptical to summarize his project by seeing Heidegger as noting "the truly remarkable and singular fact that sense is made of anything," and so proposing "to try and make sense of that."[43] The "sense" [*Sinn*] at issue is not discriminable intelligibility as such but always primordially a mode of mattering within a world that sets a horizon, serves as a possible source of mattering. The availability of beings is first of all a matter of their salience for a "concernful" Dasein. That is not a sense that we "make" but are attuned to.) This is not to say that he does not later express some reservations about the way he wants to pose the question of the meaning of Being by means of a preliminary "Dasein analytic," an interrogation of the meaning of Dasein's being for it. For example, in the 1940 Nietzsche lectures (*On European Nihilism*), he notes,

> In *Being and Time*, on the basis of the question of the truth of Being, no longer the question of the truth of beings, an attempt is made to determine the essence of man solely in terms of his relationship to Being. That essence was described in a firmly delineated sense as Da-sein. In spite of a simultaneous development of a more original concept of truth (since that was required by the matter at hand), the past thirteen years have not in the least succeeded in awakening even a preliminary understanding of the question that was posed. (N IV, 141)

He notes that this was partly the result of our habituation in modern modes of thought, such that it was inevitable that his attempt would be grouped together with philosophical anthropology or subjective idealism. But he also notes an internal difficulty, one that he now says was responsible for the incomplete nature of the book. "On the other hand, however; the reason for such noncomprehension lies in the attempt itself, which, perhaps

---

42. The interpreter who has made the strongest case for this continuity in Heidegger's thought in these terms (meaningfulness, *Bedeutsamkeit*) is Sheehan (2015).

43. Moore 2012, 472.

because it really is something historically organic and not anything 'contrived,' evolves from what has been heretofore; in struggling loose from it, it necessarily and continually refers back to the course of the past and even calls on it for assistance, in the effort to say something entirely different" (ibid.). When he explains why this occurred, he notes a danger in how the *Daseinsanalytic* was understood. "The reason for the disruption is that the attempt and the path it chose confront the danger of unwillingly becoming merely another entrenchment of subjectivity; that the attempt itself hinders the decisive steps; that is, hinders an adequate exposition of them in their essential execution. Every appeal to 'objectivism' and 'realism' remains 'subjectivism': the question concerning Being as such stands outside the subject-object relation" (N IV, 141–2).

I think that the point Heidegger is trying to make can be put this way. The major question is the question of the meaningful availability of being at all. Once that original availability is shown to be a matter of significance, such salience requires an account of the being open to such availability, Dasein. But Dasein is the being for whom its being is always at issue for itself, is not a standing subject or substance or nature, but rather "existence," to-be. The salience at issue is thus tied to Dasein's practical existence, the meaning of its being as "care." (Hence "Reality is referred back to the phenomenon of Care" BT, 255.) Only thereby do beings "show up" in their significance. But the meaning of Dasein's being can be at issue for itself either authentically or inauthentically and that bears on the way in which the question of this availability is possible. Hence the published fragment of BT. In Division One of BT, the possibility of any such nondiscursive availability is established by demonstrating phenomenologically that Dasein is Being-in-the-world, not a subject standing over against objects, and a being whose meaning is care. In Division Two, the possibility of Dasein's authentic existence as anticipatory resoluteness, and this mode of being as a matter of existential temporality is established. But as Heidegger begins to return to the question of the relation between the being open to the availability of meaningful being and the sources of such meaningfulness *for* Dasein, or Dasein's historicality, the book abruptly ends. In those closing chapters of Division Two, V and VI, he himself notes that thus far, his project is incomplete and one-sided, a comment on his book thus far that is rarely taken serious account of in commentaries on BT. What he says should "backshadow" *everything* so far: "Dasein has been our theme only in the way in which it exists 'facing forward,' as it were, leaving 'behind it' all that has been. Not only has Being-towards-the-beginning remained unnoticed; but so too, and above all, has the way in which Dasein stretches along between birth and death. The 'connectedness of life,' in which Dasein somehow maintains itself constantly, is precisely what we have overlooked in our analysis of Being-a-whole" (425).

What he means is explained further this way: "In the existential analysis we cannot, in principle, discuss what Dasein factically resolves in any particular case. Our investigation excludes even the existential projection of the factical possibilities of existence. Nevertheless, we must ask whence, in general, Dasein can draw those possibilities upon which it factically projects itself . . ." (BT, 434). Without the completion of his project in this way, it can seem that the meaningful availability of being "depends on" how Dasein as an individualized existence projects itself towards its future, and that is exactly what he is referring to in the Nietzsche lecture passage just cited. It will turn out that, rather, Dasein should be understood also to "depend on" sources of meaningfulness which it inherits rather than projects.[44]

So his later remarks on BT are hardly a rejection of the way the question of the meaning of Being was posed in BT. It is a claim that what he was trying to do was misunderstood, and as we shall see in the next chapter, in BT he originally takes even greater pains to avoid the misinterpretation, and he returns to the issue again and again in the '20s and '30s, in insisting that his approach has nothing to do with subjectivism, or subjective idealism, even as he continues to claim that being's manifestness requires a being *to whom* it is manifest, to whom it can mean something, and open to such manifesting in the way that such a being, Dasein, is. This is all not to deny that his emphasis after the war shifted from existential thrownness into a world to the problem of language. But the general theme of most relevance to the critique of German Idealism—*dependence*, and so the impossibility of Hegel's (and all of philosophy's) pure, autonomous thinking—is still quite apparent. In "Poetically Man Dwells," a 1951 lecture published in *Vorträge und Aufsätze*, we read, "Man acts as though he were the shaper and master of language, while in fact language remains the master of man" (PLT, 212).

Moreover, just as Dasein's own stake in the meaning of its own being is not theoretical, we have already seen that the enterprise of metaphysics itself, at least as Heidegger understands it—i.e., some way of illuminating the

---

44. He puts the point most clearly in HG: "It has indeed often been remarked that there cannot be an unconcealment in itself, that unconcealment is after all always unconcealment 'for someone.' It is thereby unavoidably 'subjectivized.' Nevertheless, must the human being- which is what is being thought here—necessarily be determined as subject? Does 'for human beings' already unconditionally mean: posited by human beings?" HG, 334. (Put another way, like Kant and Hegel, Heidegger does not agree that insisting that the meaning of being [or possible objects of knowledge] be considered in terms of the possible availability of being does not mean that any result in such an inquiry will yield "being only as it is available" not "as it really is.")

very availability and manifestness of the meaning of Being as such—is not primarily theoretical but requires an attunement (*Stimmung*) or orientation. So, such metaphysics must, Heidegger says, first of all get some "grip" (FCM, 7), felt or "awakened," as a practical need rather than taking up a topic or theme. This is another mark of our finitude, another denial of the autonomy of thinking, that there is no *direction* for thought to take without this precedence of practical mattering.

Admittedly, this approach creates a terminological problem for a resolute or continuity reading. There is no question that Heidegger, throughout his long career, continued to think that the problem of first philosophy (Aristotle's term), which the tradition inherited as the problem of metaphysics, is the problem of *the meaning of being qua being*, as Aristotle again puts it. Heidegger never wavers from this as *the* issue of philosophy, from his earliest speculations in 1918 until his death in 1976. That is what metaphysics *takes itself* to address. But, and here lies the source of the difficulty, what we have come to understand as metaphysics actually has never really addressed the question it poses for itself, aside from traces of an appreciation of the genuine issue in the pre-Socratics. Metaphysics has asked instead about the possible meaning of the "beings." He means the exploration of the conditions necessary for any being to be determinately what it is, distinguishable from any other being. The ancient answer to such a question was, of course, *form.* But, for reasons I go into in the following, that leaves unanswered, in all traditional metaphysics, the possible meaningfulness of Being qua Being itself (why such determinacy should count exclusively as the meaningfulness of being, its primordial significance). While in his early work, as we shall see, he was not hesitant to call for returning metaphysics to its original, fundamental question, the unthought issue, and so implies that if we succeed, we will finally have a proper metaphysics, after the mid-1930s he apparently became uncomfortable with invoking the notion of metaphysics altogether, seemingly convinced there was no effective way to pry it from its conventional meaning, or that metaphysics *as such* has never appreciated the ontological difference between these two questions.[45] He wanted a clear target for that aspect of the tradition he proposed to destroy and so named that target metaphysics as such.[46] He began to prefer various new designations for first philosophy, terms like, simply, "thinking," or

45. For example, in TB, he proposes to "cease all overcoming, and leave metaphysics to itself" (24).

46. The terminological complication is even more complex when we consider that a more recognizable concept of metaphysics is something like "a priori knowledge of substance." The *Sinn des Seins* formulation is already Heidegger's and can be said to stand for an unrealized metaphysics.

"poetic thinking," or even a "thanking" meditation—formulations we shall explore. But it is still the case that if one means by metaphysics addressing that question posed but never properly addressed, then one can distinguish a metaphysics as we have inherited it from a manner of thinking that *does* respect the ontological difference, and I will sometimes continue to refer to that as a "proper" metaphysics, a metaphysics of finitude, or even "post-metaphysical thought" when the original meaning of metaphysics is clearly meant.

Heidegger's own approach has afforded another point of contact with anglophone philosophical work—namely, pragmatism. If the general idea of the latter can be expressed by the claim that so-called philosophical problems can never be properly formulated or understood outside of practical contexts, that there must always be or always should be a practical point to any such question (as in, why would an answer to this question actually matter? What would the answer change? Is what it would change important?), then there is indeed a kindred spirit between the enterprises.[47]

Heidegger's assessment of German Idealism became more and more refined and central to his view about the fate of the history of philosophy in the 1940s and '50s. This is especially true of Heidegger's views on Hegel. His best assessment came in 1955, as a result of one of his private, invitation-only seminars on Hegel's *Logic*, later published as the essay "The Onto-Theological Constitution of Metaphysics" and included in *Identity and Difference*.

In the next chapter, I will set out what I take to be the core problem in all of Heidegger, the meaning of Being question (chap. 2)—the question he thinks metaphysics either misunderstood or ignored. In section 2, I will then turn in detail to his early assessment of Kant in the 1929 book and in his later work on Kant. This will allow us to proceed to section 3 and a consideration of the general position on idealism and finitude coming into view. Thus, in chapter 7, we will need to explore how he understood both the finitude of thinking's powers and the finitude of the object attended to, the misunderstanding of which is clearest in idealism and Hegel. This will allow us to summarize the outlines of the idealism at issue in German Ideal-

---

47. Okrent 1988 has provided one of the most compelling readings along these lines. See especially his chapter 5. Rorty 1989 and 1991 express a resolute agreement with Okrent. He agrees with Heidegger that if you start with Plato and think it all through, you will end up somehow with pragmatism, but he thinks that is not at all a bad thing. Pragmatism presupposes, but does not address, what matters in what we might achieve, and presupposes that either individual self-fashioning or the betterment of the general human condition matters. Rorty would protest that such a claim would have ignored Dewey's *A Common Faith* or the last chapter of his *Art as Experience*, but pursuing such an issue would take us far afield.

ism and especially in Kant and Hegel, the general nature of the idealism/ anti-idealism dynamic in post-Hegelian thought, and a demonstration that Heidegger himself thought of idealism in the way sketched here. We will then be able to consider Heidegger's full claim about Hegel as the culmination of philosophy (his interpretation of the *Phenomenology* and the *Logic*) (chap. 8), and we can then turn to Heidegger's proposal for a new beginning in philosophy, a "poetic" thinking (chap. 9).

2

What Is the Problem of the Meaning of Being?

Significance is that on the basis of which the world is disclosed as such. (BT, 182)

Bedeutsamkeit ist das, woraufhin Welt als solche erschlossen ist. (SZ, 143)

"Meaning" [*Sinn*] is thereby clearly delineated conceptually as that from which and on the grounds of which Being in general can become manifest and can come into truth. (N, I, 18)[1]

THE PROBLEM

The problem of "the meaning of Being" is the problem of the meaningfulness of beings—that is, beings in the way they matter. Their way of mattering is their original way of being available; they become salient in a familiarity permeated by degrees of significance; it is how beings originally show up for us in our experience. The source of that meaningfulness is the possibility of meaningfulness as such, the possible meaningfulness of Being as such. That possibility of meaningfulness question is not a transcendental possibility for Heidegger because it cannot be raised in strict distinction

---

1. See also BT: "But in significance [*Bedeutsamkeit*] itself, with which Dasein is always familiar, there hides [*birgt*] the ontological condition which makes it possible for the understanding Dasein as an interpreting Dasein [*das verstehende Dasein . . . als auslegende*] to disclose such things as 'significances': upon these in turn, is founded the being of words and language" (121, translation altered). On the invocation of "world" as the problem of the meaning of being, cf. "Let us provisionally define *world as those beings* which are in each case accessible and may be dealt with, accessible in such a way that dealing with such beings is possible or necessary for the kind of being pertaining to a particular being" (FCM, 196, my emphasis).

from the meaningfulness of beings. That is, this relation, between the general possibility of meaningfulness of Being at all, and the meaningfulness of entities, is not a matter of conceptual necessity but of what Heidegger calls "primordiality," and it is established in BT phenomenologically, not deductively. There is a profound difference between the two regimes of meaningfulness, what Heidegger calls the ontological difference. That any attunement to such possible meaningfulness has been lost, forgotten, or at best deeply obscured is how Heidegger wants to characterize our destitute time, a time of homelessness. The meaning of being has been reduced to the mere perceivable presence of beings, a kind of barely meaningful form of intelligibility.[2] In this chapter, I want to explain what I take Heidegger to mean.[3] That is, Heidegger clams that the dominant understanding of Being since antiquity has been standing presence: what is simply present or at hand there in the present and enduring through a sequence of presents. But he does not mean that this is the definition of what the word or the concept means. Such a notion is also available within a world in its significance, its meaningfulness. That meaning, and what originally discloses it, is that beings are available to us, usable by us, objects for us, material for our manipulation and control. Beings show up because their intelligibility has come to matter to us, and this in terms of their manipulability. Hence, the claim that Heidegger's question is "what it means to be" or "what it means to be a being" is far too elliptical and thus misleading. It sends us to questions of linguistic meaning or conceptual clarification, and Heidegger never tires of denying that this is his interest.[4] (There is certainly a Heideggerian sense of "what it means to be," but in his BT phase that amounts to "*what it means to me to be*, to exist," and this within a historical horizon of

2. "The essence of presence together with the difference between presence and what is present remains forgotten. The oblivion [forgetting] of being is oblivion [forgetting] to the difference between being and the being" (AS, 275). Heidegger does not distinguish his issues this way, but it would have helped had he also distinguished the question of the very possibility of availability at all (as, fundamentally, meaningfulness—a kind of meta-ontology), from the determinate horizon of all meaningful availability in an epoch (e.g., "idea," *ens creatum*, representation, etc.), from the variety of inflections of such a horizon in regional ontologies of the beings, *Seiende*.

3. To set it all out at once: this source of possible meaningfulness and so the meaning of Being as such is time, the "event" of epochal disclosure, and so available only in its historicity. I don't pretend that any of these terms are clear at this point (or that putting things this way is any part of conventional Heidegger interpretations), but it shall be the task of this book to defend the interpretation and explain the claims themselves. The most thorough staging of a confrontation between Heidegger and Hegel on the issue of temporality is De Boer 2000, and I shall be referring to her argument in the notes for other chapters.

4. BN1, 37, 53.

what it *could* mean to anyone at a time. In his later work his attention shifts somewhat from the former emphasis ("to me") to the latter ("what is and how are we open to a historical horizon?").

In his 1927 lecture course *The Basic Problems of Phenomenology*, Heidegger is unambiguous about what he considers *the* basic philosophical problem. "We assert now that being is the proper and sole theme of philosophy" (BPP, 11). Philosophy itself is said to be "the science of being" (BPP, 13). That Heidegger believes this is unambiguous. No philosopher has ever concentrated so intensely on one question for the entirety of his fifty-plus-year career. But the first question for any student of Heidegger is simply what this question concerns, which in the 1920s was said to address "the *meaning of Being*," the "*Sinn des Seins.*" Is the question of the meaning of Being even a question—that is, a question with some possible answer?

The issue is made more difficult because Heidegger is eager to qualify and to some extent marginalize the usual and much more familiar semantic ways of addressing the problem: the various senses of the word "is." (His word for such an approach is "logic," or a "logical understanding" of the meaning of Being via analysis of the copula.) Neither the "is of existence"[5] ("There are bears in those woods"), the "is of predication" ("The bears in those woods are black"), nor the "is of identity" ("That black bear is the one who ate my strawberries") is adequate as a path to such an issue.[6] They all presuppose the more fundamental meaning of Being qua Being; all already assume that bears, woods, and colors are available, and he means this to be understood as: in some meaningful way they "manifest as what they are."[7] Moreover, it is not just linguistic or semantic meaning that Heidegger excludes as his topic. That is why his issue is so hard to get a handle on. If the question is "the meaning of Being," it would seem natural to begin by appreciating that meaning is what we understand in attending to another's vocalizations, or that meaning is what we come to understand when someone's actions seem unintelligible to us until we learn what her ends are and her intentions to achieve it. Or meaning is understood in an intentionality context where it means determinate content, the meaning of something intended *as* something, such as consciousness being onto a determinate content. Then we say we understand the meaning of what she is saying or

5. Heidegger will certainly appeal to the various uses of the copula as a way of manifesting its inadequacy as the path to his question, and he will engage in detail with Kant's claim about existence and predication, but again with the same purpose.

6. Heidegger gives a lucid account of these distinctions and their inadequacy in EF, 30.

7. See Heidegger's discussion of "the board is black" and his development of several other senses of the copula in FCM, 326–333.

what she is doing, or we understand a determinate content of an intention.[8] It would therefore seem natural to understand the question as asking what someone means to say when he says something exists or declares the meaning of some action, declares it to be what it is, just *that* action, or that he is aware of that object as such-and-such. Because it is understood as such-and-such, it is meaningful, in the sense of intelligible. If we respond that Heidegger always considers such formulations are about "ontic" matters that leave the basic question unclarified, then we might think he wants to ask "what it means to be at all" in this semantic or intentional sense of meaning. But he tells us that such formulations assume the answer to the question he is trying to pose and so do not point to a way of addressing it. It assumes the question is about the criterion of existence, that something is present-at-hand or present, as he will say, or as in "a content as such" is present to consciousness.[9] Moreover, as we saw in the previous chapter, if Heidegger's lifelong claim is that forgetting the question of the meaning of being is a catastrophic event in the history of mankind, that it leads to nihilism and a predatory, self-destructive technical manipulation of the earth, then it is extremely hard to see how one could claim that this has come about because we do not have an adequate account of what we mean when we say that anything is. The forgetting of the meaning of being is "the age of complete *meaninglessness*."[10] So, any retrieval of the question must be a path towards a renewed meaningfulness of being. Accordingly, we must keep that in mind in any of Heidegger's formulations about the "problem of Being." That is what I meant by insisting on a "resolute" reading of all his work. But where do we begin?[11]

We can't begin with what is also often meant in philosophy by "the ques-

---

8. As in Crowell 2013. Crowell's illuminating study rightly raises the question of the relation of normativity of any sort of meaning—that it must always involve some sort of measure or success standard—and that can be a valuable perspective on the revolutionary theory of intentionality in BT, especially in Crowell's treatment. But given Heidegger's theory of contingency and thrownness, it is unclear whether meaningfulness can have a measure or standard, beyond something mattering at all or mattering somewhat or not at all. That is the essential mark of our finitude.

9. Again, this is not to say that such an issue, the possibility of intelligible content of intentional awareness, is not an important issue for the Heidegger of BT. But it is preliminary, a preparation for a move that involves a different register—the meaningfulness of being as such. See Crowell 2013, 9–30.

10. "The essence of modernity is fulfilled in the age of consummate meaninglessness" (N II, 178).

11. I do not mean to suggest that there are no other such readings. See Gelvin 1989, for example, 12ff. Often, however, such readings are oriented towards the "existentialist" reading of Heidegger ("the meaningfulness of my existence"), but Heidegger's ambition extends much further.

tion of being." His is not a question of ontological commitment, the question of *what* beings there are or what kinds of beings. (E.g., Is there a God? Are there minds? Are there possibilities?) And he does not ask: what makes it possible for beings to be the determinate beings they are? How can they be what they are and be differentiated from other beings? (E.g. what is it to be a mind? What is it to be a possibility?) He says his question is the *meaning of Being* and insists that this question is presupposed by all others. He does not even mean what must be true of anything at all: being itself, such that Aristotle's question—*ti esti?* What is it?—could be asked of any particular thing or kind. That is to ask the question in a way that takes its bearings from all the beings, *Seiende*, a point of orientation that also already assumes some unacknowledged answer to the meaningfulness of Being question.

What is common to Heidegger's early works—by which I mean the Marburg and Freiburg lectures, such as *The Basic Problems of Phenomenology* (1927) and *The Fundamental Concepts of Metaphysics* (1929/30), the 1929 lectures on German Idealism, the 1930 lectures on Hegel's *Phenomenology of Spirit*, and his publications from that period, like *Being and Time, Kant and the Problem of Metaphysics* (1929), and *The Question Concerning the Thing* (1935–1936, published in book form in 1962)—is his revolutionary revision of Husserlian phenomenology. This story is by now a familiar one in intellectual histories of the period. Husserl thought he had invented a method that would allow him to isolate the essential elements in any intentional attitude, any consciousness of an object being the attitude it was and any kind of content being the kind of content it was, and he thought he had developed the resources to account for the minimal conditions for the possibility of such intentional relations. Consciousness is always consciousness of something, and in any such intending in various modalities—perceiving a red block, hating a political leader, hoping for a win, loving a friend, imagining a future, believing a promise—we could distinguish a mental attitude, a mode of description, and the object (we can both love a friend, I under one description, you under another; we can both imagine Paris, you under one description, I with a particular image, but both intending Paris). This possibility, such intentionality, is prior (logically prior) to the distinct sort of theoretical spectatorship or sociological inquiry into objects undertaken by a science. The latter all presuppose the former, that consciousness *could* be onto objects in the first place. Husserl proposed a way of isolating this issue: a "phenomenological reduction" whereby the question of the existence of the intended object would be suspended (only its being for consciousness should be isolated) and a "transcendental reduction" wherein the "essences" of such stances and objects could then be found.

We need here only the main results of Heidegger's dissatisfactions. The most important is probably the most influential claim in *Being and Time*: Husserlian intentionality, and indeed all consciousness-based and representational models of intentionality, are all improperly formulated and misleading. The possibility of such intentionality should rather be understood as requiring "being in the world." A subject-conscious-of-a-distinct-object model should be replaced by an inseparable subject-object nexus, a subject always already transcended in a practical and unthematic relation to its objects. The relation is not one of spectatorship or simple perceptual awareness but "comportment" (*Verhalten*), an active engagement with the world, an involvement that is driven by how things have come to matter. *That* is how beings are primordially available to a subject. The claim is that beings are only accessible to Dasein, Heidegger's term for our openness to beings other than ourselves, "within a world," and for Dasein as the kind of being it is. What does he mean by "world"? "Let us provisionally define world as those beings which are in each case accessible and may be dealt with, accessible in such a way that dealing with such beings is possible or necessary for the kind of being pertaining to a particular being" (FCM, 196). And, "from this it follows that world properly means accessibility of beings as such. Yet this accessibility is grounded upon a manifestness of beings as such. Finally, it was revealed that this is not a manifestness of just any kind whatsoever, but rather manifestness of beings as such as a whole" (FCM, 284).

For Heidegger, world is not the totality of what there is, as in Kant, or all that is the case, as in Wittgenstein. World is a necessarily presupposed (i.e., primordial) condition for the possible availability or accessibility of beings within such a world in the first place, a horizon of possible sense or meaningfulness always within which and in terms of which beings are encountered. These are the consequences Heidegger draws from this claim. This notion of availability as deep familiarity implies a kind of immediacy in our original encounter with beings in the world, but not like the direct presence of intentional objects as in theories of a pure "given." Anything available in this familiarity is already embedded in, understood in terms of, its historical world. This means that such a being is not first encountered and then interpreted any more than a string of sounds is first heard as such and then interpreted as language. This implies a kind of immersion in the field of significances—what Heidegger, following the lead of Emil Lask in his early years, calls *Hingabe* or submission to the world, as well as in contexts he will describe as also permitting a possible reflexive attentiveness.[12]

12. See the account of Heidegger's "breakthrough" from Husserlian phenomenology to a "hermeneutics of facticity" by Kiesel 1995, 30ff, especially 49. Thus there is neither any pure givenness in this sort of attunement to significance, nor any linguistic or conceptual mediation. Dasein as Being-in-the-world avoids that issue altogether.

So, beings as such are accessible to, manifest to, Dasein *only* within-a-world. We have quite a useful contrasting example in Heidegger's treatment of animals in FCM. Animals have (in some sense of "have" that Heidegger is somewhat ambiguous about)[13] a world, even though they are "world poor."[14] That is, beings *are* "meaningfully" accessible, manifest; they show up for "comporting" animals. Beings are primordially available to animals too as significant, meaningful. The horizon of such a world of possible significance is though set by their species form. That provides something like a fixed context of relevance in which things are accessible *in their meaning* for the animal. They don't encounter or have access to mere objects, although there are plenty around. Many of them "mean nothing" for the animal (power lines, mining equipment, discarded clothing). What does mean something is what in its world is set by the life their species form requires: food, shelter, mates, prey, offspring, and so forth. But they cannot access prey or food *as such*. Their world has a minimal level of meaningfulness and a limited range of accessibility. (Heidegger says animals are "captivated" by their objects and driven by instinct, but the things that emerge as salient for them still do so because of the distinctive features of their world.) Our own comportment towards food, as such, for example, is not merely something to be eaten. We can wonder where it was grown, and if it is organic or not. We can maneuver around issues in food as food because that being can show up for us as such. He does not mean that in accomplishing our tasks, we are constantly reflecting on the beings we deal with. It is rather that *in* dealing with them "as such" a range of possibilities is implicitly available as practical possibilities when relevant, all without such explicit reflection, and not strictly set by our species requirements.

This has important implications for the whole question of what it means to understand other species, especially strange ones like bats. The main implication is that it is a mistake to consider that the right question in such reflection on understanding is "what is it like" to be a bat, as if the goal is somehow to inhabit imaginatively a bat consciousness or peer into it or successfully imagine it. For that matter, that would be a foolish way

13. "So in distinction from what we said earlier we must now say that it is precisely because the animal in its captivation has a relation to everything encountered within its disinhibiting ring that it precisely does not stand alongside man and precisely has no world. Yet this not-having of world does not force the animal alongside the stone—and does not do so in principle. For the instinctual capability of taken captivation, i.e., for being taken by whatever disinhibits the animal, is a way of being open for . . . , even if it has the character of not attending to. . . . The stone on the other hand does not even have this possibility" (FCM, 269).

14. Heidegger will later change his mind about this and decide that animals are actually "worldless."

to think about understanding another person, especially since that version of the problem ensures a skeptical answer.[15] But our understanding of animals is possible by means of our engagement with them and understanding them in such an engagement. I understand my dog's happiness in her playing and swimming, in how she goes about it, not by being able to look into her consciousness. This is not anthropocentric; I am under no illusions that we share what happiness is in her world and mine, but I understand her nonetheless to be happy in her way. The engagement is possible because we share a world with animals, with considerably more overlap with higher mammals, and with considerably less (but not an absence) with animals like bats. The sharing is evident in our engagement, and the engagement, our being attuned to their way of going on in a world, is what understanding consists in. Observing and understanding anything about bats would be impossible without already sharing with them the need for food and water, reproduction, care of the young, and the search for shelter.

To be sure, animals are "poor" in world, poor (compared to us) in what is meaningfully available to them, and we do tend to think of understanding them as a "transposition" (*sich versetzen*), but as Heidegger formulates that issue: "If we understand self-transposition into another being as a way of going along [*Mitgehen*] with this being, then it is obvious that the expression 'self-transposition' is still liable to be misunderstood in certain respects and indeed is quite inadequate with respect to the decisive aspect of the issue. The same is true of the term 'empathy' which suggests that we must first 'feel our way into' the other being in order to reach it. And this implies that we are 'outside' in the first place" (FCM, 203).

And so he claims, and it is another claim about priority:

Can we transpose ourselves into an animal? What is it that is actually in question here? Nothing other than this: whether or not we can succeed in going along with the animal in the way in which it sees and hears, the

15. "Can we as human beings transpose ourselves into another human being? We find ourselves in a different situation again compared to the first two questions. It is true that we seem to be confronting the same question as in the case of the animal. Indeed it appears much less questionable to us, indeed as not questionable at all, that in certain contexts and situations other human beings on average comport themselves to things exactly as we do ourselves; and furthermore, that a number of human beings not only have the same comportment toward the same things, but can also share one and the same comportment with one another, without this shared experience being fragmented in the process; it appears that it is possible, accordingly, to go along [*Mitgang*] with others in their access [*Zugang*] to things and in their dealings [*Umgang*] with those things. This is a fundamental feature of man's own immediate experience of existence" (FCM, 206).

way in which it seizes its prey or evades its predators, the way in which it builds its nest and so forth. For we do not question the fact that the being into which we wish to transpose ourselves does relate to other beings, that it has access to its prey and to its predators and deals with them accordingly. The question as to whether we can transpose ourselves into the animal assumes without question that in relation to the animal something like a going-along-with, a going along with it in its access to and in its dealings with its world is possible in the first place and does not represent an intrinsically nonsensical undertaking. (FCM, 203–4)

For us, "beings as such" means "as disclosed *to* Dasein," and that means *in* their significance, for a Dasein whose primordial mode of being is care (*Sorge*), a practical investment in the world, attuned to and sensitive to significance, importance, and mattering, all implicit in our comportments with beings, deeply familiar, and unthematic. Human animals also have a biological species form, but that does not determine the world for Dasein. In a very shorthand way, we can say that the background world for any possible accessibility and for their own individuation is a historical world—what Heidegger will call, using another term for openness, a clearing (*Lichtung*), not a species form. Our world is always also a specific historical world and a horizon of sense, not mere instinctual attentiveness.

Said a slightly different way: beings are manifest to Dasein *as Dasein is*, in its distinctness as a being. That distinctness is its "existence," its being as pure possibility and not as a substance or mind, and that mode of existence is practical, care (*Sorge*). Dasein is what it takes itself to be, within a world into which it is thrown, over which it has no power or influence. This means that primordial access to beings and to beings as a whole, being as such, is not originally cognitive, not the object of judgments, but requires instead what Heidegger calls a prior attunement, a *Stimmung*,[16] an orientation that stems from its primordially practical involvement, given the horizon of possible meaningfulness set by its world. Obviously, in a cognitive sense, we can know what an MRI machine is, or a molecule, a cavity, a poem. We can provide a list of identifying predicates, more or less. But since Heidegger claims we encounter anything we do always with greater or lesser degrees of involvement, it is that involvement within a world that allows meaningful access to the beings that show up in such a world. We normally do not just happen upon an MRI; we are being examined, or we are running the

16. Wellbery 2010 provides an indispensable account of the various uses of *Stimmung* in the German language, one that I have found especially valuable in understanding Heidegger's usage.

machine, repairing it, etc. Even if we are explaining it to someone, we "care" about so defining it in that context. We might say there are greater or lesser degrees of concern, ranging from whether it is yours or not yours, needed but unavailable, ugly, distasteful, irrelevant, in the way, too near, etc. This would be to say we can have various degrees of concern that various beings are available, something like varying ways of understanding the meaning of their being at all. The meaning of their being should be understood as the meaningfulness (*Bedeutsamkeit*) for Dasein of their being at all. Heidegger admits that this is a certain unique form of Idealism[17]. Things can be manifest only to a being open in its way to that manifestation, as that being is and matters. If there were no Dasein, there would be all the entities there now are, but none of them would mean anything.[18] The world is the condition of availability—what Heidegger often calls a ground for the possibility of what emerges as significant, salient for Dasein. The question of what accounts for things' existing at all is not Heidegger's question. This is clear in the opening passages of IM where Leibniz's question—"Why is there something rather than nothing?"—is quickly shown to be derivative, already relying on some answer to questions like "How do things stand with being?" or "What is the meaning of Being presupposed by any question like why do they exist at all?"

It is because of this reorientation (away from the putative primacy of mere sensory receptivity, or observation, or theoretical spectatorship) in how beings originally become available that Heidegger says so many of the other things he does. For example, that metaphysics itself is not to be understood as a conceptual clarification of the possibility of being, or that that element of its task is secondary and depends on something of existential significance. Recall again this passage, cited in the last chapter: "The concept is thus something like a determinative representation. The fundamental concepts of metaphysics and the concepts of philosophy, however, will evidently not be like this at all, if we recall that they themselves are anchored in our being gripped [*in einer Ergriffenheit gegründet*], in which we do not represent before us that which we conceptually comprehend, but maintain ourselves in a quite different comportment, one which is originarily and fundamentally different from any scientific kind" (FCM, 9).

Even in the much later (1951–1952) and highly speculative context of *What Is Called Thinking*, when Heidegger is trying to explain to his students the mysterious saying of Parmenides that it is "useful" or "needful" to say

---

17. In the sense in which "Aristotle was no less an idealist than Kant" (BT, 251).
18. See Carman's 2003 explanation of this "ontic realism."

and think being, his translation insists that the meaning of thinking, *noein*, in the passage is "taking to heart" (203).[19]

The task of metaphysics is said to be to "awaken" a fundamental attunement to the world (or to awaken us to the realization that we are always already attuned), to call to mind what might be disclosed to us in such a fundamental attunement: a way of being "onto," receptive to, what matters and the possibility of mattering that is not an issue of belief or consciousness but, as in the musical sense of being tuned, on the right wavelength, or appreciatively engaged in this field of what matters. If, say, the cleanliness of a room matters to one, one will have a belief that it is important, but it mattering in the first place is a matter of *finding* untidy rooms irritating or anxious-making, and feeling contented when the room is tidied.[20] These are not mere emotional reactions but how the beings in the world itself originally show up. At the philosophical level, this sense of "being gripped" is being intrigued not by conceptual paradoxes but by what Heidegger says, following Novalis, is the condition of all genuine philosophy: homesickness, an uncanniness at our dependence on a regime of mattering whose source is difficult to bring to light and understand, is always originally "hidden."[21] The ontologically significant states that disclose such meaningfulness as such are attunements like anxiety or boredom, where all such mattering in a sense *fails*, and so, in such a brutal contrast, the fundamentality (and contingency) of meaningfulness and manifestness as such is itself salient.[22] And Heidegger always insists that such a significance, such degrees of mattering,

19. "If we say that entities 'have meaning,' this signifies that they have become accessible in their Being; and this Being, as projected upon its 'upon-which,' is what 'really' 'has meaning' first of all. Entities 'have' meaning only because, as Being which has been disclosed beforehand, they become intelligible in the projection of that Being—that is to say, in terms of the 'upon-which' of that projection. The primary projection of the understanding of Being 'gives' the meaning" (BT, 369–70).

20. "Attunement and being attuned is in no way to be regarded as a knowledge of psychological states, but is rather a way of being borne out [*Hinausgetragenwerden*] into the specific manifestness of beings as a whole in each case, and that means into the manifestness of Dasein as such, as it finds itself disposed in each case in the midst of this whole" (FCM, 283).

21. This is the source of Heidegger's appeal to Heraclitus's famous Fragment 123 that is usually translated (not by Heidegger) as "nature loves to hide" (FCM, 27).

22. Heidegger leaves unclear what could count as an appropriately disclosing *Stimmung*, but he is clear that anxiety is not privileged. "But it is no less certain that the title of §40 (BT), which deals with anxiety, is worded as follows: 'The Basic Disposition of Anxiety as *an* Exemplary Disclosedness of Dasein.' We do not read that anxiety is *the* exemplary disclosedness of Dasein; nor it is being claimed that it is the only one" (MGI, 26). There are also explorations of Greek "astonishment," Hölderlin's "sacred grief," "wonder and terror," and other *Grundstimmungen*. See Haar 1992.

cannot be understood as a subject projecting onto otherwise meaningless entities. There are no two steps in such *Bedeutsamkeit*, or meaningfulness: an encounter with a mere object and then a subjective projection of value by an individual or community. There are not two steps because there is no such first step; Dasein is "always already" within the world of meaningfulness. It is the only way things show up for Dasein and bear on it. We can, however, take objects to be available in a way that conflicts with and covers up their actual availability. Scientism is like this. The insistence, thanks to the philosophical tradition, that things are manifest for Dasein primarily in their cognitive intelligibility is another distortion—that is, in their being rendered intelligible by "*logos*" (all of which is what is brought to that culmination in German Idealism in general and in Hegel's *Science of Logic* in particular). Everyday thoughtlessness is another (FCM, 275ff).

I should pause here to make a special point of emphasizing the direction of interpretation already suggested in the passages cited above and in many that will follow. When Heidegger insists that any question we might raise about any of the beings or any region of beings depends on, and is oriented already from, some originary implicit understanding of the meaning of Being, he does not mean a reliance on an implicit *view* of, or belief about, "what it means to be," where that is taken to raise the question of how we divide the world into those things that exist or could possibly exist and those that do not or could not, or whether we can have some sort of unfiltered access to the real. He is not proposing to exfoliate a preconceptual or, as he says, "pre-ontological" understanding of *this* division. He always says that would also itself presuppose an implied answer to the question he is most interested in asking: the meaning of Being in the sense sketched above, as meaningfulness, *Bedeutsamkeit*, and mattering as setting a horizon for what is originally available. Appreciating this fact will, as we shall see, completely alter many of the well-known construals of the problems that are taken to follow from Heidegger's question: skepticism, truth, idealism, intentionality. Heidegger is proposing to shift the main tasks of philosophy from the analysis of the concepts involved in knowledge claims, empirical experience, and moral claims to an interpretive enterprise, at the center of which are these notions of familiarity (*Vertrautheit*), meaningfulness (*Bedeutsamkeit*), and care (*Sorge*). As he tells us, a "fundamental ontology" is a "hermeneutics of facticity," and for all of the revisions in his language and approach, I don't believe he ever changed his views about the centrality or "fundamentality" of such a hermeneutics. Another reason it is important to keep this focus is that without it, it would be very hard to comprehend what Heidegger proposes as a "new way of thinking," the notion of poetic thinking already on partial view in BP. This means that there is something off-center in the numerous discussions of whether Heidegger is a realist or an idealist, or a deflationary realist, a robust realist, or a transcendental idealist, and so forth. It is almost irresistibly tempting to consider that the problem of Being is the problem of "the really real" and whether we have access to it or how, whether it "depends on us" for its sense or existence. But as I have begun to argue and will continue to argue throughout, the "problem of Being" for Heidegger is, in all his writings, the problem of the meaningfulness of Being, the correlation between meaningfulness and its availability through modalities of attunement. That is why the epistemological issue is not prominent in what follows. The manifestation of such significance, and the way in which that significance manifests itself, "happens" as a matter of mattering and is not a problem of idealism and realism. The right pathway is marked by the epigram cited at the beginning of this chapter.

Now it is easy to imagine, in the spirit of many of the things Heidegger says, an objection to this direction: that it "over-corrects" for the realism-idealism distortions and leaves us with a simple picture of a world in which some things matter and others don't, something close to the philosophical anthropology Heidegger fears he will be taken to have defended. But significance or meaningfulness as such (the problem of the meaning of Being) is a mode of the original availability of what is, not a psychological or social-normative issue.[23] And what is made available (the entities, *Seiende*) is *what is, in* their significance and so their availability, and Heidegger's way of posing the question is not meant to be leading us to anything like a determinate answer. How entities are available in their mattering is endlessly elusive, a disclosing and concealing we will have to discuss later at some length. Compare, for example, his remark in WT that "multiplicity of meanings is the element in which all thought must move in order to be strict thought. . . . Therefore, we must always seek out thinking and its burden of thought, in the element of its multiple meanings, else everything will remain closed to us" (71). And all of this is not to mention that Heidegger has no problem with an abstraction from such originary availability in the service of measurement, causal explanation, subatomic particle research, and so forth. "Whether such access to the real" is possible is not his question because it does not address the original availability of meaningful being, and if it is so taken, nihilism results.

As noted, my proposal for a resolute reading is that if we keep our eyes

23. It is true that normative issues are involved in the experience of a practical engagement model of intentionality. In any engaged project, Dasein is committed to the success conditions of such an enterprise, and this means Dasein has committed *itself* to a norm. But what the norm requires is not up to me to decide. That is "always already" a matter of the world into which one is thrown. Cf. Crowell 2013.

on the long continuity of this way of proposing the question in Heidegger's career, we will be better able to appreciate what he is trying to say about German Idealism, Kant, and Hegel. Heidegger's question is not about the content of the concept, Being, but rather about the meaningfulness of our engagements and comportings; or, in the philosophical register, about the possibility of such meaningfulness and its availability in our everyday dealings. (There can be a psychological question about whether what we think matters to us, as we might report it, is "what really matters to us," but that is not Heidegger's concern and does not involve the problem of realism.)[24]

"Manifesting," in the sense we have been using it, is to be understood as an emerging, as showing up, beings as "announcing themselves" (*sich melden*) or becoming salient. He means "to emerge out of concealment," appearing in their significance as such from a kind of background hiddenness (the hiddenness of insignificance), unconcealed by virtue of Dasein's engagements in the public world. This is why in his early work he claims that the most original and insightful understanding of Being was *phusis*, the Greek word often translated as nature. "*Phusis* is Being itself, by virtue of which beings first become and remain observable" (IM, 15).

> We shall now translate *phusis* more clearly and closer to the originally intended sense not so much by growth, but by the "self-forming prevailing of beings as a whole" [*sich selbst bildenen Walten des Seienden im Ganzen*]. (FCM, 25)

As Heidegger increasingly insists throughout the '30s, manifestness in this sense is an *event*, an *Ereignis*, the central topic of his *Beiträge*. For one thing, significance, *Bedeutsamkeit*, can wax and wane, emerge in a different way in a different historical world, so it must be an emerging event, not a standing state of affairs. Beings *come* into view given the world within which they are encountered, and in the light of Dasein's projects within that world. All of this even as he constantly concedes the enormous difficulty of somehow

---

24. This is not to say that there are not many passages in Heidegger that either seem to address such an issue (there are certainly many in which he rejects both characterizations as a way of addressing the problem) or offer up the language of realism and idealism in ways that suggest a possible view on the issue when it is posed in that way. This is clear from the illuminating and careful readings of Carman, Blattner, McManus, Rouse, Haugeland, Dreyfus, and many others (and in their various complex disagreements with each other), but my claim is that the Idealism Heidegger is interested in rejecting is "Hegel's culmination," that this has to do with the autonomy and self-grounding claims of rationality (as I will attempt to begin to show in the next chapter on Kant), and involves a far more radical rejection of the post-Platonic rationalist metaphysical and epistemological tradition than can emerge in such treatments.

getting into view that allows anything at all to come into view in its significance, as it matters. (More on this below.)

There are, of course, regions of such beings, which call for differentiated
modes of attentiveness and so different modes of accessibility and differentiated kinds of significance. There are tools, equipment, weapons, other
human beings, nature, art objects, cities, books, and so forth, but they are
all beings, and so all, despite their differences, assume an understanding of
beings as such and worldhood as such as the condition of their availability,
and so are all subject to a common interrogation of the possibility of such
significance. Beings don't have this familiar signification in isolation but
within a horizon of possible meaningfulness—that is, within the world.

The world is the condition for the possible accessibility of beings as such,
but the world can never become an object, a being, in the world. In that
sense it is not available in that way within the world. We want to know what
the worldhood of a world consists in such that anything that can be accessed
as a being depends on such a prior horizon, but we must reckon with this
element of our finitude. As he claims: "We can never look upon the phenomenon of world directly. It is true that even here we could extract some
content from a given interpretation of the phenomenon of world without
reference to its indicative character, and set it out in an objective definition
which could then be passed on. But this would deprive the interpretation of
all its reliable power, since whoever seeks to understand would not then be
heeding the directive that lies in every philosophical concept" (FCM, 298).

That is, the problem of worldhood of the world in effect *names the problem of the meaning of Being as such*. And so, likewise, as the condition for
such meaningfulness, its availability is as disclosed in some kind of opening
up or unconcealing event, not as the content of any judgment nor as empirically encounterable within the world. The combination of the world's centrality and relative cognitive unavailability is what produces what Heidegger
refers to as a kind of homesickness, an uncanniness at our being always
subject to such a world into which we are thrown, but which we cannot redeem, make sense of theoretically, or directly articulate. The source of how
things have come to matter collectively at a time is hidden but must be unconcealed. This is so even though, to repeat the most important point, such
worldhood is not a source we have any extra-worldly access to. Anyone for
whom anything matters knows that such mattering cannot be understood
as the result of any prior reflection on what ought to matter,[25] and if there is

25. It is, of course, possible that someone might think that she ought to be the sort of
a person to whom opera matters and then engage in a project of self-education, exposure,
and so forth, until finally she genuinely enjoys opera. But in that case, what was originally

some general horizon for the possibility of anything mattering at a time, any attempt to thematize it or render it the content of a judgment would always presuppose it and must be intra-worldly. In a way parallel to his notion of thrownness in BT, we always already find ourselves in a world, in a horizon of possible mattering, and this mark of our finitude should be reflected in metaphysics: "Rather, the understanding of Being, its projection and its rejection, happens in Dasein as such. 'Metaphysics' is the basic happening for the incursion into the being" (KPM, 170).

A fundamental attunement like boredom can allow a glimpse, a blink-of-an-eye (*Augenblick*) insight. "In this fundamental attitude, from which none of us may consider ourselves free, what is overlooked from the outset is that the fundamental character of existence, of human existing, lies in resolute disclosedness [*Entschlossenheit*]. Yet this resolute disclosedness is not some present at hand condition that I possess, but on the contrary is something which possesses me. However, this resolute disclosedness is what it is as such only and always as the moment of vision [*Augenblick*], as the moment of vision of genuine action" (FCM, 295). And as we shall explore a bit more later, art works can also serve, together with historical crises and fundamental attunements, as moments of such disclosure. "Poetry, creative literature, is nothing but the elementary emergence into words, the becoming-uncovered, of existence as being-in-the-world. For the others who before it were blind, the world first becomes visible by what is thus spoken" (BP, 171–172).

It is also the case that any such emergence, if it is to be disclosed, requires a responsiveness from Dasein, a kind of thinking Heidegger will call in IM a gathering, a focusing and development of possibilities, as when the Platonic philosophical world emerged and eventually the horizon of meaningfulness as *logos* (understood as *ratio*) prevailed. This is exactly the kind of disclosure, the emergence of a horizon of significance, that paradoxically obscures and even denies its own conditions for such a possible disclosure, assuming instead as original what is derivative or "founded," as Heidegger puts it. This would be the assumption that an access to beings as substances, continual subsistence through time, itself understood as a measurable sequence of nows wherein our responsiveness is modeled on sight (*eidos*), and the question of meaningfulness are either lost or treated as the result of reflection and projection (a move that ignores the conditions under which reflectiveness itself came to matter in such a primordial way). Here is how Heidegger describes what such a disclosure calls on us to do:

_____

important was not opera but being the kind of person who loves opera, and *that* sort of mattering was not originally the result of reflection.

What is originary and primary is, and constantly remains, the full undifferentiated manifold out of which, from time to time and in particular cases and discursive tendencies of the assertion, only one meaning or one predominant meaning is referred to. The originary yet unarticulated and unaccentuated multiplicity of what being already means in advance in each case becomes a particular meaning via limitation, whereby the whole multiplicity that is already inter alia understood is not eliminated, but precisely also posited. (FCM, 333)[26]

In the following, I will be relying heavily on this construal of Heidegger's project—that at its center is this concern with the availability of beings in their significance, that this is what he is after in asking for the meaning of Being: its meaningfulness. This means that when he mentions the "originary yet unarticulated and unaccentuated multiplicity of what being already means," he is not talking about the need for a criterion to clearly demarcate what exists from what doesn't exist. He notes frequently that there would certainly be entities without Dasein, and he repeats that Dasein's mode of being is care. Moreover, when he is discussing in FCM what he considers a "fundamental" attunement, boredom, he is describing what he calls a disclosive event, *disclosive of the meaning of Being,* and that can be manifest in boredom precisely because of the massive failure of any investment in, commitment to, or care about anything at all in the world. In what he calls "fundamental boredom," beings do not show up as what there are in any salience of significance but in what he calls a kind of "emptiness," "indifference," "being held in limbo," "being left in the lurch" (*Im-Stich-gelassen*), in being's "refusal" of our involvement. For example, "rather the 'it is boring for one'—this 'it is thus for one'—has in itself this character of manifesting how things stand concerning us. This attunement brings us ourselves into the possibility of an exceptional understanding. Attuning and being attuned have the intrinsic character of a making manifest, though this does not exhaust the essence of attunement" (FCM, 136). Given that the emphasis here on our primary access to the meaning of Being as such is an attunement, not any theoretical claim, and given this focus through boredom, it is clearly the

26. The enormous influence of Heidegger on his students in Marburg and the early Freiburg years with respect to this issue can be noted in this remark by one of them, Leo Strauss: "There no longer exists a direct access to the original meaning of philosophy, as quest for the true and final account of the whole. Once this state has been reached, the original meaning of philosophy is accessible only through recollection of what philosophy meant in the past, i.e., for all practical purposes, only through the reading of old books" (Strauss 1980, 157). For Heidegger the "books" at issue are simply even older than those prized by Strauss.

case that Heidegger is tracking how things "mean" to us ("how things stand concerning us") as a matter of mattering, a kind of mattering that could contingently collapse and thereby reveal itself.

Our initiation into any historical world is primarily an initiation into this regime of mattering. When we learn a language as children, not only do we learn intuitively the rules of grammar but we learn in a different way the pragmatics of the language: what point there would be in saying such a thing in such a context, what effect an expression might be expected to have, how aspects of rhetoric work, when it is better to say nothing. Language use is normative not only grammatically but in the matter of its proprieties. That is, we are implicitly attuned to proprieties, or meaningfulness and significances, in daily exchanges with others. (Being so attuned is not incompatible with disregarding or challenging such assumed norms. In fact, it is a necessary condition for doing so.) Likewise, when we learn a task, like cooking, we learn the normative proprieties of the art: what utensils are for, how best to use them, what makes for good seasoning, good time management, best techniques, *mis en place*, etc. We learn to understand the relation between eating and dining, and the place of food and cooking in the rituals of family and social life. In this and in many other domains, all the beings we encounter are encountered within a world in which public proprieties have come to prevail, and we are onto these not by having beliefs about them or as a result of explicit evaluations but through being in a world, coping with the other beings and other Dasein, in our *Verhalten,* as Heidegger keeps saying: comportment, a practical mode of access everywhere normative.

Moreover, the greatest possible contrast Heidegger wants to draw is between his approach and a way of dealing with beings that is common to modern science, capitalist consumerism and its reduction to exchange value, and everyday thoughtlessness, all of which involve what Dahlstrom has called "the logical prejudice,"[27] that only what is fit to be the content of an assertion can count as a being. The result is a kind of leveling of meaning to mere presence and a prioritizing in our involvement of only one dimension of care, efficient mutual satisfaction of interest.

Let us count up one by one the various meanings that we have interpreted by paraphrase. The "to be" said in the "is" signifies: "actually present," "constantly present at hand," "take place," "come from," "consist of," "stay," "belong," "succumb to," "stand for," "come about," "prevail," "have entered upon," "come forth." It is still difficult, and perhaps even impossible, because it goes against the essence of the matter, to extract

27. Dahlstrom 2011a.

a common meaning as a universal generic concept under which these modes of the "is" could be classified as species. However, a definite, unitary trait runs through all these meanings. It points our understanding of "to be" towards a definite horizon by which the understanding is fulfilled. The boundary drawn around the sense of "Being" stays within the sphere of presentness and presence [*Gegenwärtigkeit und Anwesenheit*], subsistence and substance [*Bestehen und Bestand*], staying and coming forth. (IM, 96)

The result in everyday life: "We board the tram, talk to other people, call the dog, look up at the stars, all in the same way—humans, vehicles, human beings, animals, heavenly bodies, everything in the same uniformity of what is present at hand" (FCM, 275).

Somewhat paradoxically, this event, what being has come to mean, "what is present at hand," is a complex denial of its meaningfulness, complex because it involves a forgetfulness of original availability and also because it requires a meaning bestowal (a subjective imposition), useful for us. Being as standing reserve, mere material for technological manipulation, or a kind of meaninglessness,[28] has emerged *as* its significance. And this prevails even while our experience in the world everywhere manifests saliences of significance that belie the dominant notion of being as present at hand subsistence and substance, constantly belie clock time in the daily experience of authentic temporalizing.[29]

This distinction is not altogether clear. It seems quite possible to consider the entities that Heidegger treats as the objects of "the theoretical attitude" in general not as meaningless entities just "there," standing before us, but objects of practical engagement and so interpretation with a significance tied to a particular sort of attunement to a kind of sense in the world. This is not to say that for some purposes, even Dasein itself "can and with some right and within certain limits be *taken* as present-at-hand" (BT, 82), but that too would be undertaken for some purpose and so within a world of such interconnected purposes. Science can certainly be understood like this—not as the abstraction of all practical concern but as a particular sort of practical comportment, as Rouse (1985) has argued quite compellingly. As Rouse has pointed out, Heidegger's own later critique of the technological worldview would seem to require this. Within such a world, now our world, entities are available because of a particular worldly attunement, which he

28. This meaninglessness is what Heidegger calls, with increasing frequency in the '30s, nihilism.

29. "Authentic temporalizing" is obviously a vast independent topic in Heidegger. The best account known to me is Blattner 1999.

calls manipulability or "disposability," asserting that even the scientific attitude itself could be considered an aspect of such worldliness.[30] However, Heidegger's main point is that the present-at-hand seems to be such that an engagement with mere substances and their properties is *treated* as if it *weren't* a worldly interpretation. We are engaged in a practical comportment that we take ourselves to be avoiding, to be aspiring to "the view from nowhere." This would be like saying that what has come to *matter* most in our late-modern world is a "*not* mattering" world-relation. When we realize the obvious, that such a claim still falls within the "meaning-mattering-as-availability" regime Heidegger has argued for, the incoherence of the position is clear, as well as its phenomenological falseness. That is, as a claim about mattering, as it understands itself, it has no phenomenological "attestation" or at least none that can claim "primordiality," and therefore is what Heidegger will later call "willful" and distorting if such a claim about primordiality is asserted. The paradox in all of this is that such a claim to primordiality can come to be *taken* as primordial, can emerge in a historical world as a distorting but nevertheless "factical" attunement. (This would be the same sort of initially paradoxical claim that in this world, Dasein's ownmost "being itself" emerges as *not* being itself, in its "subjection" [*Botmäßigkeit*] to the They *das Man* [BT, 164].)

So it is not science but a misunderstanding of science's enterprise that promotes a forgetfulness of our dependence on an original orientation from Being's meaningfulness.[31] A more existential approach to science[32] and empirical knowledge is denied out of worries about Idealism and a commitment to naturalism and realism. So, the distortion is real, even if it is also a misunderstanding and a "misattunement." And a distortion blocks an appreciation of genuine availability, especially when the claim about fundamentality is made.

I should also signal here that, especially with respect to Hegel, we will have to revisit the issue of a logical prejudice and examine whether Hegel is guilty of it. After all, Hegel relies in the *Phenomenology* on such nondiscursive moments of "disclosure" as the struggle for recognition, which is certainly not an exchange of judgmental claims. The fact that for both, at least from a relatively high altitude, the distinctiveness of a human life emerges

30. This is clearly the case in QCT, 27, v 32.

31. See McManus's discussion in chapter 6 (2012), especially his compilation of relevant passages in Heidegger (138).

32. In seeking the ontological genesis of the theoretical attitude, we are asking which of those conditions implied in Dasein's state of Being are existentially necessary for the possibility of Dasein's existing in the way of scientific research. This formulation of the question is aimed at an existential conception of science (BT, 4087).

in a confrontation with and response to one's own death is another point of deep similarity, another nondiscursive form of disclosure.[33] The experience of forgiveness in the morality chapter (which "concludes" that struggle) and the disclosive role of religious experience, prior to its transformation into theology, and the appeals to literary moments like Diderot's *Rameau's Nephew* as in some sense "disclosive," are further points of contact. For Hegel, moments like this are, however, incomplete, subject to the kind of abuse he worries about with appeals to conscience (one man's disclosure is another man's delusion), and he relies on no such experiential base in the SL. But at this point it is an open issue.[34]

MANIFESTING AS SUCH

My hope is that with this fairly high-altitude sketch of Heidegger's basic approach in view, we can now proceed to try to deepen our understanding of various elements of it. For example, he writes,

> We said that world is the manifestness [*Offenbarkeit*] of beings as such as a whole. And we have already pointed out that something enigmatic emerges from such a characterization: namely this "as such," beings as such, something as something, "a as b." It is this quite elementary "as" which—and we can put it quite simply—is refused to the animal. . . . Perhaps it is superfluous to point out that this "as" is also essential in Latin—the qua of *ens qua ens*—and especially in Greek—the ᾗ of ὄν ᾗ ὄν. (FCM, 287)

This passage confirms our emphasis on the problem of the worldhood of the world as the meaning of Being problematic, and it is important to note that according to Heidegger it is also possible for *a being* to be manifest as such, as what it is, as well as "beings as such as a whole." But the general larger significance of the latter, of "*manifestness of beings as such as a whole*" as a formulation of the basic question, is signaled by his telling us that he wants thereby to understand the ancient problem of *being qua being* (their version of the basic problem) in *this* sense of manifestness. (That is, in a special sense. Elsewhere, Heidegger will want to distinguish what he here calls manifestness as the mode of "ontical truth," the manifestness of

---

33. This is noted by Taminiaux 1991, xvi.

34. In MGI, when Heidegger is trying to explain Schelling's notion of the will and focuses on the inherent striving of the understanding, he seems aware of this other dimension in Hegel. He quotes Schelling favorably, "the understanding [is] properly the will in the will," and glosses it, remarkably, as "(Reason! Kant, Hegel, but the will of love)" (69).

beings as the beings they are, from disclosedness of Being, or ontological truth. See EG, 103.)[35] What is that sense? We know from BT that the way in which the question of the meaning of Being as such gets any kind of grip on Dasein is not as the result of judgmental claims. The manifestness of beings as such as a whole cannot be understood as the content of any "as such" judgment. That is the "apophantical as" (BT §44, 266–267) and cannot be original because it depends on a prior "hermeneutical as." The way in which the problem of being as such shows up for us is what we are trying *to point to*, as Heidegger sometimes puts it, by discursive means, but the meaning should not be thought of in terms of discursivity—again, the cardinal sin of the metaphysical tradition, culminating in Kant and Hegel.

There is a natural, intuitively plausible way of construing how we are to think of this distinctive power or capacity human animals have—the capacity to attend to a reason or an ocean or any being *as such, as* what it is, not just unreflectively dealing with it *being* what it is. We do have this capacity to attend to any singular being or kind of being as such, according to Heidegger, but it is derivative. Any such reflection assumes something: that the beings in question are already "manifest," or meaningfully accessible. They have shown up, appeared, are now available. If we ask: How do we explain this? What makes this manifestness possible? What does it mean? Is there anything more to say than just that there are beings that may be interacted with, perceived, used, wondered at, thought about, explained? Heidegger insists there must be, because this is just to say *that* they are manifest; it is not to ask about manifestness as such.[36]

35. "Unveiledness of being first makes possible the manifestness of Being" (EG, 103) (Enthülltheit des Seins ermöglicht erst Offenbarkeit von Seienden [GA 9, 151]).

36. None of this implies that there are not ontologically acceptable contexts appropriate for the apophantical "as such." For example, one way to draw a line between the working of reason in the sensory capacities of human animals and those of nonhuman animals is presented by John McDowell in his 2009 essay "Cognitive Capacities in Perception."

> That wording ["responsiveness to reasons as such"] leaves room for responsiveness to reasons, though not to reasons as such, on the other side of the division drawn by this notion of rationality between rational animals and animals that are not rational. Animals of many kinds are capable of, for instance, fleeing. And fleeing is a response to something that is in an obvious sense a reason for it: danger, or at least what is taken to be danger. If we describe a bit of behavior as fleeing, we represent the behavior as intelligible in the light of a reason for it. But fleeing is not in general responding to a reason as such. (128)

McDowell goes on to say that this "as such" is what allows human animals to "step back" sometimes when they see danger approaching and reflect on whether that danger is a sufficient reason to flee or not. Cf. Heidegger in his *Fundamental Concepts of Metaphysics* lectures: "The lizard basks in the sun. At least this is how we describe what it is doing, although

But however natural, for Heidegger we would be "erring," as he puts it, if we thought of this rendering explicit as fundamental, and the error is the most important and consequential one in the history of philosophy. It would be the same error to think that what we should do to address the basic question is to see what everything that is has in common just by being. Such an attending would already presuppose an answer to the question in hand; Being's original availability would not be able to provide it.

Heidegger certainly realizes that his basic question seems to invite us to treat such manifestness as itself another fact about something in such a world, and so "of" or "in" that world; say *that it (whatever it is) is,* not what it is as such, or what manifestness as such amounts to, but that it simply exists and can be interacted with. There is such a distinction that's important to Heidegger ("that-being" versus "what-being") but not in quite this sense. A clearer sense of the question he wants to attend to is *how* the being may be said to be at all, to be manifest—that is, closer to what he is after. For example,

> Every being has a way-of-being. The question is whether this way-of-being has the same character in every being—as ancient ontology believed and subsequent periods have basically had to maintain even down to the present—or whether individual ways-of-being are mutually distinct. Which are the basic ways of being? Is there a multiplicity? [And then the question Heidegger means to ask as far and away the most important.] How is the variety of ways-of-being *possible* and how is it at all intelligible, *given the meaning of Being*? (BP, 18, my emphasis)

So, we begin with a difference between the beings, there being beings around, their being available for perception or use, and their assumed (prior, "already") manifestness as such, not just manifest as such a distinct being. *Is* this a distinction? Again: is not something just *being what it is* the same thing as it being manifest, available? The contrary assumption must be that something can be as it distinctly is but not be appropriately available or manifest to the one being for whom beings can be available as such: the human being. If it is, then that availability must be explained as to its possibility; it is a distinct question, and, according to Heidegger throughout his career, rarely recognized as such in the history of metaphysics. It has been forgotten. Availability, understood as emerging into view, into manifestness, must be distinguished here from what Heidegger calls, in his critique

---

it is doubtful whether it really comports itself in the same way as we do when we lie out in the sun, i.e., whether the sun is accessible to it as sun, whether the lizard is capable of experiencing the rock as rock. Yet the lizard's relation to the sun and to warmth is different from that of the warm stone simply lying present at hand in the sun" (FCM, 197).

of Aristotle's *ousia* or substance, "*Verfügbarkeit*," or "disposability"—what is just there before us, *Vorhanden*, present-at-hand, to-be-disposed-of (or not) by us. There is a deeper sense of availability than that assumed by such a notion of disposability, presence, and obscured by that "errant" construal (BP, 109). This is one of the continuous themes in the history of metaphysics according to Heidegger, and he even attributes this construal of being as disposability to Plato because Plato names the source of the "light" by virtue of which things are manifest as ideas as itself an idea—the idea of the Good. Heidegger interprets that to be a confusion of the present-at-hand with presencing (as we shall see, another term for emerging, showing up) and an interpretation of such a source idea, "the good," as "good *for us*" in the sense of "usefulness," material for use, disposable. As in the Nietzsche lectures: "Through Plato's interpretation of idea as *agathon*, Being comes to be what makes a being fit to be a being. Being is shown in the character of making-possible and conditioning. Here the decisive step for all metaphysics is taken, through which the a priori character of Being at the same time receives the distinction of being a condition" (N, IV, 169).

This characterization is consistent with a different interpretation of the Good: that Plato means to signal that the cosmos is receptive to our attempts to know it, and so we can live well in the light of such knowledge—good to us, not for us in Heidegger's sense—but he doesn't pursue such a reading. He rather makes the same point about "disposability for our production" in several figures—in Kant, for example. Using Kant's *Lectures on Metaphysics* (a questionable source for Kant's own ideas), he says, "The primary and direct reference to the being of a being lies in the production of it. And this implies that being of a being means nothing but producedness [*Hergestelltheit*]" (BPP, 150).

To reiterate the point made earlier: beings are available for animals, for example, but not as such, only in a way strictly circumscribed by their determinate being—within "a fox world" or "a bird world," for example. That is why animals are "world poor." Only a very restricted range of beings "show up," are salient or manifest, and certainly not "as such"; even less does "manifestness as such," or beings as a whole emerge. Further, something can be what it is—an unrealized possibility, an essence just considered as such—without existing, and perhaps in this sense not being manifest. But this way of thinking would again just treat such manifestness (as existing in matter of fact) as another fact, and a fact must also be already manifest to be available as what *it* is. The question of manifestness is just pushed back. As we move deeper into Heidegger's domain, we will see that there is also some distinctive experiential attentiveness to "manifestness as such" (let us use this phrase for a while), without that attentiveness being propositional, predicative, or even linguistic. What would that be? We should note again that such attentiveness would not be to *the being as such*—an ocean *as an ocean*, say, or a book as what it is: a book. While this is certainly possible, Heidegger always treats this as what he calls an "ontic" and derivative concern. The attentiveness is supposedly to something else, manifestedness of the being as such, as being. The point of the attentiveness is that in the everyday and, for Heidegger, in all of Western philosophy, we do not know what we mean when we simply note that something, whatever it is, is manifest as what it actually is, endures, or is still alive or occupies space—or, to broach a large topic for him, "happens" to be.

And, in line with the thought that the "as such" in "manifestness as such" need not be explicitly attended to in order to be a feature of our experience of the world, he writes:

> Being is projected upon something from which it becomes understandable, but in an unobjective way. It is understood as yet preconceptually, without a logos; we therefore call it the pre-ontological understanding of being. Pre-ontological understanding of being is a kind of understanding of being. It coincides so little with the ontical experience of beings that ontical experience necessarily presupposes a pre-ontological understanding of being as an essential condition. The experience of beings does not have any explicit ontology as a constituent, but, on the other hand, the understanding of being in general in the pre-conceptual sense is certainly the condition of possibility that being should be objectified, thematized at all. It is in the objectification of being as such that the basic act constitutive of ontology as a science is performed. (BPP, 281)

So again, he means that a being's being manifest as what it is forces the question: What is manifestness as such? How is it possible? We have now added the idea that there is some sort of experiential attentiveness to such manifestness and that this attentiveness is "preconceptual," and that will form one of the most important points of contrast with the German Idealists.

ALTERNATE FORMULATIONS

Some of Heidegger's other formulations may help. One comes from a slightly later period, even after what is supposed to be a decisive turn away from phenomenology (to "thinking") marked by the 1930 lecture in Marburg and Freiburg, "On the Essence of Truth." It is not quite decisive since he is still employing what seems a phenomenological approach in the Nietzsche lectures of the 1930s and 1940s.

> For anyone who at the end of Western philosophy can and must still question philosophically, the decisive question is no longer merely "What basic character do beings manifest?" or "How may the Being of beings be characterized?" but "What is this 'Being' itself?" The decisive question is that of "the meaning of Being" [*Es ist die Frage nach dem Sinn des Seins*], not merely that of the Being of beings. "Meaning" [*Sinn*] is thereby clearly delineated conceptually as that from which and on the grounds of which Being in general can become manifest as such and can come into truth. (N I, 18)

This echoes the language of *Being and Time*. "Basically all ontology . . . remains blind and perverted from its ownmost aim, if it has not already first clarified the meaning of Being and conceived this clarification as its fundamental task" (BT, 31).

So the question is not what some being is, or what it is as such, but what it "means" for it to be at all. By "meaning" here he does not mean linguistic meaning (he says that all linguistic meaning is founded on ontological meaning), and he does not mean meaning in the sense of purposiveness, as in "what is the meaning of his defection?" or "what is the meaning of life?" At a minimum he means that "manifestness as such" can be "understood" in the prediscursive sense suggested above, or we can understandingly, meaningfully comport with, deal in some way with, such manifestness, or, as he will say in this period, be "attuned" (*gestimmt*) to it, be onto it in such a nondiscursive but differentiated, open way. Manifestness, here understood as meaningfulness, can be as such manifest and in some way understood intelligibly as such.[37] This emphasis on meaning is the basis for Heidegger's argument against transcendental phenomenology and his case for a new "hermeneutical phenomenology." As he puts it in BT: "Our investigation itself will show that the meaning of phenomenological description as a method lies in interpretation. The *logos* of the phenomenology of Dasein has the character of a *hermeneuein* through which the authentic meaning of Being,

37. In the language of *Being and Time*: "But in significance [*Bedeutsamkeit*] itself, with which Dasein is always familiar, there lurks the ontological condition which makes it possible for Dasein, as something which understands and interprets, to disclose such things as 'significances' [*Bedeutungen*]; upon these in turn is founded the Being of words and language" (BT, 121).

and also those basic structures of Being which Dasein itself possesses, are made known to Dasein's understanding of Being. The phenomenology of Dasein is a hermeneutic in the primordial signification of this word, where it designates this business of interpreting" (37).

Here Heidegger clearly means to refer to our deep, unthematic familiarity with everything around us that matters (*that* sort of "intelligibility," its making sense, always already interpreted in order to matter), so unthematic and deeply assumed that we rarely take note of it. Hearing a worrisome noise in my car, listening to a lecture, boiling an egg, trying to explain long division to my son, gazing at the stars, bidding on a job, hearing a voice calling my name, perceiving a train going by, being in pain, looking for a book—all these forms of comportment with and within the lived world are familiar encounters, meaningful in this sense, or if not, then they also make sense as unfamiliar within some frame of possible future inquiry. They are all manifest within the world of our concerns, and we can, in various contexts ranging, as we shall see, from anxiety to boredom to art works, be directed to an attentiveness to manifestness as such, not the manifestness of some region of being or singular entity but the manifestness, the meaningfulness of anything at all, of beings as a whole. This means both that the very condition of manifestness as such can be available, as well as what makes such manifestness determinately what it is in some epoch.[38] It is *because* of our prediscursive understanding of what it is to be manifest that everything is so familiar, that all appears within a world. (Of course, we need working sensory and neurological systems for any such manifestness to be possible, but the entities in the world are not originally experienced as, are not familiar as, mere sensory objects. That requires a serious abstraction from intra-worldly significance.) This can still seem like a relatively vacuous reformulation of the fact that all the things that are are "available to us" as the beings they are (how could it be otherwise? It seems just to amount to *what it is* to say that the entities *are*), except for two aspects of this way of framing the question. First our pre-discursive, pre-ontological sense of such manifestness as such, meaningfulness as such, must also be understood as also a kind of absence of sense—at least determinate, assertible sense. (This introduces one of the most significant and constant ideas in Heidegger: that any *unconcealment* is always at the same time a *concealing*, and much more will need to be said about this since it is a major component

38. The short answer for the former is "time"; the latter, in the various historical epochs that Heidegger attends to, ranges over "idea," "*ens creatum*," "representation," logos, and material for technological manipulation

of his later understanding of finitude). Second, whatever manifestness as such amounts to, it changes historically, and so the terms, as it were, of our familiarity change as well.

Another term: Heidegger will often also note that being should be considered a "presencing" (*Anwesende*) of being (BP, 307), not something present at hand. By making this distinction, he means that any being present to us (which Heidegger thinks we usually and thoughtlessly attend to as merely present-at-hand, *vorhanden*)[39] is so only as a *result*, as derivative of and founded on, this presencing, *coming* to presence, or originally manifesting or appearing, or showing up meaningfully. As just noted, he will soon complicate matters enormously when he also insists that any such presencing, or manifesting, is also a concealing, an absenting, but for now the distinction between merely being present and presencing (on which such being present is said to depend) is what he wants. He is fully aware that the distinction he is insisting on is elusive. "The ambiguity of the *on* (Being) designates both what is present as well as presence itself" (HBE, 162). He is no less clear on the importance of the elusive distinction. "If we think of the nature of metaphysics in terms of the emergence of the duality of what is present and its presence out of the self-concealing ambiguity of the *on* (and it will henceforth be necessary to think of it in this way), then the beginnings of metaphysics coincide with the beginnings of Western thought" (HCE, 107).[40]

Although Heidegger is not always consistent about "the" beginning of Western metaphysics, this summary remark from the Nietzsche lectures is fairly typical.

> According to the meaning of the matter under consideration, the name metaphysics means nothing other than knowledge of the Being of beings, which is distinguished by apriority and which is conceived by Plato as idea. Therefore, meta-physics begins with Plato's interpretation of Being as idea. For all subsequent times, it shapes the essence of Western philosophy, whose history, from Plato to Nietzsche, is the history

---

39. "Being, being-actual, or existing, in the traditional sense, means presence-at-hand" (BPP, 109).

40. Exactly what Heidegger wants to say here is elusive since the very beginnings of Western thought, the pre-Socratics, do not coincide with the beginning of metaphysics, which he attributes to Plato and Aristotle and which he wants to overcome. This sensitivity to "presencing" as something very much not itself "present" would indicate that he means the pre-Socratics. He seems to mean that when the question of what makes possible or allows a being to be manifest, present, prevailing, is "idea," or when beingness is understood as *ousia*, then metaphysics is born. But he could also mean, and often seems to mean (for example, in WM), a sense of "metaphysics" as it should have been and now can be.

of metaphysics. And because metaphysics begins with the interpretation of Being as "idea," and because that interpretation sets the standard, all philosophy since Plato is "idealism" in the strict sense of the word: Being is sought in the idea, in the idea-like and the ideal. With respect to the founder of metaphysics we can therefore say that all Western philosophy is Platonism. Metaphysics, idealism, and Platonism mean essentially the same thing. (N2, 165)

I think we should interpret "idea" here as a more general term than what is named in Plato as the "theory of ideas," the account of "most real" entities, immaterial objects, but should see the reference as pertaining to the founding metaphysical assumption noted in the previous chapter: the meaning of Being is to be intelligible, knowable, and subject to a logos. This is the way that Heidegger reads Plato's commitment to ideas—a level of generality that makes virtually all rationalist philosophy afterward post-Platonic.

In both his 1929 *The Fundamental Concepts of Metaphysics* lectures and his 1935 *Introduction to Metaphysics*, he adds another participle to make his point. In both lectures he is making the case for one of his unusual translations, in this case for the Greek words *phusis* and *phuein* not as nature or growth but as *being* and the verb not as *growing* but as what he calls prevailing (*walten*). The first quotation we have seen before: "We shall now translate *phusis* more clearly and closer to the originally intended sense not so much by growth, but by the 'self-forming prevailing of beings as a whole' [*sich selbst bildenen Walten des Seienden im Ganzen*]" (FCM, 25). And, "*Phusis* means this whole prevailing that prevails through man himself, a prevailing that he does not have power over, but which precisely prevails through and around him—him, man, who has always already spoken out about this" (FCM, 26).

The same language, with more twists and qualifications, occurs in his *Introduction to Metaphysics*. He tells us first that "*phusis* is Being itself, by virtue of which beings first become and remain observable" (IM, 15). The structure of the problematic is unusually clear here. There are beings, and this alone supposedly raises the question of what makes possible their manifesting themselves, their availability, their prevailing. He does not mean "what makes possible their having come into existence?"—as if a causal question (that would assume some sense of what it is for something to have come to be available), and he does not mean "how is it that they are determinately what they are?"—a question that might be answered by "their form" or "their essence." He also does not mean something epistemological: how is it possible to *know* such beings, to make truth claims about them? He is quite explicit that that is not the fundamental mode of availability. He means how is it that they are *available* as *beings* at all, that they are encounterable, and in some way meaningfully? (To anyone trained in philosophy, it will seem inevitable that the only possible answer to such a question must have to do with our concepts, our ability to distinguish properties and substances, our having come to learn what a thing is called. All of Heidegger's efforts from start to finish involve trying to undermine this bias, and it is this errancy that culminates in Kant, German Idealism, and Hegel in particular.) When we put it this way, we can say that Heidegger's question does not make any sense except as asking also about the being for whom things are so familiar. There is no question of meaningful familiarity as such except for Dasein, the only being for whom its being and Being itself is at issue. Without Dasein, then, there are beings, and there would be a number of facts that would be true of such beings—what exists, what kinds exist, what might exist but does not—but there would be no Being qua Being, manifestness as such, Heidegger's version of the sense any available being originally makes. The question of the meaning of Being, the core question of metaphysics, is always as much a question about Dasein as it is about entities. Heidegger's question is not "what is there?" but "what allows" beings to be manifest? *We* encounter the beings, always assuming they are encounterable—that they are something, not nothing. The beings are encounterable for us; that is the assumption. What is that assumption? Later he will say, "Being means that which, as it were [*gleichsam*], 'makes' this a being instead of nonbeing, that which makes up the Being in the being, if it is a being" (IM, 33). In BT, he put the point this way: Being is "that which determines entities as entities, that on the basis of which entities are already understood" (BT, 25–26). And in IM he says with his usual flourishes, "Now what does the word phusis say? It says what emerges from itself (for example, the emergence, the blossoming, of a rose), the unfolding that opens itself up, the coming-into-appearance in such unfolding, and holding itself and persisting in appearance—in short, the emerging-abiding sway [*Walten*, prevailing]" (IM, 15).

This sense of *prevail* in ordinary use would be familiar in contexts like "justice finally prevailed" or "a tone of anger prevailed in the discussion." Here, the sense being intimated is more like *abiding*: an abiding presencing, something like a holding forth, a primordial enduring familiarity, tied up with Dasein's attunement, Dasein's pre-discursive sense of what matters.[41] That may seem an arcane way of putting it, but as we shall see when we ap-

41. See IM, 30.

proach the topic of the finitude of thought, that relation between being and non-being becomes very important to Heidegger.[42]

At other points, notably in his 1929 Kant book, Heidegger writes that finite intuition can "take in" (*hinnehmen*) what there is only because what there is "announces itself" (*sich melden*), that intuition "lets" being announce itself as it is (KPM, 18), or that it must "offer the possibility of announcing itself" to already existing being (KPM, 19). Or, coming closer to Kant's own language, finite knowledge can "make manifest" "the being which shows itself, i.e., the appearing, appearance" (KPM, 21). Heidegger is quite explicit in this book that when Kant tries to show that no empirical knowledge, no way for any experience to be onto any object, would be possible without a priori conditions (pure concepts, pure intuitions, and the productive imagination), Kant is in his language attesting to the dependence of all ontic knowledge of the beings on what is always already assumed, a certain disclosive engagement with Being qua Being. The language there is appropriately Kantian—not so much about Being making itself available but about our role, our "openness" in that availability being possible.

> A finite, knowing creature can only relate itself to a being which it itself is not, and which it also has not created, if this being which is already at hand can be encountered from out of itself. However, in order to be able to encounter this being as the being it is, it must already be "recognized" generally and in advance as a being, i.e., with respect to the constitution of its Being. But this implies: ontological knowledge, which here is always pre-ontological, is the condition for the possibility that in general something like a being can itself stand in opposition to a finite creature. Finite creatures need this basic faculty of a turning-toward . . . which lets-[something]-stand-in-opposition. In this original turning-toward, the finite creature first allows a space for play [*Spielraum*] within which something can "correspond" to it. (KPM, 50)

In IM, that availability is glossed by reference to *Being and Time* and the language there of the "disclosedness" (*Erschlossenheit*) of Being, another word we can add to our growing list. He says, "Disclosedness means: the openedness [*Aufgeschlossenheit*] of what the oblivion [*Vergessenheit*]

42. Another interpretation would be that in some historical epoch, there is a dominant meaning of Being that prevails in the sense that it pushes aside or renders unavailable, even unthinkable, any other alternative.

of Being closes off and conceals" (IM, 21). And while he mentions onto-logical knowledge, we have to keep in mind that he means originally a pre-discursive "attunement" and nothing assertoric. Such disclosedness is the precondition for any ontic uncovering. A general attunement to the mean-ingfulness of being as such is in the background of every apprehension of an entity. Perception, for example, is an uncovering, a manifesting of a being as it is, but which presupposes an original disclosive attunement. He puts the point this way in BP:

> Not only does its uncoveredness—that it is uncovered—belong to the entity which is perceived in perception, but also the being-understood, that is, the disclosedness of that uncovered entity's mode of being. We therefore distinguish not only terminologically but also for reasons of intrinsic content between the uncoveredness of a being and the disclos-edness of its being. A being can be uncovered, whether by way of per-ception or some other mode of access, only if the being of this being is already disclosed—only if I already understand it. Only then can I ask whether it is actual or not and embark on some procedure to establish the actuality of the being. (BP 72)[43]

It should also be noted that, although this question can sound abstract and academic in the extreme, his extraordinary claim is that everything of significance in a human life turns on the issue. Heidegger goes very far here. The forgetting of the question is called a "darkening," which he describes this way: "The essential happenings in this darkening are: the flight of the gods, the destruction of the earth, the reduction of human beings to a mass, the preeminence of the mediocre" (IM 47). Even Russia and America are entangled in the metaphysical question: "Russia and America, seen meta-physically, are both the same: the same hopeless frenzy of unchained tech-nology and of the rootless organization of the average man" (IM, 40).

This is so, such that, "To ask: how does it stand with Being?—this means nothing less than to repeat and retrieve the inception of our historical-

43. See Haugeland's modal understanding of this ontological difference, the distinction between disclosedness and discovery or uncovering (2013, 194ff). The former, involved in our understanding of Being, involves grasping beings in terms of a distinction between what is possible and impossible for them, whereas the latter involves claims about the be-ings that can be either true or false (196). This is an important distinction, is in Heidegger, but cannot, I think, be read as exhausting the problem of the ontological difference. The basis on which the former distinction can be made at all is left out of the formulation, as well as the fraught problem of nonbeing or concealment. Cf. Heidegger on the difference between the uncoveredness of entities (*Entdecktheit*) and the disclosure (*Erschlossenheit*) of the whole that makes the former possible (BT, 263).

spiritual Dasein, in order to transform it into the other inception. Such a thing is possible. It is in fact the definitive form of history, because it has its onset in a happening that grounds history" (IM, 41).[44] But this raises other issues we will have to return to. For now, we need to return to canvasing his various attempts to explain his problem, and why it is the one and only problem for philosophy.

We almost have as much as we need to understand the next phase of the question: our relation to, access to, engagement with, or, in his preferred early term, comportment (*Verhalten*) towards and with Being qua Being. We should continue to note though Heidegger's language about the issue in other publications. Perhaps the most well-known passages come from his influential work *On the Origin of the Work of Art*, first delivered as a series of lectures in Vienna and Frankfurt in the 1930s and then reworked for publication in 1950 and 1960. Here is a typical formulation: "And yet: beyond beings—though before rather than apart from them—there is still something other that happens. In the midst of beings as a whole an open place comes to presence. There is a clearing. Thought from out of beings, it is more in being than is the being. This open center is, therefore, not surrounded by beings. Rather, this illuminating center itself encircles all beings—like the nothing that we scarcely know" (OWA, 30). In this passage, Heidegger also broaches the question of our access to Being (this "more in being than is the being"), as opposed to the beings so illuminated in such a *Lichtung*. "The being can only be, as a being, if it stands within, and stands out within, what is illuminated in this clearing. Only this clearing grants us human beings access to those beings that we ourselves are not and admittance to the being that we ourselves are" (ibid.).

The notion of such a clearing or lighting up is a metaphorical way of talking about the event of coming to be manifest, emerging out of the anonymity of possible objects of attention as something that matters (because of Dasein's careful absorption in a world), but the metaphor is both useful and somewhat misleading. It is useful because it emphasizes something of great importance, but it is very difficult to get a handle on. A clearing is not an object as such in our field of vision. It is the absence of any object, an openness that enables, makes space for, objects in their familiarity, meaningfulness. When using the language of worldhood, the analogy is that of a horizon of possible meaningfulness and its not being available *within* such a horizon. It can be referred to as an absence or emptiness, even though strictly speaking

---

44. Cf. "Is Being a mere word and its meaning a vapor, or does what is named with the word 'Being' hold within it the spiritual fate of the West?" (IM, 45). Or, in WM, metaphysics "is neither a division of academic philosophy nor a field of arbitrary notions. Metaphysics is the fundamental occurrence in our Dasein. It is that Dasein itself" (96).

what is being referred to is a nonbeing, a void, and just because of that it "allows" beings to appear. To continue the metaphor, trees and animals of course appear and are manifest in the dense thickets of a forest too, but in a way that makes it very difficult for us to attend to what makes possible their emergence as the beings they are, at least not with the heightened clarity that the notion of a clearing shows us. In fact, it is the contrasting notion of such a thicket that confuses things. Even there, there must be some space, emptiness, a clearing of some kind, lighting of some kind, for beings to be available as what they are. (I mean this metaphorically, not just as perceivable.) Hence the "only this clearing" claim above, even when there is no easy way to attend to such a clearing (which difficulty is actually the normal course of things in everyday life).

The metaphor is misleading for three reasons. His remarks indicate both that such a clearing, in all its metaphorical dimensions, is a condition for beings, ordinary *Seiende* appearing. "Only this clearing grants us human beings access to those beings that we ourselves are not." *And* they indicate a site or some condition of availability for the meaning of Being itself. As he is well aware, this means that confusion can easily arise when we speak of beings being made available because of a clearing. "There is a clearing. Thought from out of beings, it is more in being than is the being." This latter should not be claimed to be of equal significance. Obviously, the former must somehow depend on the latter, and his series of remarks may just contain an ellipsis, an assumption that the former is possible only because the latter has "already" been "given."[45]

Second and more importantly, it is too static an image and does not embody the temporal dimension Heidegger wants to emphasize. He wants finally to say that such an ultimate ground for the availability of anything at all changes over historical time, and so such a possibility makes things available in radically different ways. This is the beginning of the idea of Being (Being qua Being, not beings) as an *Ereignis*,[46] *Geschehen, Geschehnis,*

45. Wrathall 2005 reports that it was only in the 1928 lectures *Einleitung in der Philosophie* that Heidegger began invoking the "clearing" or "openness" language of unconcealedness (*Unverborgenheit*) to discuss the disclosure of Being, and that between 1926 and 1948 he would write both about the unconcealement of beings and of Being. He also notes that Heidegger's marginal notes were quite critical of that confusion (341).

46. *Ereignis* is one of the most contested terms in the later Heidegger. It is largely a post-BT technical term of art and has been translated as everything from the everyday meaning of "event" to "appropriating" to, in the forbidding text from 1936–1938, *Beiträge zur Philosophie: Vom Ereignis*, as "enowning." (The first English translation was *Contributions to Philosophy: From Enowning*. It was retranslated as *Contributions to Philosophy (Of the Event)*, trans. Richard Rojcewicz and Daniela Vallega-Neu [Bloomington: Indiana University Press, 2012]. I use and much prefer the latter translation.) For a history of Heidegger's

as a happening or event and so because ultimate, without a possible logos, but the ground of any logos, itself groundless; that is, a *mere* happening. Commentators sometimes have been misled by the relatively theological-sounding language that the later Heidegger uses to make this point, when he insists on the "mittance" (a common translation of *Seinsgeschick*)[47] or bestowal or "gift" of being. As noted previously, when he notes that the availability or familiarity of beings has a condition for its possibility, he means to emphasize in this sense that beings are *made* available in distinct ways across historical time; how beings are available in their "familiarity" changes across historical time because they are made available in different ways at different times (in different "clearing-locations," I would assume, or as illuminated by different sorts of light), in a way that cannot be taken in by any logos (as ratio) because any determinate logos is "grounded" in how any beings are made available at a time. This is a source or ground that cannot itself be made available in any logos because it must serve as the source of any availability at all. Being does not *do* anything or *give* any gifts. These are metaphorical ways of insisting that for beings to be available to us, they must be *made* available by a kind of illumination that is "beyond being" because it is itself not any being, into which we find ourselves contingently thrown. But such is the distinct historical "emptiness"—and herein the paradox: both distinct, a determinate moment, like the technological framing in modernity, and empty, even abyss-like—necessary for beings to be available at all.[48] (Hence the formulation we saw above: "This open center is, therefore, not surrounded by beings. Rather, this illuminating center itself encircles all beings—like the nothing that we scarcely know" [OWA, 30].)[49]

Given all of this, although Heidegger does not make this distinction, he would seem to be referring to three different ontological levels. There is

---

various usages, see Polt 2005. Whatever translation may be most apt, I take the term in general to be at least an indicator that whatever "gives" being, it is utterly contingent, itself groundless.

47. For example, PR, xvii and xviii.

48. We don't decide that contemporary art objects—Hollywood films, graphic novels, downloaded songs—now show up originarily as commodities. After a certain point in the late nineteenth century, this began to happen and finally prevailed. A contrasting memory of what had been available as a Bach fugue allows, by this contrast, manifestness as such to become salient.

49. Note this formulation from FCM: "This transformation lends a properly primordial historicity to the occurrence of the history of philosophizing, a historicity which makes its own demands (sacrifice, being overcome). We cannot comprehend this historicity and will never be able to get a grasp of it if, for instance, we associate it with the notion of history derived from the sensational historical accounts we find in the newspapers. The historicity of the history of philosophy, and correspondingly, albeit in quite a different way, the historicity of the history of art and of religion are intrinsically and wholly divergent" (FCM, 175).

the clearing or lighting process itself, the most general notion of possible manifestness as such. There is then what appears to be a historical inflection of this rendering available, like *ens creatum* or representationalism or "standing reserve," but which is not a true rendering available, since it actually makes unavailable the true nature of what makes the available available. And then there are the beings available as the beings they are, given such a "dispensation" historically.

The most dramatic word for this picture of an ever-shifting source of availability would simply be *chaos*.[50] As he puts it in POR, "The *Geschick* [destiny] of being, a child that plays, shifting the pawns: the royalty of a child—that means, the arche, that which governs by instituting grounds, the being of beings. The *Geschick* of being: a child that plays" (POR, 113).

This would mean a wholly contingent shifting from beings available as substantial in one period, "enduring through some sequence-of-nows-conception-of-time," to, in another, beings available as created beings, to beings available only as represented for a subject, to being available only as material for technological manipulation. These possibilities are not like regional ontologies, the way entities show up as what they are given in the delimitation of a specific world, like the world of music, or the world of politics, wherein entities are available as what they are only in such delimited worlds and are relatively nontransferable. They are rather all attempts at a determination of Being as such, *simpliciter*, where that, as manifestness or meaningfulness, is always Dasein-inflected, asked as only "for Dasein." However, all of these represent moments of manifestness as such that also work to obscure any proper comportment towards *there being such manifestness*. These various modalities in how beings can be said to be at all *sound* like responses to the basic question, accounts of manifestness as such, but Heidegger will want to say that they all presume without acknowledging they assume, manifestness *as such*, and so, in being offered as fundamental, actually obscure true fundamentality. In other words, the "concealing" in these cases is or promotes a kind of being-forgetting (*Seinsvergessenheit*). The Greek notion of *ousia* (which Heidegger insists is already connected to property, material for use, disposability), the medieval focus on *ens creatum*, the post-Cartesian notion of represented-being, and the technological orientation all involve a kind of concealment (and therein lies a crude summary of Heidegger's entire history of metaphysics)[51] that must be different

50. This is something emphasized at length in Rosen 1993.
51. "Crude" is the operative word. Heidegger's remarks about the "epochal" phases of the "history of Being" are clearly not meant to be anything more than shorthand characterizations of public "worldly," implicit orientations at various times. His whole project resists

from the inevitable and, one might say, ontologically appropriate sort of "concealing" (more a kind of elusiveness) in the "work of art"—a Greek temple, say. And even when we have in view properly such a picture of utterly contingent dispensations, the focus seems to be on something Heidegger also wants to take back, even as he provides such characterizations, as when he is driven, in his 1955 essay *Zur Seinsfrage,* to graphological extremes in writing "~~Sein~~."

However, it must be said that Heidegger's occasional discussions of these epochal inflections of the metaphysical tradition post-Plato do not seem to be very important to his project, at least not comparted to what they are all inflections of, the "metaphysics of presence." That is, he makes no real attempt to justify these divisions, to show us what might have prompted these crises or how what they prompt might be said to be responsive to the crises. They are suggested somewhat casually, and one gets no sense, as one does, say, with the later Foucault, that there are just massive and completely discontinuous and incommensurable shifts in historical worlds, that we are subject to radical contingency in horizons of possible meaningfulness. This is because he does not think we are so subject. For one thing, in Heidegger's treatment, these historical worlds, horizons of possible significance, are immensely complicated networks of interconnected meaningfulness. It is the interconnectedness (a kind of meaningfulness holism) and the enormous stake persons have in the comforts of ordinariness in such worlds that create the great weight that makes this sort of possibility (fickle epochality, let us say) impossible. Much more importantly, there is also, according to Heidegger, despite rare crises of meaningfulness, like the tragic closure of the possibility of the ancient Greek form of life, or Nietzsche and the advent of modern nihilism, still a remarkable (declensionist) *continuity* in Heidegger's account. Plato and Aristotle set us in a direction we have found it impossible to free ourselves from—the metaphysics of presence, the primordial mattering of intelligibility, knowing, which shows up even in Nietzsche's claim to have freed us of metaphysical illusions. It is not even the case that this continuous orientation itself should be said to be "contingent," at least if we mean arbitrary or mysterious. It is existentially motivated by an attempt at a reconciliation with the world through the exercise of reason, a project that culminates in Hegelian self-consciousness and the implication

---

formulaic summaries of possible sources of meaningfulness in thematic terms. These shorthand summaries sound like commonly held "beliefs" and that is the farthest thing from Heidegger's intentions. Any determinate thematic articulation of meaning always already depends on a source beyond articulation in that way, even though, nevertheless, not wholly unavailable (as in, for example, the experience of artworks).

of which is the late modern technological world, almost literally the attempt to *make* the world our own.[52]

This also speaks to the "critical" potential of Heidegger's approach. What he wants to claim about the ultimate (if not existential) groundlessness of this metaphysical orientation has a normative consequence that Heidegger clearly thinks is catastrophic, a dimension brought out best by "Heideggerians" such as Marcuse on "One-Dimensionality" and Arendt on "thoughtlessness."[53] It is also manifest in his explicit linking of consumerist capitalism with the implications of the metaphysics of presence. That is not a dimension we will pursue here, but it has an important bearing on what might be possible if we manage to recover, to remember, what we have forgotten. The absence of any acknowledged, genuine source of meaningfulness has a political dimension, even, perhaps especially, when it is not acknowledged.

To be sure, it would be reasonable to express some skepticism that Heidegger's account of modernity itself, especially in his later Nietzsche lectures, as a "metaphysical" problem, could be defended.[54] But this skepticism would be due to an insufficient understanding of what Heidegger meant by construing his question about the *Sinn des Seins* as a question of *Bedeutsamkeit*, significance, and to a misplaced confidence in the inescapably self-reflective character of any orientation or attunement to the meaningfulness of Being. The question could be framed this way: on Heidegger's assumption that we live in "destitute times," a situation of anomie, deracination, and "homelessness," is it plausible to claim that this should be understood as somehow or other a consequence of the ontological assumptions dominant in the West since the ancient Greek enlightenment, specifically a continuous assumption that the meaning of Being is "standing presence"? Stated that way, it seems highly implausible. But it all depends

52. Rorty 1991 sees a tension in Heidegger between an extreme historicism, historicism "all the way down" or a historicism that envelops Heidegger's own position as a mere historical happening, and some stance "outside" of such a historical location from which the truth of such radical historicity might be known or was intimated in the writings of the pre-Socratics, between what he calls "contingency" and "belatedness." He thinks Heidegger in his development changes his mind from the latter (the earlier ontological-ontic distinction) to the former and so to the distinction between primordial and secondary. The view defended here is that he does not change his mind and always defends his own view of possible "transcendence." An interpretation of a text is itself a text but that need not send us off into infinite and indeterminate "text-less" interpretability. An attunement to the primordial is a resonance with the obscurity of the sources of possible and actual meaningfulness, and an attunement to the difference between them. It is to be "gripped" by the elusiveness of this source and to live out the implications of this orientation.

53. Marcuse 1964; Arendt 1978.

54. I did myself in Pippin 1999.

on how the latter claim is understood. If we are asking a question about the major "steering mechanisms" of society, the power to shape the direction, organization, and fate of a society, it would seem much more plausible to appeal to the forces of global finance capitalism, the consumerist culture it requires, and the vast unintended consequences of technology than to "metaphysics." But if the question concerns the available sources of meaningfulness in a society, sources that can inspire and sustain a living commitment to the shared projects of that society, and if Heidegger means to account for the absence of such sources in the late modern West, then it might be that the latter sort of account must be assumed for the commitments to the former sort of account to have gotten a grip in the first place. And the explanatory direction need not just go one way or the other but can be mutually explanatory. In that case, and given what Heidegger means by "metaphysics" as the question of the possible meaningfulness of Being, his insistence on its importance does not at all sound implausible.

ERRANCY (*IRRE*)

This position means that in the late modern world, beings have become "available" in some sense (*verfügbar*, disposable) but, it would appear, meaninglessly, merely as whatever "lies before us," is "at hand." Nothing is ever originally available to us as such present-at-hand beings, but remarkably we have come to experience the world through some sort of willful blindness thanks to which in our everyday world, what should be closest to us, the familiarity of the world as *pragmata*, is furthest from us. (In WP, Heidegger notes that "the destitute [or starving, *darbend*] time is no longer able to experience its own destitution [*Durft*]" [91], or in BN, he notes that the "devastation of spirit [*die Verwüstung des Geistes*] is taken for spirit itself" [178].) And what is furthest is taken to be closest.[55] The question of the meaning of Being has been not only forgotten but *suppressed,* layered over with some putative "neutral" posing of observing subjects against present at hand substances. Everything we have said about genuine availability in emerging significance and Dasein as care still holds, but some kind of "errancy" has occurred, errant especially since present-at-hand entities still do "mean something" for Dasein, material for manipulation to serve human ends. And although this historical shift is sometimes treated by Heidegger as if it were the result of some willful, hybristic subject, it is nevertheless a historical shift, something that happens, and its dominance as a kind of pseudo or ersatz world is now maintained in bad faith.

55. "Common sense misunderstands understanding." BT 363.

But errancy, how being has misleadingly come to show up (to seem to show up), is a topic in itself and touches on one of the most complex in Heidegger, his account of truth. In IM, he puts it this way. "The space, so to speak, that opens itself up in the interlocking of Being, unconcealment, and seeming, I understand as errancy [*Irre*]. Seeming, deception, delusion, errancy stand in definite relations as regards their essences and their ways of happening, relations that have long been misinterpreted for us by psychology and epistemology, relations that we therefore in our everyday Dasein barely still experience and barely recognize with adequate perspicacity as powers" (IM, 115). But what could it mean to say that this is not a matter of epistemology? How could a disclosive moment of unconcealment seem to be what it is not? Does it mean that the assertion, "beings are substances perduring through time," merely what lies before us at hand, is false? But Heidegger tells us that ontological truth is *aletheia,* that unconcealment, uncovering what is hidden, and while he does not reject truth as correctness, correspondence, he insists it is not the mode of truth appropriate ontologically. How does errancy fit in with that view?

We need to recall first that Heidegger's claim that ontological truth is unconcealment, *aletheia,* is meant to contrast with what he has identified as by far the greatest "errancy" in the Western philosophical tradition: the priority of logos as ratio in the understanding of the meaning of Being. By *logos* he means most generally a theory of pure thinking, all possible thinking with any object other than thought itself, the results of which are taken to determine, ground the possibility of, what could be (from Plato's Ideas to Kant's categories). As we have seen, this ultimately means that being must be understood as what could be the content of an assertion. The meaning of Being is then understood to be intelligibility or knowability, and the corresponding notion of truth is what Heidegger calls "correctness," correspondence with the beings about which assertoric claims are made. This will, he thinks, inevitably lead to the construal of being as mere presence at hand. By contrast, Heidegger insists that such a notion of truth cannot be fundamental because it clearly relies on a prior disclosure, an unconcealment that an assertion depends on and points to. This original "uncovering" must count as primordial truth. So, about the conventional view, Heidegger asks: "However, we would still like to raise one question. What does 'logic' mean? The term is an abbreviation for *episteme logike,* the science of logos. And logos here means assertion. But logic is supposed to be the doctrine of thinking. Why is logic the science of assertion? Why is thinking determined on the basis of assertion? This is by no means self-evident" (IM 127). But there is an obvious answer to Heidegger's question. The assumption behind the priority of logos is that *only* an assertion can be a truth-bearer, can be true or false. And if true, then an assertion says how things are, corresponds with being.

But, as in the famous critique by Ernst Tugendhat,[56] if Heidegger responds to this by claiming that such asserting presumes a prior "disclosure," then, contrary to what Heidegger says, truth must still reside in some assertion *about* what is disclosed. An event cannot itself be true or false. There is no truth claim without a contrast with falsity, and a disclosure by itself is just that, a manifestation that, we have to say, could disclose something true or could only seem to. This would be to distinguish meaning from truth, and to link meaning with what it *would be* for the assertion to be true. If there is a form of Dasein's openness that is originally receptive to this disclosure, should we not ask what would distinguish a spurious disclosure from a genuine one, if not that an assertion that it was genuine could be true or false?

It is important that Heidegger treats the disclosure as an event and, in the context of BT, where the primary focus is on aspects of the disclosure whereby the meaning of Dasein's being can be said to be available to it, and important that he would insist on the experiential specificity and first-personal quality of the event. The meaning of one's being is one's "ownmost." In that context, there are many cases where there is clearly something to be understood, but it would not be understood if it were formulated propositionally and simply delivered to the person. Psychoanalysis would be easy if, after a session or two, the analyst were to proclaim to the analysand, "You hate your father and you feel terrible about it." Such knowledge can only be arrived at first-personally and in various diverse ways it is hard to summarize. Getting someone to understand a poem can be like this; in fact a great deal of teaching is such an attempt to "awaken," to use Heidegger's word, an experiential openness to a disclosure that can range from the trivial to life-altering, all of which require coming to the disclosure first-personally. (Telling the student the meaning of the poem in a series of paraphrases is not teaching.) This is not surprising. In phenomenological terms, what it is like to strive or fail or love or hate, what it is like for a world to bear on the possible course of a life, are all not available for reflection third-personally or by observation or by interviewing people. And so in cases like these (where the meaning of Dasein's being is at issue), a propositional formulation would get us nowhere; its truth condition would have to be the disclosure itself. And in the domain of greatest importance to Heidegger, how things matter, how much they matter, why they matter, and so

56. Tugendhat 1970.

forth—the primary mode of availability in the everyday world—is available to us only in disclosures, not as objects of propositional attitudes.

And second, the phenomenon in dispute should not be held hostage to whether a genuine disclosure can be detected from a spurious one, as if there should be a method to do so or clear confirmation conditions. There might have to be a reliance on such a disclosure even if this distinction cannot be clearly made or only with great difficulty. Heidegger could not be more explicit about this than in his 1936 essay on Hölderlin.

> The word as work therefore never directly offers a guarantee [*Gewähr*] as to whether it is an essential word or a delusion [*Blendwerk*]. On the contrary—an essential word often looks in its simplicity like an inessential one. And what on the other hand presents itself in its finery as the look of the essential is only said by rote or repeated. Thus is language ever obliged to place itself in a seeming [*Schein*] produced by itself, and thereby threaten what is uniquely its own—true saying. (EH 37)[57]

He appears to mean that there can be something like or parallel to bivalence *in the disclosure itself.* In fact, he thinks that any disclosure of any significance is always accompanied by a concealing, is never just straightforwardly manifest. The disclosure of the meaningfulness of Being involves the partial emergence into presence from obscurity or hiddenness into disclosure, and this is not the result of true judgments but their condition, and that emergence is never complete. It is especially important that the disclosure is a disclosure of meaningfulness, something that does not play the role one might expect in the criticisms of Heidegger. Meaningfulness could be expressed, but not determinately as some matter of fact, as when we ask, without a clear referent, "what it meant to a person" that her child is estranged, or that his circle of friends all died in the war. If we ask such a question, we do not expect a list of assertions. Very often we expect some sort of narrative. This copresence of uncovering and concealment clearly admits of all sorts of ambiguities in and qualifications on what is disclosed.[58] The event itself then should not be said to be simply true or false, as if every

57. He is of course here talking about literary interpretation, but the same challenge posed for interpretation by any "seeming" bears on the issue of a genuine versus a merely seeming disclosure, which is the heart of the controversy about truth.

58. See Rorty 1991: "Only when we escape from the verificationist impulse to ask 'How can we tell a right answer when we hear one?' are we asking questions that Heidegger thinks worth asking. Only then are we Dasein, because only then do we have the possibility of being *authentic* Dasein, Dasein which knows itself to be 'thrown'" (44). Rorty's point is undermined somewhat when he himself asks how we know that something counts as "primordial" (43).

putative disclosure in a fundamental attunement or artwork is necessarily true in the sense of statable in true judgments. Or at least we should say that there is potentially something genuine and something obscuring in every such disclosure and the presence of something "genuine" could be said to be a form of truth. The issue of the original meaningfulness of being in any historical world is simply not statable in propositional terms, and its availability in literature and life is a matter of interpretation, not cognition, attunement not assertion. (In criticism and interpretation, the ideal cannot be paraphrase, but a way or re-creating the experience of reading the poem, say, or some way to awaken in one's audience what it is to read the poem attentively.) In fact, Heidegger is encouraging philosophy to think of itself as hermeneutic, a matter of interpretation, not essentially cognition or analysis. The meaning of terms or concepts as a subject of analysis and clarification is one thing; the meaningfulness of beings is another.

However, in BT's discussion of skepticism and truth (§43 and §44) and in his 1925–1926 lectures on *Logic: The Question of Truth*, Heidegger also wants to make a more general "logical" point about the primordiality of disclosive truth over propositional truth. (He says explicitly that he is not denying the notion of truth as correctness, or trying to replace it with unconcealedness, but is trying to raise the issue of promordiality and so dependence.) Since Dasein, as Being-in-the-world, is always already "alongside" entities within the world, always already pre-reflectively familiar (and in a primarily practical comportment) with elements of its world, there is no force to the question of how an isolated subject could ever be said to reliably "reach out to" an entity by knowing it, much less how some putative inner state could be said to correspond to some external object. Instead any propositional formulation and assertion must be said to presuppose a "context of significance,"[59] a context which already forms a horizon of possible meaningful (that is, relevant, appropriate) assertoric formulations about the world. Such a context is not one Dasein has a mediated relation "to"; hence all the formulations about Dasein *being* its disclosedness (*Dasein ist seiner Erschlossenheit*, BT, 171), that it is the "clearing" where such disclosure happens.

This is the sense in which Heidegger wants to claim that propositional truth presupposes unconcealment. The simplest sense of this is the unavoidable contextual horizon for the meaningfulness of assertion. It is possible

59. McManus (2013), whose position shares features with Carman's (2003), has a good discussion of how this context presupposition bears on the question of both propositional truth and a more original disclosive truth. I think that bearing has more to do with the primacy of the meaning/*Bedeutsamkeit* issue developed here than his appeal to "cognitive tools" for active engagement with the world. See also Carman's critique of Wrathall's deflationary interpretation of the issue, 259–263.

that while teaching ¶44 in BT, I suddenly assert "The capital of Columbia is Bogotá." My students would have understood the assertion, but they would not, in the sense Heidegger is interested in, have understood me. And it is this contextual orientation from meaningfulness, what Carman (2003) calls "hermeneutical salience" (254) that is behind Heidegger's qualification on what he otherwise agrees with, Husserl's critique of psychologism (BT, 259–260).

And since any such disclosure, some "attuned" sense of contextual relevance and appropriateness, is never possible without also concealment, while there cannot be any such thing as a false disclosure, there can be no genuine disclosure, or a sense of such a contextual meaningfulness that disorients, obscures, mis-attunes.[60] The forgetfulness of the question of the meaning of being results. A version of such disclosive falseness or merely putative disclosure is given several times in BT. For example:

> At the same time our interpretation of understanding has shown that, in accordance with its falling kind of Being, it has, proximally and for the most part, diverted itself [sich . . . verlegt] into an understanding of the "world." . . . The interpretation of Being takes its orientation in the first instance from the Being of entities within-the-world. Thereby the Being of what is proximally ready-to-hand gets passed over, and entities are first conceived as a context of Things (*res*) which are present-at-hand. "*Being*" acquires the meaning of "*Reality*." Substantiality becomes the basic characteristic of Being. (245)

And,

> Entities have not been completely hidden; they are precisely the sort of thing that has been uncovered, but at the same time they have been disguised. They show themselves, but in the mode of semblance. Likewise what has formerly been uncovered sinks back again, hidden and disguised. *Because Dasein is essentially falling, its state of Being is such that it is in untruth.* (264)[61]

60. See in his LO: "I cannot be deceived when it comes to uncovering those 'simple' beings which are always there, because here the only possible uncovering is a direct having of those beings. By the very nature of the case, the uncovering comportment towards beings that is required if I am to be deceived is the uncovering and having of the being itself" (155).

61. This all raises the question of the right way to state in Heidegger's name the relation between uncovering and "assertion," the vehicle of propositional truth. This is a problem because even false assertions have content, are about something and that means for Carman (2015) that all assertion must be a form of uncovering; even false assertions can be said to disclose "seemings." But Heidegger says not that true assertions just are the uncovering of an entity itself (266), but, as Carman quotes, an assertion "lets" the entity be seen in its un-

Further, that this is not a form of constitutive idealism, as if truth is whatever Dasein takes to be disclosed to itself, as if Dasein's experience as such counts as a truth about Being, is clear already in BT: "In so far as Dasein is its disclosedness essentially, and discloses and uncovers as something disclosed to this extent it is essentially 'true.' Dasein is 'in the truth.' This assertion has meaning ontologically. It does not purport to say that ontically Dasein is introduced 'to all the truth' either always or just in every case, but rather that the disclosedness of its ownmost Being belongs to its existential constitution" (263). This is why he can say in EnP, commenting on his own claim, "'Dasein is in truth' does not imply a bad relativization of truth to man, but rather the other way around" (155).

Would it not still be the case that what it would be to *make* such a distinction is the work of possibly true or false assertions? We might be tempted to say so if we forget, as is, I think, often forgotten in the discussion around Tugendhat and his critics, that another of Heidegger's most radical innovations is his insistence that our access to such a disclosure, the mode of being of Dasein "open" to such an unconcealment, is not cognitive, at least not as that notion is commonly understood. Correspondingly, we should not think of the content of any disclosure as being of the sort that could have propositional form. The condition for the possible accessibility of the meaning of Being is *Stimmung*, attunement, and being attuned, being "gripped" by something mattering, is not an object of "seeing" something of significance, *that* it is significant. Likewise, what we are attuned to is a register of meaningfulness or mattering that can't be determinately identified in a way required by judgment, can't be qualified or even directly characterized. In the matter of mattering, what matters, how much, compared to what, and so forth are impossible to set out neatly in discursive form, at least without greatly distorting how we are onto such matters at all.

Accordingly, it is important to keep in mind Heidegger's own examples of what he means by the event of unconcealment. There is a striking example in BP, when he cites and comments on a passage in Rilke's *The Notebooks of Malte Laurids Brigge*. (We shall return to this passage in more detail in chap. 9.) Here is some of the passage from Rilke. Malte is considering

---

coveredness; that is, once uncovered (BT 261). He also often notes that *logos* as *apophansis* is letting something be seen in its uncoveredness by "pointing" to such an uncoveredness (BT, 56), not by accomplishing the uncovering. So it seems to me misleading to say that semblance or seeming is itself "a mode of uncovering, a kind of truth" (273). We can't be said to uncover a semblance or a concealing, because precisely as semblance it is not "uncovered" as concealing. That is why it is a semblance. This is not to deny what Sheehan (2015) points out: that any disclosure of what turns out to be a mere seeming nevertheless does disclose something meaningful "as something I can understand" (62). This seems to me the right way to put the point.

some old homes in decrepitude, some torn down, some barely standing, their insides exposed.

> But most unforgettable were the walls themselves. The tenacious life of these rooms refused to let itself be trampled down. It was still there; it clung to the nails that had remained; it stood on the handsbreadth remnant of the floor; it had crept together there among the onsets of the corners where there was still a tiny bit of interior space ... There stood the noondays and the illnesses, and the expirings and the smoke of years and the sweat that breaks out under the armpits and makes the clothes heavy, and the stale breath of the mouths and the fusel-oil smell of fermenting feet. There stood the pungency of urine and the burning of soot and the gray reek of potatoes and the strong oily stench of decaying grease. The sweet lingering aroma of neglected suckling infants was there and the anguished odor of children going to school and the sultriness from beds of pubescent boys. (BP 172–3)

About which, Heidegger says:

> Notice here in how elemental a way the world, being-in-the-world—Rilke calls it life—leaps toward us from the things. What Rilke reads here in his sentences from the exposed wall is not imagined into the wall, but, quite to the contrary, the description is possible only as an interpretation and elucidation of what is "actually" in this wall, which leaps forth from it in our natural compartmental relationship to it. Not only is the writer able to see this original world, even though it has been unconsidered and not at all theoretically discovered, but Rilke also understands the philosophical content of the concept of life, which Dilthey had already surmised and which we have formulated with the aid of the concept of existence as being-in-the-world. (BP 173)

It is impossible to imagine that what Rilke has Malte experience could be reformulated in assertoric judgments, just as it is extremely difficult to state what the "content" of the disclosure is beyond the description of an old building. Rilke is evoking the manifestation of the living past presence of Dasein and its concerns, cares, in the beings in the world, and evoking the mood of human life and decay "there" in the objects. In such a context, truth as genuineness, this awakening of an attentiveness to the saturation of lived meaning in the wall (now dead), any contrary insistence of propositional correctness as the only measure of its truth seems wildly irrelevant.

Heidegger makes a similar point when, in his 1925 seminar on Plato's *Sophist*, he introduces Aristotle's distinction between *techne* and *phronesis*, and follows, with some qualifications (Heidegger thinks *phronesis* is also a sort of making, of deeds) Aristotle's prioritization of *phronesis*, commonly translated as practical wisdom, knowing what to do. Such a knowing has no logos; no formalization is possible, no method. Knowing what to do is highly contextual and its wisdom cannot be formulated in an assertion. It is simply to do what the practically wise person would do. *Phronesis* is not theoretical knowledge of the good but knowing what to do; the knowledge is practical knowledge only if it issues in an action, not an assertion about what is to be done. Heidegger says that the final object of *phronesis* is Dasein itself. Of course, a determinate action results from the exercise of such wisdom, and that can be described, but the deliberation and the practical knowing itself is not a form of propositional knowledge (PS 34–36).

So we have now a series of attempts, not at all exhaustive, to pin down the distinctive way in which the question of the meaning of Being can be formulated. As:

Manifestness as such
Presencing
Availability
Meaningfulness
Pre-discursive familiarity/intelligibility
Phusis
Prevailing
Disclosedness
Openedness (*Aufgeschlossenheit*)
Announcing itself/appearing
Clearing (*Lichtung*/lighting)

And this gives us a way of understanding how Heidegger approaches the history of philosophy. There are beings available for us for our comportment towards them. How is this possible? In Plato, the answer would be: by virtue of any being's participation in an idea. The meaning of Being is *eidos*. This, though, treats Being as another being and raises the question of the availability, the mode of access, the being or the disclosedness potential, of the Ideas (and so the "third man" problem, among others).

Or in Descartes, a being is available by being represented. The meaning of Being is being representable in clear and distinct ideas. For Heidegger, this produces only confusion and equivocation; Being is *res cogitans*, *res extensa*, and God, and the mode of Being itself throughout all such substances is unclarified. Or, as he puts it: *cogito ergo sum*. But Descartes never enquires into the *sum*.

In Kant, beings, objects, are available as objects of sensory experience. Such are the beings. But Kant also asks: how are objects of sensory experience even possible? This requires an a priori account of the meaning of objectivity, the possibility of the experience of objects as they are. Objectivity is understood as necessary unity, and unity is understood as unity in any continuous apperceptive consciousness, dependent on sensory givenness for its content.

This is the unity of *I think*: the conditions necessary for the *I think* to accompany any one continuous consciousness. This, then, is the meaning of Being: the transcendental unity of apperception of a sensation-dependent finite being, open to the world in just that one way, sensorily.

But, creating a famous equivocating complexity, this does not exhaust the meaning of Being in Kant, for beings may also be posited in a practical register by pure thinking, by reason and its requirements for practical coherence. Hence there are posited beings, the freedom and immortality of the soul and a just God.

For Hegel, Being is the Concept. The meaning of Being is intelligibility, and the basic condition of intelligibility is set by the self-determining and autotelic spontaneity of pure thinking—thinking itself in its necessary "*Denkbestimmungen*," determinations of thought, the systematic totality of which is the Idea.

SECTION TWO
Heidegger's Kant

3

Being as Positing

There are three main foci in Heidegger's Kant interpretation. Each focus is given pride of place in three different works, although there is naturally a good deal of overlap, and the themes he highlights are all interrelated. The first issue arises at the beginning of the 1927 lecture course on *The Basic Problems of Phenomenology*, in section 8, "Phenomenological analysis of the explanation of the concept of being or of existence by Kant." There, he introduces the notion of the meaning of being as, for Kant, positing, *Positio* or *Setzung*. This is taken up and much more fully developed in a 1961 essay, "Kant's Thesis about Being," published in *Pathmarks* (*Wegmarken*), a collection that appeared in 1976. In each of the three major discussions, Heidegger's interpretation takes its bearings from Kant's famous denial that existence is a predicate. This sentence is the one he focuses on: Kant's denial and his (often neglected) positive claim about what existential predication involves. "'Being' is obviously not a real predicate; that is, it is not a concept of something which could be added to the concept of a thing. It is merely the positing of a thing, or of certain determinations in and for themselves" (A, 598/B, 626).

(There are also, in *Basic Problems*, two intriguing and rich sections on Kant's practical philosophy [§13 and §14], which are somewhat independent of his main concerns in his major statements on Kant but which make several important points that we will discuss at the end of chapter 5 below. They bear on the general issue of finitude.)

The second aspect is discussed in his 1929 book *Kant and the Problem of Metaphysics*.[1] In this work, he argues that *The Critique of Pure Reason*

1. Much of the book is a distillation of his lecture course the year before, *Phänomenologische Interpretation von Kants 'Kritik der reinen Vernunft'* (GA 25).

should not be interpreted as the neo-Kantians and positivists did, as the "shattering" of metaphysics, and certainly not as a work of epistemology, but actually as a "laying the foundation of metaphysics." And he means metaphysics as he understands it, as an inquiry into the meaning of Being. To this end, he interprets Kant's Copernican Revolution, which states that we strive to show not how concepts conform to objects but how objects conform to (pure) concepts, as the principle of his own concept of fundamental ontology. That is, the claim that all experience or empirical knowledge of objects can be shown to depend on a priori conditions for the possibility of such experience is for Heidegger the equivalent of the claim that ontic knowledge presupposes ontological knowledge (even if, for Heidegger, nondiscursively formulable), that any knowledge of the beings assumes a knowledge (of some sort) of the meaningfulness of Being (the primordial basis of anything showing up as a being but which does not itself show up as a being). This ultimate presupposition in Kant is the "a priori synthesis," and so Heidegger interprets *that* as the meaning of Being for Kant. (He could just as easily put this by saying the "transcendental unity of apperception" is the meaning of Being for Kant; and in fact he later does.)[2] With this established, he wants to applaud Kant for appreciating the finitude of thinking—in Kant its dependence on sensible and pure intuition—also note the hidden importance of the imagination in Kant's project, and yet also demonstrate that Kant has not broken free of the prior metaphysical tradition but remains solidly within its assumptions. (This is the goal of all his Kant interpretations.)

The third site for Heidegger's Kant interpretation arose from a course he gave in the winter semester of 1935–1936 on "Basic Questions of Metaphysics." His book based on these lectures, *The Question Concerning the Thing: On Kant's Doctrine of the Transcendental Principles*, was finally published in 1962. Here, Heidegger's focus is again ontological. The first *Critique* is said to be concerned with the thingness of a thing, what makes up its thingness, and what makes possible what is required for it to be a thing, but now Heidegger wants to show much more explicitly how much Kant missed or ignored in investigating this issue. For the Kantian meaning of

2. "However, the basic condition of knowing as knowing is the ego as 'I-think.' Hence Kant continually inculcates that the ego is not a representation, that it is not a represented object, not a being in the sense of an object, but rather the ground of the possibility of all representing, all perceiving, hence of all the perceivedness of beings and thus the ground of all being. As original synthetic unity of apperception, the ego is the fundamental ontological condition of all being. The basic determinations of the being of beings are the categories. The ego is not one among the categories of beings but the condition of the possibility of categories in general. . . . Thus the ego is the fundamental ontological condition, the transcendental that lies at the basis of every particular a priori" (BP 128).

Being—"projected a priori," as Heidegger puts it—is not at all derived but a necessary a priori condition, is the equation of anything and so anything essential to its thingness, with a mathematized conception of nature, Newton's conception, according to which "the thing is material, a point of mass in motion in the pure space-time order or a corresponding order of such points" (QT, 34). (In the language we are using, this is what primordially matters.) This means that Kant treats our immediate familiarity with the world as an unimportant issue, since real knowledge of what really is resides in mathematical physics, and how ordinary things show up in ordinary experience is of no account. (This is the equivalent of his critique of Hegel for dogmatically insisting that determinacy is necessarily the mark of any being, thereby foreclosing any genuine inquiry into the meaningfulness of Being.) Along the way, Heidegger offers a subtle account of how the nature of judgment must be reinterpreted in the light of its dependence on intuition and cannot be considered in its traditional sense, with a sensible source of content simply "added on," and he presents a detailed interpretation of Kant's section on the principles.

There is also an extensive discussion of Kant in his 1930 lecture course *The Essence of Human Freedom: An Introduction to Philosophy*. The subtitle is quite accurate. The lectures present an exceptionally lucid and accessible account of Heidegger's position on philosophy and of his own position in *Being and Time*, and an equally lucid summation of Kant's position on the essence of freedom. For once, there is no extensive creative confrontation with Kant but a relatively standard undergraduate lecture exposition of Kant's major positions, especially on Kant's treatment of cosmological or transcendental freedom (the possibility of spontaneous causality) and practical freedom (the fact of reason, established through the experience of the moral law). Inevitably, there is one major Heideggerian variation on Kant's formulations in which Heidegger claims that not only is freedom a problem of causality, but causality is itself a problem of freedom (that causality is an originary "self-binding," "the giving of the law unto oneself" [EF 207]). But he does not discuss there the issue that will emerge as significant below— the finitude of pure practical reason—and so these lectures do not bear on the issues we are discussing.

Heidegger's summary of the Kantian argument against the ontological proof for the existence of God—that existence is not a real predicate—is relatively straightforward and conventional. But he notices two unusual things about Kant's formulation of his conclusion that traditionally go unnoticed. Most summaries of the argument say that Kant showed that existence is not a predicate, does not and cannot function like a predicate, that a hundred possible thalers is not, *qua thalers*, any different in content from a hundred actual thalers. But Kant does not say, Heidegger notes, that existence is not a predicate (in some sense it is) but a *real* predicate. Recall the crucial Kantian passage: "'Being' is obviously not a real predicate; that is, it is not a concept of something which could be added to the concept of a thing. It is merely the positing of a thing, or of certain determinations in and for themselves" (A, 598/B, 626).

And second, Heidegger wants to explore the implications of the remarkably Fichtean formulation that anything actual must be understood to be "posited," that being, the meaning of being, is "positing." This sort of formulation is regularly misunderstood in summaries of Fichte as some sort of intellectual intuition in which objects come into existence by being thought. And it sounds in this case too like radical idealism: that anything not posited by a subject, thought by a spontaneous intellect, does not exist, and that which does exist exists because it is thought. Heidegger's clarification of what is actually going on in the formulation avoids that implication and indirectly helps out with Fichte.[3] It also reinforces the fact that Heidegger's interest in Kant and in all other historical figures is not some criterion of existence but the meaningfulness of any being. The significance of any being, in his Kant interpretation, is its availability as the object of judgments, or positings.

The notion that being is not a real predicate is connected by Heidegger with the distinction between reality and actuality, which Heidegger frequently makes, and so is connected with the scholastic discussion, especially in Thomas, of the essence/existence issue.[4] That is, some feature can be rightly predicated of an essence independent of considerations about whether anything with such an essence exists. This is true of any analytic exfoliation or synthetic addition to conceptual content. "But for Kant the word 'real' still has its original meaning. It means that which belongs to a *res*, to a substance, to the substantive content of a thing. . . . Reality is for Kant not actuality but rather substantiality. A real predicate is such as belongs to the substantive content of a thing and can be attributed to it" (P 341).

This interpretation leaves out a lot, especially any discussion of how Kant might understand essential predication and its accompanying notion of necessity,[5] but his main interest is in showing that even if being is no *real* predicate, we do know something more about a stone (even if not more about what it is to be a stone) when we know, in addition to knowing what

3. I defend Fichte against the charge of mind-dependence idealism in Pippin 2000.
4. Thomas 1968.
5. See Graubner 1972 and Kant's discussion of "forma dat esse rei" in his 1796 "Von einem neuerdings erhobenen vornehmen Ton in der Philosophie" (AK, Bd. 8, 404).

its essential properties are, like "heavy," that it exists. (Heidegger claims that Being, understood in its various modalities, including actuality, is not a real predicate but is a "transcendental [ontological] predicate" [P, 353].) That counts as some sort of predication, and the sort is: "is posited." (In Heidegger's terms, this means: conforms to the conditions of its availability, ultimately understood by Kant as "perceivable" and so possible contents of judgments.)[6] Most of the essay takes up what this might mean. Without telling us much here about what he thinks the concept of representation involves, he goes another step forward by claiming: "In representing we place something before ourselves, so that it, as thus placed (posited), stands over against us as object. Being, as position, means the positedness of something in representational positing" (P, 343).

Position or positing is treated throughout as *judging*,[7] the discursive form of representing, and Heidegger is claiming that for Kant the only sense we can make of something being or existing is by understanding being as the object of a judgmental positing or a claiming that something exists or exists as such and such. Again, the topic is the meaning of Being, and Heidegger is noting that for Kant such a meaning must be the way any being can be said to register on our discriminating faculties, basically our powers of perception or assisted perception, and thereby be a fit object of a judgmental positing. That is what counts most of all. In Heidegger's own terminology, this means that the meaning of being as existence is the present-at-hand, *Vorhandensein*. That is what it means to be. (He certainly never suggests that something exists *because* it is thought in a judgment.) He notes, "Its [the understanding's] basic feature is positing as synthesis. Positing has the character of proposition, i.e., of judgment, whereby something is placed before us as something, a predicate is attributed to a subject by the 'is'" (P, 347). That is, Being is understood in terms of our capacity to determine whether or not something exists or exists as such and such. "Existence consequently expresses a relationship of the object to the cognitive faculty" (BP, 45). What it means for something to exist is for an assertoric judgment that it does exist to be possibly true or false. Heidegger shows how early Kant developed this position, not only in the 1763 essay *The Only Pos-*

6. "When Kant says that being equals perception, then in view of the ambiguity of perception this cannot mean that being equals perceiving; nor can it mean that being equals the perceived, the entity itself. But also it cannot mean that being equals perceivedness, equals positedness. For perceivedness already presupposes an understanding of the being of the perceived entities" (BP 314).

7. Heidegger varies his references to this activity between the logical notion of judgment (*Urteil*) and its linguistic and communicative expression, assertion (*Aussage*). See Schear 2007 for a fuller account.

sible Ground of Proof for a Demonstration of the Existence of God (Heidegger quotes from that work: "The concept of positing or asserting [*Position oder Setzung*] is completely simple and identical with that of being in general" [P, 341]), but also from several undated notes from the *Nachlass*.

Heidegger can seem to be staying too close to Kant here, as if he is accepting Kant's assumptions about a transcendental analytic (reason's analysis of the concept of pure reason). To some extent he does, but it is occasionally useful to remind ourselves that he sees himself still as providing a phenomenology. At the beginning of the 1927 lecture course on *The Basic Problems of Phenomenology*, in section 8, what is announced is a "*Phenomenological analysis* of the explanation of the concept of being or of existence by Kant." And his most extensive engagement with Kant, from which most of his other comments derive, is his 1927/1928 Marburg lecture course, "Phänomenologische Interpretation von Kants Kritik der reinen Vernunft." It must in fact be a phenomenology if we remember that it is only via a phenomenology that the question of the meaning of being (and not the conditions for empirical and pure knowledge of being) can arise. This in effect already seals the deal for Heidegger because he thinks it is easy to show that the meaning of being or of any being does not show up for us, manifest itself, as the possible content of assertoric judgment, or simply "the perceivable." "What it is like" for Being to come to matter as it does is not as the result of the application of any concept of mattering, nor by simply assuming that all that fundamentally matters is knowing what exists and what does not.[8]

From Kant's point of view, there is nothing particularly problematic about this focus in general. As long as we assume that this capacity is an *objective* power, that for beings whose thinking is necessarily discursive, existence must be understood in terms of that determining power, *the power objectively capable of determining what exists or what exists as such and such.* We have the power to determine objectively when something exists or not, and so what there is can be understood as what this power can determine. For Kant, nothing is thereby left out, or relativized idealistically, given that the understanding is an *objective* power. That is, the concept of something existing beyond our capacity to determine in principle if it exists (or if we

---

8. We should recall a passage cited earlier. "The fundamental concepts of metaphysics and the concepts of philosophy, however, will evidently not be like this at all, if we recall that they themselves are anchored in our being gripped [*in einer Ergriffenheit gegründet*], in which we do not represent before us that which we conceptually comprehend, but maintain ourselves in a quite different comportment, one which is originarily and fundamentally different from any scientific kind" (FCM, 9). This is the sentiment that will eventually surface in Heidegger's treatment of Kant, however much he admires Kant's emphasis on finitude.

cannot but believe it exists) is an empty notion. It would be like specu-
lating on in principle undiscoverable invisible fairies at the bottom of my
garden. Such a claim by Kant is no more problematic than "being is being
the value of a bound variable," or Kant's own later discussion of modality,
where actuality is understood as "that which is bound up with the material
conditions of experience." Everything changes, however, when we add that
this power of positing is *finite*, as we shall see. The principle that "existence
must be understood in terms of our determining power" can acquire quite
a different meaning, depending on what is meant by this finitude.

Heidegger, of course, realizes what he had so emphasized in his 1929
book on Kant: that thinking alone, the activity of the understanding in isolation, can have "reference" to an object only under the main condition of
its finitude, its dependence on sensible intuition. "But this positing can only
posit something as object, i.e., as something brought over against us, and
thus bring it to a stand as something standing over against us [*Gegenstand*],
if something that can be posited is given to our positing through sensuous
intuition, i.e., through the affection of the senses. Only positing as positing of an affection lets us understand what, for Kant, the being of beings
means" (P, 346).

But Heidegger then draws out the implications of this dependence for
the nature of judgment itself, as a matter of logic. This dependence means
Kant is right, consistent with what he famously remarked at B140 in section 19: "I have never been able to accept the interpretation which logicians give of judgment in general. It is, they declare, the representation of a
relation between two concepts." Kant's complaint is that the nature of this
relationship is not explained, and the formulation especially misses that, as
a matter of logical form, the notion of judgment must include as a necessary element "that wherein positing a predicate of a subject is grounded"
(P, 347). This means that the Kantian conception of judgment must be as
he states it in this passage, and it is quite a radical reformulation of the logic
of judgment, one decisive for Hegel. "I find that a judgment is nothing but
the manner in which given modes of knowledge are brought to the objective unity of apperception. This is what is intended by the copula is. It is
employed to distinguish the objective unity of given representations from
a subjective unity."

"Given modes of knowledge" are primarily sensible intuitions, both empirical and pure, and so the structure of judgment must be understood as involving as a *ground* the relation to an object that *provides* the understanding
with the material for the unity necessary for apperceptive unity in experience. This *can* be put by saying that Kant "subjects" any question about the
meaning of any being or the meaning of being in general to the subjective

requirements of the transcendental unity of apperception; in effect under-standing being as what is required by apperceptive unity. Whether it should be put that way is what we must explore.

Heidegger then begins to hint at what he finds problematic in Kant's understanding of being. He notes that in all the formulations since 1763, no matter how important the revisions and expansions in the first *Critique* were, "*one thing, however, remains untouched*. It is the guiding thread to which Kant holds in setting up and clarifying his thesis on being: namely, that it must be possible for being and its modes to be determined from their relation to the understanding" (P, 349; italics in original).

As noted above, as long as the understanding is understood as an ob-jective power, this simply means that, as in the postulate, conforming to the material conditions of experience simply states that what exists can be known to exist, and the concept of an unknowable or unintelligible exis-tence, or even a modality of existence that cannot be captured in the discur-sive form of judgment, is an idle and irrelevant speculation. But Heidegger wants to begin to suggest that this latter speculation is not necessarily idle and irrelevant, and that there is actually no good reason to assume that subjecting, as it were, the problem of the meaning of being to the restric-tions of a discursive understanding will produce anything other than typical metaphysical errancy, a subjectivism and so a blindness to the meaningful-ness of Being as such. For one thing, this approach limits our understanding of the mode of being of the perceiving subject to its cognitive capacities, a restriction that will raise inevitably the problem of the possible transcen-dence of subjectivity in the object and how the interior psychic world could connect with an objective world—something Heidegger thinks requires that we think of such a subject as another present-at-hand entity itself—and this is all a problematic Heidegger wants to reject rather than answer. The primordial mode of being of Dasein is not primarily as a perceiver but being-in-the-world.[9] ("The statement that the comportments of the Dasein are intentional means that the mode of being of our own self, the Dasein, is essentially such that this being, so far as it is, is *always already dwelling with the extant*" [BP, 65; my emphasis].)

He also gives clear indication that this is how he thinks of Kant on posit-ing in a brief appositive in a quotation from Kant. He is explaining how for Kant, transcendental apperception is "the guiding thread of the determi-

---

9. His premise is a familiar one by now. "What is it that belongs to an uncovering of a being, in our case the perceptual uncovering of an extant entity? The mode of uncovering and the mode of uncoveredness of the extant obviously must be determined by the entity to be uncovered by them and by its way of being" (BP, 70).

nation of the concepts (categories) and the basic principles of the being of beings," and he notes, "It is this way because [here he starts quoting Kant] 'the first pure cognition pertaining to the understanding' [i.e., the decisive stamping (*die maßgebende Prägung*) of the being of beings] is the principle of the original synthetic unity of apperception" (§17, B, 137).[10] There is no "*maßgebende Prägung*" in Kant's texts, and so Heidegger's appositive is tendentious.[11]

It is tendentious because Heidegger has not dealt with Kant's claim to have shown in his Transcendental Deduction that the conditions for the possibility of experience *are* at the same time conditions for the possibility of objects of experience (although Heidegger is well aware of this claim), and this not because the understanding "stamps" its form onto formless matter, but because Kant takes himself to have demonstrated that all that relation to an object, a determination of any being, *can amount to* is the objective unity of an apperceptive synthesis.[12] We should recall Kant's famous letter to Herz that sets the stage for the critical period. Kant had certainly realized that he should not have simply assumed that the forms of thought are, without further ado, the forms of being, that this must be *demonstrated*. And there is no indication that he thinks that demonstration will show that the mind imposes a form on a formless matter. (In fact, as we shall see in the next section, he backs off this claim and tries to show that we cannot isolate our cognitive capacities—and so the possibility of cognition itself—from our distinctive mode of being as a whole; if we do, we will not properly understand even the cognitive function.)[13] That would hardly be a demon-

10. The full quotation (Heidegger does not indicate his ellipsis) in the Guyer-Wood translation is: "The first pure cognition of the understanding, therefore, on the whole of the rest of its use is grounded, and that is at the same time also entirely independent from all conditions of sensible intuition is the principle of the original synthetic unity of apperception" (B, 137).

11. For an argument against construing either Kant's theoretical or his practical philosophy as a kind of "impositionism," see Pippin 2014.

12. Heidegger certainly appreciates that this is what Kant was trying to do: "What makes an experiencing possible at the same time makes possible the experienceable, or rather experiencing [an experienceable] [*Erfahrbare bzw. Erfahrene*] as such. This means: transcendence makes the being in itself accessible to a finite creature" (KPM, 84). But "makes possible" seems to have for him (he is not consistent about this) this unilaterally impositionist dimension.

13. This is not in itself a point ignored by Kant, although he makes something different out of it. "Plato noted very well that our power of cognition [*Erkenntniskraft*] feels a far higher need than that of merely spelling out appearances according to a synthetic unity in order to be able to read them as experience, and that our reason naturally exalts itself to cognitions that go much too far for any object that experience can give ever to be congruent,

stration about the forms of being. The deduction is not about "stamping" but about demonstrating that there cannot *be* any intuited content (i.e., any cognitively relevant content) that is incongruent with the required a priori conditions of experience, of empirical knowledge, or, generally, cognitive intelligibility. The argument is not only that experience would not be possible unless a rule a priori determined what could count as objective time order, but also that an intuited manifold *itself* must offer up a possible distinction between, say, subjective and objective succession, or experience would also be impossible. But Heidegger is simply asserting that this unity is "subjective" and imposed. As he says,

> But the legitimate use of the understanding depends on the following: that thinking continues to be specified as representational thinking that posits and judges—i.e., as positing and proposition by virtue of transcendental apperception, and that thinking remains related to affection by the senses. Thinking is ensconced in human subjectivity, which is affected by sensibility, i.e., is finite. "I think" means: I connect a sensuously given manifold of representations by virtue of a prior glance toward the unity of apperception, which articulates itself into the limited multiplicity of pure concepts of the understanding, i.e., categories. (P, 350)

There is quite a lot, most of it simply assumed by Heidegger, packed into "Thinking is ensconced in human subjectivity" (*Das Denken ist eingesenkt in . . . endliche Subjektivität des Menschen*). "Sunk" in a subjectivity (a more literal and appropriately graphic translation) suggests "trapped," "restricted within," "cannot get out of," and Heidegger has only asserted, not defended, this interpretation of the passages he cites. Of course, any content of thought must *be* thought *by* a thinker to be such a content, but why does thinking it mean content is trapped inside internal or subjective episodes of thought? Perhaps a contrary interpretation would not stand full critical scrutiny across the whole text of the *Critique*, but Heidegger is not dealing with the plausible claim that for Kant the understanding is determining what *must objectively* be thought together with what, not that what must be thought together with what is determined by *whatever* the understanding unilaterally requires and imposes or stamps onto intuitions. As Kant puts it at B138: "The synthetic unity of consciousness is therefore an *objective* condition of all cognition, not merely something I myself need in order to cognize an object but rather something under which every in-

---

but that nonetheless have their reality, and are by no means merely figments of the brain [*Hirngespinste*]" (CPR, B370/A314).

tuition must stand in order to become an object for me, since in any other way, and without this synthesis, the manifold could not be united in one consciousness."[14]

The understanding must determine *objective* unity or there could not be a unity of experience across time, a continuous "I think." But that claim is certainly not equivalent to: the I must achieve a unity of consciousness somehow or other, and any unity among intuited elements that achieves this counts as objective. Rather, only an objective determination of time order, a representation of objective succession, can allow the distinction from a mere succession of representations that would constitute an unacceptable subjective unity of apperception. The pure principles for this unity are not derived from experience, are "prior," but they are not to be understood as subjective dispositions (that is Hume, not Kant). They are the rules for *any* thinking that can be onto objects by any thinker. They are not "our" rules. They are "human" and finite only because we are among the creatures who cannot create the objects thought by thinking of them. That is an exclusion that does nothing to isolate this requirement as a unique feature of the human species. It is a requirement for any non-divine thinking being.

Once Heidegger has slipped in his "*eingesenkt*" characterization, the full import of what he wants to claim can be stated. For he wants to say that far from having freed us from metaphysics, and despite Heidegger's own demonstration in 1929 that Kant had laid the foundation for a metaphysics of Being (which we will consider shortly), Kant still remains firmly ensconced, let us say, in the metaphysical tradition that Heidegger thinks has betrayed us. "The age-old prevailing meaning of being (constant presence [*ständige Anwesenheit*]) . . . is preserved in Kant's critical interpretation of being as the objectness of the object of experience. . . . The substantial means nothing other than 'the concept of object in general, which subsists in so far as we think in it merely the transcendental subject apart from all predicates'" (A, 414; B, 441; P, 351). So, even if the qualification we are insisting on is true, Heidegger is right, up to a point, that at the end of the day, objectness in Kant's sense is the primordial meaningfulness of Being.

In the background here is a lot of material in BT, especially his insistence that it is not perceivability that defines availability but Being-in-the-world, and that means via comportment. This is more explicit in BP. (He is discussing Fichte's example imperative, "Think the wall.") "There is already a constructive violation of the facts, an unphenomenological onset, in the request 'Think the wall.' For in our natural comportment toward things we

14. To be fair, with that last phrase, Kant does seem to be reverting to "what I myself require."

never think a single thing, and whenever we seize upon it expressly for itself we are taking it out of a contexture to which it belongs in its real content: wall, room, surroundings" (BP, 162). Any being is only available to "circumspective concern," so Heidegger thinks there is nothing ontologically valuable in something like a "theory of perception."[15]

Heidegger certainly realizes that for Kant the "transcendental subject" is not meant to be a psychological or metaphysical subject, and while he deals extensively with the limitations of "logic" for metaphysics (the insufficiency of the discursive form for any authentic engagement with being as such) he does not much deal with the possibility of such a *logical subject*.[16] This is not to say that Heidegger is completely wrong about the (also Hegelian) claim that Kant's idealism is finally subjectivist, but he mislocates the subjectivizing moment. Ironically, and this is the important point, it lies in the very feature that Heidegger shows links the subject with being, the pure and indeed wholly subjective forms of intuition. It does not lie in the transcendental unity of apperception.[17]

I should note that this is not something like an error or simple misinterpretation by Heidegger. He is uninterested in the idealist implications of the pure forms of intuition because he does not think Kant's arguments for their subjectivity work. In his 1925/1926 lectures *Logik. Die Frage nach der Wahrheit*, he notes that Kant's case assumes "Cartesian dogmatism."

---

15. Heidegger must be "setting up" this issue since he gives us a very different example of a comportment toward a "wall": the Rilke passage from *The Notebooks of Malte Laurids Brigge* that we discussed in chapter 2.

16. To anticipate the next section, consider this remark:

> The concept of pure reason and the unity of a pure, sensible reason become the problem. Inquiring into the subjectivity of the subject, the "Subjective Deduction," leads us into darkness. Therefore, Kant does not refer to his *Anthropology*, not just because it is empirical and not pure, but rather because in and through the execution of the ground-laying itself, the manner of questioning regarding human beings becomes questionable. (KPM, 150)

Cf. the discussion in Taminiaux 1991, 98–103. (Taminiaux thinks the passage is problematic because Heidegger will say that *any* self-understanding that takes its bearing from things is "inauthentic and improper" [101; 107]. His larger point is that the naïve ontology of the Greeks, which, for Heidegger, realized the priority of *Zuhandenheit* to *Vorhandenheit*, must be wholly overcome, lest even works of art come to be regarded as ready-to-hand, tools. But Heidegger always intended the practical circumspective concern in BT to be a preliminary and limited example of *Bedeutsamkeit*, not to exhaust the notion, and Taminiaux's subsequent discussion of Heidegger's freeing himself completely from the assumptions of Greek metaphysics and starting a new path [say with OWA] makes, I think, too much of an idea of a break.)

17. See chapter 2 of Pippin 1989.

This is the basic thesis of that dogmatism. What is given first, and fore-most, and prior to anything else—i.e. what is given a priori—is the *ego cogito*. . . . Kant has correctly and phenomenologically shown . . . that space and time are given prior to any specific spatial or temporal thing. . . . But it does not follow that whatever is earlier than something else has to be a *cogitatio*. But Kant in fact draws this conclusion. In directing himself to the phenomena, Kant sees that space and time are something given antecedently as the conditions of the possibility of understanding any manifold at all. But on the basis of Descartes' dogma this means: Because it is a priori, what is originally given in this way prior to something else must be subjective, must be a *cogitatio*. (L, 278)[18]

As a student of Husserl, Heidegger is certainly aware of the objections to any psychologistic account of judgment, and his suggestions about "stamp-ing" and being "sunk" in subjectivity do not trade on any such psycholo-gizing. Moreover, from BT on, Heidegger often objects to any interiorized or Cartesian account of judgings as mental acts alone. Judgment too is a mode of public comportment towards entities, a modality of being-in-the-world, and not originally an inner episode. But he appears to think that Kant, without the notion of being-in-the-world, still wedded to the view that our primary understanding of Being and the beings is cognitive, has still not escaped Cartesianism of some sort. Occasionally, as at BT, 200–201, he appears to think that locating the intelligibility of being in judg-ment unavoidably transforms the objects of judgment into mere present-at-hand entities.[19] Given the claim that the primordial, fundamental, or original meaning of *beings* is as *pragmata*, equipment, ready-to-hand, our fundamental mode of comportment towards beings is engaged and unre-flective use, and any interruption of such unreflective use, such as a cogni-tive judging, must lose any grip on this primordial meaning and primordial comportment in favor of a present-at-hand substance. This would seem the basis for his charge about Kant's errant metaphysics, that Kant preserves the meaning of being as "constant presence," which Kant's treatment only covers up or disguises.[20]

18. As cited by McManus 2012, 114. The translation is his.
19. Schear 2000 argues that the most one can rightly infer from this passage and others is that judging has a certain tendency toward a present-at-hand, contemplative or theoretical interpretation. In the case of Kant, Heidegger would then be suggesting that this tendency is not only not resisted but embraced. See the concise summary of his interpretation, 154–155.
20. This is a standard summary of existential primordiality in Heidegger's early ac-count, but there are other passages with a different slant. In FCM, in a passage we quoted a small part of previously, he suggests that our everyday interaction with beings other than ourselves is not for the most part unthematic, engaged coping but that "most proximally"

Unless there is such a link between judgment as such and being as constant presence or the substantial, this mere link to a thinking subject, in the way Kant links the three modalities of being to the experiencing subject, would not appear to justify any claim to a distortion or unthinking appropriation of the core metaphysical tradition. Heidegger himself treats the modes of being and the modes of Dasein's access to beings as two sides of the same coin. The fact that we can interrogate the meaning of being by interrogating our modes of access to being, or that interrogating the meaning of being can illuminate the only possible access (*our* access, a human subject's access) to such a meaning, do not indicate either that we are subjecting the meaning of being to what our finite mode of access can allow, and so "stamping" being with the subject's distinctive, finite requirements, nor that we are, because of this reciprocity, "sunk" in a Cartesian subjectivity. And, at least in this essay, Heidegger does not rest his argument on any necessary connection between judgment as such and the present-at-hand kind mode of being.

Moreover, Heidegger is focusing on Kant's treatment of cognition, ultimately scientific cognition of the Newtonian world, and it would not be fair to Kant to insist that he understands this cognitive or judgmental modality as either exclusive or even privileged. It is simply the topic he is writing about in the first *Critique*. In fact, a good case can be made that one of Kant's contributions to philosophy is his demonstration that our primary and most significant mode of comportment towards being "as a whole" is not cognitive but practical, the experience of the moral law, our own status as free subjects, and our sensitivity to the beautiful and the sublime. In that context, it would be fairer to Kant to concede that within the parameters of the problem posed by the *Critique*—how can there be synthetic a priori judgments?—his understanding of the connection between self-conscious judging and objectivity is deliberately circumscribed and cannot be under-

---

what we take ourselves to experience are present at hand entities: "This character of beings as something simply present at hand in the broadest sense cannot be insisted upon too strongly, because this is an essential character of beings as they spread themselves before us in our everydayness and we ourselves are also drawn into this widespread presence at hand. It is the fact that beings can be manifest in this levelled out uniformity of the present at hand which gives to human everydayness its peculiar security, dependency, and almost inevitability, and which facilitates the ease with which we necessarily turn from one being to another in everydayness, and yet the specific manner of being that is in each case entirely essential to beings is never acknowledged in its importance" (FC, 275). In these lectures, any appropriate way of dealing with beings is said to require a transformation of Dasein, something that is the result of an awakening, which itself is said to be the goal of Heidegger's philosophizing and quite difficult to achieve.

stood as a "thesis about being" as much as a "thesis only about whatever being *is* cognitively accessible."[21]

Heidegger would doubtless not accept this qualification and would argue that Kant *has* given pride of place in any question about *reality, being as such*, to cognitively accessible reality, and that priority reveals Kant's indebtedness to the metaphysical tradition. Kant certainly does want to give priority to the practical in the manner suggested above, but that priority is based not on some original disclosure of meaningfulness but on what we cannot but believe about our moral vocation. And such a profound requirement of reason, the very core of our inestimable worth, the source of our dignity, just cannot be a postulate without depriving it of any fundamentality or weightiness. As we shall see several times in Kant and Hegel, Heidegger's question—what is the meaning of Being? What is the meaning of my Being?—is difficult if not impossible to raise from within either the critical or speculative project. Heidegger would also no doubt charge that even in the practical context, the foundation for any ontological implications remains logic, as the consistent, identical architectonic structure of the other critiques demonstrates. And all of this is to be contrasted with an approach that Kant would not accept as primordial. That is, for Heidegger, being simply is not positing in the senses we have discussed but "presencing," in the sense of salient emerging, "revealing," that "being means letting be present" (P, 362). And even within a putatively restricted domain of cognition alone, Kant has left the crucial questions unthought or addresses them in ways that obscure. "Thought must ask: What, then, is called being, such that it can be determined by way of representational thinking as positing and positedness? That is a question that Kant does not ask, just as he does not ask the following ones: What, then, is called being, such that positing can be determined by the structure of form and matter?" And Heidegger concludes from this: "Being, in the sense of enduring presencing, is dominant in Kant's thesis about being as positing, and also in the entire realm of his interpretation of the being of beings as objectivity and objective reality" (P, 360).

As we have noted, this treatment of Kant is only one aspect of quite a complicated mix of criticisms and enthusiasms, distancing himself from Kant and embracing him at the same time. Most of the embracing occurs in his 1929 book *Kant and the Problem of Metaphysics*, to which we now turn.

---

21. There is obviously a connection between this move and what was suggested at the end of the last chapter. The same problems arise.

4

Kant as Metaphysician

In *Being and Time* and the lecture courses *The Basic Problems of Phenomenology* and *The Fundamental Concepts of Metaphysics*, Heidegger had rejected a conception of metaphysics as a contemplative or strictly theoretical enterprise—that is, as an a priori account of some fundamental level of reality inaccessible to empirical experience. Kant had done so as well, of course, insisting on shifting our attention in any attempt at philosophical knowledge, which he defined as synthetic a priori knowledge, to the nonempirically determinable "subjective" conditions for the possibility of empirical experience. In this way, he thought that philosophy, an a priori science, could still determine in advance what could be a real object—if only a real object of sensible experience, and this by showing that "the conditions for the possibility of experience are at the same time the conditions for the possibility of objects of experience" (A, 158/B, 197).

It is uncontroversial to say that Heidegger rejects both enterprises as inadequate for any inquiry into the only question that should matter to metaphysics: what is the meaning of Being? This is because both approaches must already ("errantly," as he would put it) assume an answer to such a question—the answer that Heidegger calls *ständige Anwesenheit*, standing presence or substantial perdurance through time, with time understood as a sequence of nows. This is inadequate because it can be shown to be secondary and artificial (no one ever encounters any object as standing presence as such, or no object means that in its original availability), and so such presence is not the original and primary manifestness as such that we seek and that any other conception must presuppose. "Being, in the sense of enduring presencing, is dominant in Kant's thesis about being as positing, and also in the entire realm of his interpretation of the being of beings as objectivity and objective reality" (P, 360).

In making this case, he is also insisting that the availability of being as such both requires a kind of thinking or thinking attentiveness in our being-in-the-world, and a thinking *about* such thinking that is not, cannot be, exclusively conceptual and cognitive in the traditional sense. The original thinking or apperceptive comportment in which being as such is manifest also requires a kind of attunement that is prereflective and preconceptual, and one in which inevitably Dasein has a stake, in which its own being is at issue for itself as a task, not an intellectual problem. And any *account* of this comportment, the thinking on such a possibility, the thinking going on in the lectures and the first Kant book, must also not be a mere intellectual analysis. We can no more "understand" such an attunement from a sideways on or third-person perspective than we can understand romantic love, or jealousy or anxiety or boredom, by a descriptive, third-person account. Accordingly, Heidegger describes what he is doing as an attempt to "awaken an attunement" we must already implicitly have but have not attended to.

Or, as he puts it: "More essential by far than the acumen and rigor of conceptual incisiveness (which we may also need and which has a special character of its own compared to scientific thought) is the seriousness with which we strive to keep these questions on the right path. This is necessary if they are to serve the task which is given over to philosophizing: not to describe the consciousness of man but to evoke the Dasein in man" [*sondern das Dasein im Menschen zu beschwören*] (FCM, 174).

There is thus in one way a deep similarity with the project of idealism outlined in the last chapter. At least it could be put this way: metaphysics is a thinking on thinking (acknowledgeable availability in the most general sense) that is just thereby an illumination of being itself, of the possibility of meaningful being *as* availability, manifestness. Although Heidegger would disagree with this formulation, it is fair enough to see here something of the "logic as metaphysics" thesis he will oppose throughout his early career, if we expand the notion of logic to include apperceptive comportment. That is, in his famous formulation that resonates in various ways in Hegel's metaphysics, the conditions of the possibility of experience are at the same time the conditions for the possibility of objects of experience. On a plausible reading of Kant this knowledge of the necessary constituents of any "phenomenal reality" is not knowledge of something other than reality as it is in itself (say, subjectively constructed objects) but those limited aspects of *reality* that we, as finite beings, can know. That

limitation concerns the way our finite, human forms of intuition restrict
what of the available world we have sensible access to, but on this view
the result can count as a limited metaphysics, an a priori knowledge of
the real. The reason Heidegger would disagree is that his version of this
thinking on thinking is very different from Kant's program of reason as
spontaneity, as autonomously setting its own limits and possibilities, and
even more different from Hegel's account of thought's "infinity," its capacity for a self-grounding self-sufficiency and so its "absolute" status (the
elimination of these Kantian intuitive limitations as psychological). In Hegel, the *Logic*, the "science of pure thinking," appears as an account of all
possible account-giving, but it is just thereby, without any second step, an
account of all the "accountables," and the accountables count as all there
could be: Being. Heidegger's view has a structural similarity (no Dasein, no
meaningfulness) but is different because the original attunement and the
attempt to awaken an attunement (his version of our passive relation to the
world) involves an acknowledgment of a profound dependence. "Logic is
consequently to be grasped as the system of pure reason, as the realm of
pure thought. This realm is truth, as it is without a veil, in and for itself. . . .
Can there be more compelling proof for how little the metaphysis which
belongs to human nature, and hence how little 'human nature' itself, is
self-evident?" (KPM, 171). We cannot engineer, bring about, or convince
ourselves that we ought to have any such attunement, and thereby bring it
about. Any illumination of it requires that it *be* awakened, brought out as
always already attuned. The implications of this dependence are vast and
according to Heidegger wholly unappreciated.

However, while all the above is roughly accurate, Heidegger would dispute the characterization of Kant as one-sided and incomplete. There are
various dimensions to Kant's project, various tendencies and temptations
he would say, and in his 1929 book, *Kant and the Problem of Metaphysics*, he wants to show that Kant's appreciation for the finitude of thinking
and the implications of such finitude are far more radical than has been
appreciated. Kant finally, in this account, did not carry through those implications, and Heidegger is not really interested in "Kant interpretation,"
but he teases a great deal out of Kant that illuminates his own relation to
idealism.

By this point, it should surprise no one that Heidegger was so attracted
to a book called "The Critique of Pure Reason." Consider this remark from
his 1927–1928 seminar on the *Critique*. "When, a few years ago, I studied *The
Critique of Pure Reason* again and read it against the background of Husserl's
phenomenology, it was as if the scales fell from my eyes, and Kant became

for me an essential confirmation of the correctness of the way I was seeking" (PhK, 292).[1]

That title could, without distortion, be considered the title for Heidegger's own enterprise if its positive implications were more Heideggerian. But that positive dimension for Kant is first of all the possibility
of synthetic a priori knowledge, in a way that could be called Kantian first
philosophy or metaphysics. But in the conventional reading, as noted, synthetic a priori knowledge concerns the subjective conditions for the possibility of empirical experience, not a metaphysical knowledge of reality. That
is the Kantian revolution. And Kant is famous for denying the possibility
of ontology, claiming that the proud name of ontology must give way to
the humbler analytic of the understanding (A, 247/B, 303). The results of
that analytic limit knowledge to empirical experience and a mathematized
conception of nature, applicable to the empirical world because of the pure
form of subjective intuition: space.

But in this book, as opposed to *The Question Concerning the Thing* and
his criticism of the treatment of being as the present at hand in *Kant's Thesis
about Being*, in KPM Heidegger does not so much concentrate on Kant's
empiricism and scientism. His enthusiasm is about finitude in Kant's account, the insufficiency of pure thinking on its own as any measure of the
real, and the implications of such finitude for all of philosophy. In line with
this, and his own metaphysics of finitude, he insists that the *Critique* has
nothing to do with epistemology. Rather, it "lays the foundation for metaphysics," the only metaphysics now possible: an inquiry into the meaning
of being, given such finitude. This, of course, means that his approach is
already orthogonal to, even foreign to, Kant's project. He is framing the
Kantian project in terms of not our possible a priori knowledge of being but
the availability of the meaningfulness of being.

He gets started with his Heideggerianizing of Kant right away by ap-
plauding in his own way Kant's famous Copernican revolution.

Through the Copernican Revolution, the "old" concept of truth in the
sense of the "correspondence" (*adaequatio*) of knowledge to the being is
so little shaken that it [the Copernican Revolution] actually presupposes
it [the old concept of truth], indeed even grounds it for the first time.
Ontic knowledge can only correspond to "beings" (objects) *if this being*

1. It should be noted, though, that in the fourth edition of KPM, the 84-year-old Heidegger said that his original interpretation was indefensible because of so many foreign concepts imposed on Kant. He would appear finally to agree with Cassirer's famous 1931 review.

as being is already first apparent [offenbar], i.e., *is already first known in the constitution of its Being.* Apparentness of beings (ontic truth) revolves around the unveiledness of the constitution of the Being of beings (ontological truth); at no time, however, can ontic knowledge itself conform "to" the objects because, without the ontological, it cannot even have a possible "to what." (KPM, 8–9)

This is quite a variation on Kant. Kant certainly does not think that our access to the constitution of the Being of beings is by means of some unveiledness or disclosure, as Heidegger understands it, and we always have to remember that by the Being of beings and ontological truth, Heidegger does not mean the accessibility of the "really real" but the "*Sinn des Seins.*" This constitution of Being for Kant, what makes possible its availability at all, are the table of categories, which Kant thinks he can derive from the logical forms of judgment in the Metaphysical Deduction, and the pure forms of intuition, space and time, which, as an analysis of the concepts of space and time can show, can be nothing other than pure subjective forms of intuition. However, since it is very unclear how Kant performed such a categorical derivation, and also very clear that it is not by mere inspection of the nature of judging as a mental activity or as a mere inheritance of some settled table, there is some leeway here. But there is no moment in Kant that holds that the Being of beings is a matter of disclosure. Its categorical structure is the result of a "metaphysical deduction," "guided" by the "thread" (*Leitfaden*) that Heidegger wants most of all to dispute—that all thinking is judging. The result of the subsequent transcendental deduction is justified as the meaning of the beings of experience (categoriality), the only possible way there could be objects of experience that show up in our experience meaningfully. All of this is circumscribed by the assumption, which Heidegger for a while passes over for his own purposes, that the meaning of Being for Kant is its knowability, the content of which are the categories, moments of the transcendental unity of apperception, inflected by our forms of intuition. Heidegger temporarily adopts the language of the knowability of Being in order to get to what he regards as deeper issues in Kant.

And on the other hand, what Heidegger is trying to say about Kant is quite right—first that a priori knowledge does not "conform to objects" as in traditional metaphysics, where pure reason conforms to immaterial entities, but objects must conform to synthetic a priori judgments establishing their possibility. There can be no objects of experience otherwise. That is, the very possibility of available objects as such—of beings, of meaningful, intelligible beings—must be *first* established. That is the true Kantian revolution. And moreover, despite his earlier interpolation of *maßgebende*

Prägung into the text as the way this happens, here he realizes that is far from the standard epistemological perspective—that is, that subjective forms of experience are imposed on the material deliverances of sensation to produce phenomenal objects, which then cannot be said to be things in themselves and must be understood as different objects.

That cannot be what objects conforming to knowledge amounts to, because without establishing the possibility of meaningful intuitability, there is nothing that could conform to such subjective conditions; those conditions delimit the possibility of objects at all. There can be no undifferentiated mere matter of sensation that is then in a second step shaped by pure concepts. If such a manifold is undifferentiated and indeterminate, there is nothing determinate that could call up, let's say, the appropriate shape. The material of sensation would then be pure materiality, undifferentiable from any other moment. We recall what he has been saying several times in a Kantian vein: at no time can ontic knowledge *itself* be said to conform "to" the objects because, without the ontological condition, it cannot even have a possible "to what." Here is the way he puts the point in his language:

> This bringing-forth of the determination of the Being of the being is a preliminary self-relating to the being. This pure "relation-to . . ." (synthesis) forms first and foremost the that-upon-which [*das Worauf*] and the horizon within which the being in itself becomes experienceable in the empirical synthesis. [Heidegger is here talking about the a priori synthesis that is said to "project" the field of possibility within which entities could show up.] . . . Hence, transcendental knowledge does not investigate the being itself, but rather the possibility of the preliminary understanding of Being, i.e., at one and the same time: the constitution of the Being of the being. (KPM, 10)

Having introduced the issue of metaphysics this way, Heidegger presents the heart of his interpretation, or rather his unearthing what he believes to be of significance in Kant's approach though not fully appreciated by Kant himself. "In order to understand *The Critique of Pure Reason*, this point must be hammered in, so to speak: knowing is primarily of intuiting. From this it at once becomes clear that the new interpretation of knowledge as judging (thinking) violates the decisive sense of the Kantian problem. All thinking is merely in the service of intuition. Thinking is not simply alongside intuition, 'also' at hand; but rather, according to its own inherent structure, it serves that to which intuition is primarily and constantly directed" (KPM, 15–16).

This is not exactly Kant's position. It would be more accurate to summarize it as: knowing is always a thinking intuiting and an intuiting think-ing. But this emphasis is a decisive feature of Heidegger's interpretation, and in one sense it is simply Kant's own restatement of the famous motto that thinking without intuition is empty, and intuitions without thinking are blind. (As we shall see, Heidegger will want to interpret the "originary" thinking in the uptake of intuitions as the work of the imagination—*that* sort of "thinking," not, originally, judging or judgmental form.) Further, he makes the very good point that thinking's dependence on intuition for genuine content (beyond the semantic content of the pure concepts of the understanding—viz., subject-predicate, or "bearer of properties but never itself a property" or antecedent-consequence, or "necessary connection") must mean that the whole question of what pure thinking is, what judg-mental forms in relation to any object are, *must go beyond "general logic."* That is, pure thinking insofar as it can be said to have some purchase on ob-jects other than thought (in Heideggerese "as constitutive of the meaning of Being")[2] is not possible without this dependence on intuition, understood as *a feature of pure thinking itself.* (Cf. "according to its own inherent struc-ture" in the quotation above.) Thinking itself must be understood in the light of this dependence, not by "adding on" its dependence on intuition. Here is another formulation: "Now if Kant calls this pure, self-orienting, self-relating-to our thoughts [*unseren Gedanken*] then 'thinking' [*Denken*] this thought [*Gedankens*] is no longer called judging, but is thinking in the sense of the free, forming, and projecting (although not arbitrary) 'conceiv-ing' [*Sichdenkens*] of something. *This original 'thinking' is pure imagining"* (KPM, 106, my emphasis). What exactly this amounts to will be clear only when we come to Heidegger's view about the centrality of the imagination in the first edition.

The faculties, that is, are logically differentiable but never separable.[3] That Kant himself means us to understand that a focus on general logic alone as constitutive of the basic formal structure of thinking as such is in-adequate is clear in that passage Heidegger cites in *Kant's Thesis about Being* that we discussed above. Again: "I have never been able to accept the inter-pretation which logicians give of judgment in general. It is, they declare, the representation of a relation between two concepts" (B, 141).

Kant's complaint is that the nature of this relationship is not explained, and the formulation especially misses that, as a matter of logical form, the

2. Always remembering that, to get to what Heidegger thinks is important in Kant, he is bracketing any question about the fact that the meaning of being in Kant is knowability, a possible object of knowledge. What happens in his later work is that he realizes he should never have done that, and he removes the brackets.

3. See Pippin 2005 for an explanation of this claim.

notion of judgment itself must include as a necessary element, something he expresses this way in *Kant's Thesis about Being*: "that wherein positing a predicate of a subject is grounded" (P, 347). This means that the Kantian conception of judgment itself must be as he states it in the passage a bit later, and it is quite a radical reformulation of the logic of judgment, one decisive for Hegel as well. It makes very difficult any strict separation between general and transcendental logic. The passage is worth repeating. "I find that a judgment is nothing but the manner in which given modes of knowledge are brought to the objective unity of apperception. This is what is intended by the copula is. It is employed to distinguish the objective unity of given representations from a subjective unity" (B, 141).

But the obvious oddity of Heidegger's view is that he does not stress what this "inseparability" means *for the doctrine of intuition*; he does not direct the reader's attention to the implications of the claim that intuitions without thinking, as Kant understood thinking (its roots in general logic), are blind and cannot, isolated and considered abstractly in themselves, be said to be anything that thought can be "in the service of."[4] As noted, this will be addressed and to some extent cleared up when Heidegger comes to his account of the role of the imagination, but Heidegger is clearly uninterested in the consequences of Kant's position for the role of concepts in empirical knowledge and the restriction of a priori knowledge to possible objects of sensory experience. The problems of sensory deliverances and accounting for perceptual content are simply not, one has to say, Heidegger's problems. What for Kant was a dependence on intuited sensory content and even a dependence on pure forms of intuition for a priori knowledge are not discussed by Heidegger as leading to Kant's final position on "the meaning of being"—that is, a dependence on spatio-temporal substances and synthetic activity, and a mathematized physics bearing on the world of spatio-temporal objects because of the necessary condition of pure formal intuition. (This will, though, become a prominent theme and a source of strong critique in *The Question Concerning the Thing*.) That sort of dependence Heidegger treats instead as thinking's dependence on a modality of "availability" that means to include, but hardly is exhausted by, sensory receptivity. Of course, Heidegger is aware of this departure from the letter of Kant's text. His hermeneutical principle is explicitly to understand the philosopher better than he understood himself, to think what is "unthought" in the philosopher's thinking, to engage in an *"Auseinander-*

---

4. Of course, if intuitions are interpreted as Heidegger (not Kant) wants, as the original availability of meaningful being, then *that* is something thought can be said to be in the service of, to depend on.

setzung" with figures in the history of philosophy, an interpretive confrontation rather than a commentary. He even freely admits that Kant insists on a reciprocity between thinking and intuiting,[5] but he proposes forging ahead anyway with his claim for the priority of intuition, as in this passage: "In contrast to this, however, we must maintain that intuition constitutes the authentic essence of knowledge and that, *despite the reciprocity of the relationship between intuiting and thinking,* [intuition] does possess authentic importance. This stands out clearly, but not just on the basis of Kant's explanation. . . . Rather, only with this interpretation of knowledge is it also possible to grasp what is essential in this definition, namely, the finitude of knowledge" (KPM, 16, my emphasis).

His translation of the issue of sensory deliverances into the much broader issue of availability and dependence is clear as he begins to analyze what he thinks is involved in the Kantian doctrine of synthesis. "Accordingly, the synthesis of thinking and intuiting accomplishes the making evident of the encountered being as object. [*Dementsprechend vollzieht die Synthesis von Denken und Anschauen das Offenbarmachen des begegnenden Seienden als Gegenstand.*] We will therefore call it the veritative synthesis which makes [something] true ([or] evident). This [synthesis] coincides with the above-mentioned "bringing-forward" of the relevant determinateness of the beings themselves. [*Wir nennen sie daher die wahr-(offenbar-)machende, veritative Synthesis. Sie deckt sich mit dem obengenannten 'Beibringen' der sachlichen Bestimmtheit des Seienden selbst.*]" (KPM, 20).

(The "veritative synthesis" is the full truth claim made by a judgment [I judge or assert that Socrates is white, say], and it is said to presuppose an original unifying—essentially, the proposition that will be asserted (Socrates is white), what Heidegger calls the predicative synthesis, and the original experience of the synthetic connection, which he calls the apophantic synthesis [the perception of Socrates's whiteness or as white]. That is, Heidegger is not claiming that Kant is committed to any direct, purely pas-

---

5. For example,

"Only through their union can knowledge spring forth." The unity of their unification is nevertheless not a subsequent result of the collision of these elements. Rather, what unites them, this "synthesis," must let the elements in their belonging-together and their oneness spring forth. If finite knowledge, however, has its essence precisely in the original synthesis of the basic sources [*Grundquellen*] and if the laying of the ground for metaphysics must push ahead into the essential ground of finite knowledge, then it is inescapable that the naming which indicates the "two basic sources [*Grundquellen*]" already suggests an allusion to the ground of their source [*ihren Quellgrund*], i.e., to an original unity. (KPM, 25)

This is foreshadowing of what Heidegger wants to claim about the imagination, the original source.

sive givenness of sensory data. He realizes that this uptake requires activity, but he is preparing for the importance of the imagination's activity in that uptake.) What is important in the passage is the beginning of the many circumlocutions Heidegger uses (*Offenbarmachen, wahr-offenbar-machende, Beibringen der sachlichen Bestimmtheit*) to draw Kant's views on our dependence on intuition closer to Heidegger's own view on our dependence on an original manifestation or meaningful disclosure that cannot itself be the product of thinking. Sensible intuitions are simply what we "take in," *hinnehmen* (the translator uses "taking in stride"), and the whole issue of sensible materiality is avoided, at least in 1929. This all again depends on the premise that perceptual availability is not "original," and that means any other determination can be said to depend on that original availability.

The same transformation goes on with Kant's claim that we know only appearances. On the one hand, Heidegger adopts what has come to be known in the last fifty years as the "two aspect" view of Kant's idealism rather than the "two object" view. He quotes approvingly the *Opus Postumum*, which makes just such a claim. "In the *Opus Postumum* Kant says that the thing in itself is not a being different from the appearance, i.e., 'the difference between the concept of a thing in itself and the appearance is not objective but merely subjective. The thing in itself is not another Object, but is rather another aspect (*respectus*) of the representation of the same Object'" (KPM, 23).[6] On the other hand, Heidegger gives this issue a predictable gloss. In this case, the issue of the intertwining of revealing and concealing comes to the fore. "Rather, the expression 'behind the appearance' expresses the fact that finite knowledge as finite necessarily conceals at the same time, and it conceals in advance so that the 'thing in itself' is not only imperfectly accessible, but is absolutely inaccessible to such knowledge by its very essence. What is 'behind the appearance' is the same being as the appearance. Because it only gives the being as object, however, this appearance does not permit that same being to be seen fundamentally as a thing which stands forth" (KPM, 23).[7]

This again does not take on board the basis of Kant's idealism in the claim that it is the *subjectivity* of the forms of receptivity, space and time, that "idealize" what can be said to be known (and not categorical form), excluding the thing as it is in itself, and so he ignores the importance of something like that claim for Kant's moral theory and practical metaphys-

6. This is what I meant above by a "plausible reading" of Kant's limitation of knowledge to phenomenal reality.

7. In the conventional view, even in most two-aspect interpretations, the thing in itself is not imperfectly accessible; it is completely and utterly inaccessible in any cognitive experience.

ics. But Heidegger's understanding of this finitude also has his own non-Kantian critical qualification. It is *"because* it only gives the being *as object"* that the availability of the beings as "that which stands forth" can be said to be concealed as well as in some limited sense revealed. Any possibility of the question of the meaning of Being is avoided. This goes even further into Heidegger's dissatisfaction with the restriction on the original availability of beings as "standing presence," substantial perdurance in time and extension in space, rather than as manifest in its meaningfulness and so as necessarily a being-in-the-world. This is pure Heidegger and not Kant, but it is the seed of the criticism that becomes explicit in QT and this is integral to his sweeping claim about German Idealism as the culmination of this view of the meaning of Being since Plato and so of philosophy itself.

And pointing out these circumlocutions is not necessarily a criticism of Heidegger, given what he is trying to bring out in Kant. If he is right that, say, the perception of a stone being warmed by the sun can never be isolated as a distinct experiential event (except by an abstraction that always has its own practical purpose), that no one originally "takes in" beings in their world in that isolated sense (and if they think they do, much is "concealed"), then the door is open for an interpretation of Kant that allows for the possibility that we do not first of all experience *ourselves* as objects of inner and outer perception and so could open the question of the practical reality of our being free beings, with others available as well as originally, not secondarily, free beings or persons. And once that door is open, there is no reason not to extend such an interpretive trajectory further.

This all brings us to the two most important elements of Heidegger's interpretation: his account of the role of the imagination, and his enthusiasm for Kant's treatment of the pure concepts as modes of time consciousness. As we have seen, the problem we face is accounting for the unity of pure concepts and pure intuitions. He first consults Kant's answer:

> Transcendental logic, on the other hand, has lying before it a manifold of a prior sensibility which the aesthetic offered to it in order to provide material for the concepts of pure understanding. Without this material, those concepts would be without any content and therefore would be entirely empty. Now space and time contain a manifold of pure a priori intuition, but at the same time they are the conditions for the receptivity of our mind-conditions under which alone it can receive representations of objects and which therefore must also always affect the concept of these objects. And yet, the spontaneity of our thought requires that this manifold first be gone through in a certain way, taken up, and bound

together in order to produce knowledge. This act I name synthesis. (A, 77/B, 103)[8]

Heidegger calls this a superficial way of putting the issue. There can be no pure manifold as such, lying ready for conceptual determination. Since we are talking about pure, not empirical intuition, this would just be a projected dispersal of possible temporally successive undifferentiated sensory material, and a "manifold" of projected spatial possibilities and impossibilities, the latter established most clearly by geometric constructability. But the possible elements of any pure intuition must already be "held together" somehow to be available at all (they don't hold themselves together), but not by a predicative synthesis (that already requires a manifold determinate enough to provide a content for such a synthesis) and not just as simply "lying there" before the mind. And Heidegger thinks that when Kant gets more precise about what is going on, we have our answer to the question of a hidden source for the possibility of a unity of intuitions and concepts.

He introduces the claim with Kant's general formulation.

What must first be given to us—with a view to the a priori knowledge of all objects—is the manifold of pure intuition; *the synthesis of this manifold by means of the power of the imagination is the second*, but even this does not yet yield knowledge. The concepts which give unity to this pure synthesis, and which consist solely in the representation of this necessary synthetic unity, furnish the third requisite for the knowledge of a proposed object [*eines vorkommenden Gegenstandes*], and they rest on the understanding. (A, 78/B, 104, my emphasis)

So what is responsible for the possible availability of beings in their givenness, what makes possible something that can be thought about, is the work of the imagination. And Heidegger is right about Kant's somewhat mysterious appeal to pure imagination. He is quite explicit about this. For example:

The imagination is therefore also a faculty of a synthesis a priori, on account of which we give it the name of productive imagination, and, insofar as its aim in regard to all the manifold of appearance is nothing further than the necessary unity in their synthesis, this can be called the transcendental function of the imagination. It is therefore certainly strange, yet from what has been said thus far obvious, that it is only by means of

8. I have used the translation provided in KPM.

this transcendental function of the imagination that even the affinity of appearances, and with it the association and through the latter finally reproduction in accordance with laws, and consequently experience itself, become possible; for without them no concepts of objects at all would converge into an experience. (A, 123)

And, "Both extremes, namely sensibility and understanding, must necessarily be connected by means of this transcendental function of the imagination, since otherwise the former would to be sure yield appearances but no objects of an empirical cognition, hence there would be no experience" (A, 124). Or most simply put, "We therefore have a pure imagination, as a fundamental faculty of the human soul, that grounds all cognition a priori. By its means we bring into combination the manifold of intuition on the one side and the condition of the necessary unity of apperception on the other" (A, 124). Accordingly, when Kant says the following—"The same function which gives unity to the various representations in a single judgment also gives unity to the mere synthesis of various representations in a single intuition which, expressed generally, is called the pure concept of the understanding" (A, 79/B, 105)—we know that that function is the imagination, operating as a mode of a priori synthesis, however strange that may sound.

Consider where we are at this point. We have no right to claim that beings as they are are simply and immediately available to us in pure sensory givenness, neither at the empirical level nor the level of pure intuition. That would be dogmatism; we need to understand their *possible* availability to a being uniquely open to engaging, comporting towards, and understanding them, and in Kant this means conceptualizing them. But this cannot be a matter of a given undifferentiated sensory manifold being simply subject to the requirements of thinking them, as if stamped with a conceptual form. And we are talking (with regard to pure imagination) about ontological knowledge. The possibility of manifestness as such. The question is: how we can a priori determine the possible availability of objects (a kind of projection [*Entwurf*],[9] an *imaginative* projection that we now learn must have always already occurred) and so we need to be able to do justice to both the role of any sensible manifold in that availability and the thinkability of that manifold.

Hence, we arrive at this "same synthesis" claim. We need a way of understanding how we can originally be attentive to the belonging together of elements of the manifold—synthetically take them in—in a way that makes it

9. See BT, 145, 385.

possible that they can be conceptualized. There must be a way of attending to a kind of unity in the manifold that is the same function, synthesis (in its imaginative dimension), as the conceptual synthesis, all without anything being "imposed." And this means we must understand the role of the imagination in mediating pure intuition and pure concept.

So how does the pure, productive imagination work? It seems most natural to think of the work of the imagination as what Kant calls the reproductive imagination in empirical experience, reproducing past elements in a succession and "keeping track" by imagining, anticipating, the future succession. The imagination considered as a function in an a priori projection of possibility is harder to conceive. How sensory contact makes available objects at all is something Heidegger seems simply to assume and has no interest in since it does not affect how beings meaningfully show up for Dasein. Perhaps the best way to put this is to say that for Heidegger the question of how we could be in any way "onto" beings other than ourselves is a question for him not *limited* to sensory deliverances in empirical intuition, that the deeper question is the possible availability of meaning for beings in-a-world. So, he begins to translate the Kantian problem into his terms so he can answer this question as he seeks to formulate it. This is part of his attempt to show that the question of the possibility of sensible intuition within the whole question of possible intentionality is also his problem, the problem of being's original, meaningful availability in the first place, and that Kant (hazily, I suppose one has to say) realized this in the first edition.

A finite, knowing creature can only relate itself to a being which it itself is not, and which it also has not created, if this being which is already at hand can be encountered from out of itself. However, in order to be able to encounter this being as the being it is, it must already be "recognized" generally and in advance as a being, i.e., with respect to the constitution of its Being. But this implies: ontological knowledge, which here is always pre-ontological, is the condition for the possibility that in general something like a being can itself stand in opposition to a finite creature. Finite creatures need this basic faculty of a turning-toward . . . which lets-[something]-stand-in-opposition. (KPM, 50)

The revealing phrases here are *pre-ontological* and *lets-[something]-stand-in-opposition* (*Endliches Wesen bedarf dieses Grundvermögens einer entgegenstellenlassenden Zuwendung-zu*). The "basic faculty" is the imagination, and it is "pre-ontological" because it is the exercise of a nondiscursive, nonconceptual imagining. (The word above for "recognized" is "*erkannt*" [normally "known"] in advance, but Heidegger puts it in quotes to indicate that we are not talking about discursive knowledge.) Despite his terminological variations, Heidegger is also happy to return to a more strictly Kantian formulation to pose the problem he is preparing to address. "This a priori unified whole made up of pure intuition and pure understanding 'forms' the play-space for the letting-stand-against in which all beings can be encountered. With regard to this whole of transcendence, it is a matter of showing how (which here means, at the same time) pure understanding and pure intuition are dependent upon one another a priori" (KPM, 54). So the setup for his answer about the work of the pure, productive imagination can be summarized this way. If we are out to prove that pure concepts of the understanding are objectively valid for all possible objects of experience, we think we have shown that there could be nothing in the deliverances of sensibility that was not subsumable under the categories.

We have seen that one problem is how we could have some access to all possible delivered objects, an infinity of them. The answer was the pure forms of intuition, space and time, the forms of outer and inner sense and so the forms of anything possibly received. But this means we must provide an explanation for how concepts, which are abstract, general, rules of the understanding, *could* be thought together with sensory materiality, especially in directly encountered particularity. We just said that the answer is supposed to be the form of all intuition, time. But we still need to say how the dimensions of temporal moments (*Augenblicke* in Kant) fit together with pure generals, when the problem is posed at the a priori level. They must have "something in common," Kant says, something that partakes of the generality of concepts and the form of the concrete materiality of sensible particulars in time. Kant's answer is that we can *imagine* these pure concepts in their possible bearing on the material of any intuition. That imagining process is called a schematism. And that means imagining a pure concept in terms of its temporal dimensions, an act of the pure or transcendental imagination.

Note here that, with respect to contemporary discussions inspired by McDowell's interpretation of Kant and McDowell's own philosophy, we should say that nothing would run afoul of Heidegger if we insisted in his name that "conceptual capacities are active in the deliverances of sensibility." In fact, he says frequently not that our uptake of the sensible world is "mindless," *non*conceptual, or *purely* intuitive but that the understanding and intuition are one faculty. So again, there is no dispute if we do not forget that Heidegger's notion of this access is a question always about the meaning of Being, not discursive determinacy. In the context of Heidegger's concerns, he would insist that while no one actually, originally, perceives a black rectangle at a certain distance from the perceiver, has black-rectangle impressions that it then construes or conceptualizes as a blackboard, but originally experiences a blackboard in a classroom within a nested set of purposes, it is possible to frame the question in terms of the role of concepts. Concepts are certainly actively involved in this original perceptual encounter. That is, what we would have to say is that concepts like hammer, nail, and board are at work; as such, they are understood as such in the use of hammers, but not *primarily* in a classificatory way, not as predicates of judgment or as classificatory in a way that would render our relation to beings as possible objects of judgment, as substances enduring in time. Concepts must play some role in making available the hammers as *pragmata*, items of use—the items, after all, are recognized as what they are, and no use would be otherwise possible—and in a way that does not invoke our checking with some "how to use a hammer rule," the concept, as necessary for such use. The key point (and the one that, on both sides, makes the controversy secondary to Heidegger's concerns) is that the primordial phenomenon is our experience of meaningfulness, the familiar role of any such object in a world of already assigned significances (all a matter not of perception but "attunement"), and concepts play their role in the service of their place in "worldliness." But this obviously raises a question. If concepts are not involved as predicates of possible judgments in such uptake, and are "involved," how are they involved? This is the difficult problem Heidegger is addressing somewhat indirectly in the appeal to the pure imagination.

That issue he poses this way: "The transcendental power of imagination is hence the ground upon which the inner possibility of ontological knowledge, and with it that of *Metaphysica Generalis*, is built" (KPM, 90). More radically put: both intuition and understanding are *derivative* functions, distinguished within an original unity, which is the activity of the imagination, "pure" because it operates at the a priori level in the absence of the object. What he appears to mean by *derivative* is that there could be no role to play for the understanding and intuition conceived as distinct capacities, were there not an original imaginative projection of a horizon of possible encounterable beings, a projection informed by the categories and spatiotemporal formality but in the service of this imagined projection. (As we shall see, he means an imagined "*Spielraum*," free play of temporal possibilities as the horizon of possible meaningfulness.) He can mean by this only that the original projection is imaginative because it does not result in some horizon of possible objectivity but meaningful availability that ultimately he must think of (at this period of his writing) as pragmatic availability, dependent on being-in-the-world. (He does not make his ultimate goal in his Kantian translations clear in the book; he just keeps hinting.)[10] These functions play their role in the service of such available meaningfulness, or for Dasein as always already in-the-world.

For example: "As pure apperception, the understanding has the 'ground for its possibility' in a 'faculty' which 'looks out in an infinity of self-made representations and concepts.' The transcendental power of imagination projects, forming in advance the totality of possibilities in terms of which it 'looks out,' in order thereby to hold before itself the horizon within which the knowing self, but not just the knowing self, acts" (KPM, 108).

Heidegger quotes from Kant's *Anthropology* lectures to make his point about everything in the service of this available access. (Quoting from *Anthropology* and then discussing a nonempirical version of anthropology is one of those hints about where he is heading—a big one.) Having already clarified the inseparability of understanding and intuition and their both being in the service of the imagination, he puts it this way: "'The power of imagination (*facultas imaginandi*) [is] a faculty of intuition, even without the presence of the object.' Hence, the power of imagination belongs to the faculty of intuition" (KPM, 90).[11] (We always have to remember that Heidegger has repeatedly claimed that the powers of understanding and intuiting are not separable, even though intuiting has priority. This is the point of the discussion above, that concepts are involved in any sensory uptake but in the service of a more original projective power.) So, Heidegger feels

10. Occasionally the link between his own project—that all of this is ultimately about the meaning of Being—is explicit.

For that reason, what is formed therein can likewise never essentially be "mere imagination" in the above sense. Rather, in general it is the horizon of objects formed in the transcendental power of imagination—the understanding of Being—which first makes possible something like a distinction between ontic truth and ontic appearance ("mere imagination"). (KPM, 97)

11. Heidegger is quoting Kant, *Anthropologie in pragmatischer Hinsicht, Werke*, vol. VIII, §28, 54. As evidence that he means to point us to his own formulation of a *Daseinsanalytic* as truly laying the foundation of metaphysics, see:

And yet, did not the first attempt to grasp the Kantian ground-laying more originally, namely, the going-back to its anthropology: break down? Certainly, insofar as it was shown that *Anthropology* offers to the interpretation of knowledge and its two sources was brought to light in a more original form precisely through *The Critique of Pure Reason*. But from that, all that now follows is that the *Anthropology* worked out by Kant is an empirical one and not one which is adequate for the transcendental problematic, i.e., it is not pure. That now makes the demand for an adequate, i.e., a "philosophical anthropology" for the purpose of a laying of the ground for metaphysics, even more pressing. (KPM, 144)

justified in continuing to elaborate this "original" role of the imagination in being onto beings, the activity from which the understanding and spatial and temporal intuitions can be said to descend. "This 'formative power' is simultaneously a 'forming' which takes things in stride (is receptive) and one which creates (is spontaneous). In this 'simultaneously' lies the proper essence of its structure. But if receptivity means the same as sensibility and if spontaneity means the same as understanding, then in a peculiar way the power of imagination falls between both" (KPM, 91). So, he feels allowed to conclude further: "The imagination forms the look of the horizon of objectivity as such in advance, before the experience of the being. This look-forming [*Anblickbilde*] in the pure image [*Bild*] of time, however, is not just prior to this or that experience of the being, but rather always is in advance, prior to any possible [experience]" (KPM, 92).[12]

Any sensible reception occurs in temporal succession. The units of that succession are moments, *Augenblicke*. It is hard to specify a priori in advance what the discrete units of that succession are or how they belong together. One sees a house, then a yard, then a plane flying overhead, and hears a chain saw running, and one cannot coherently take in the world, prior to judging, "taking a stand" on anything, by simply receiving the mere succession as if moments of some extended object. An object consisting of these elements as parts or moments is mere fantasy. And one does not have to take in a house, then its roof, then its side wall for that coherence to be possible. In taking in the series, I am already, and here we have to say projectively imagining, the house with its elements, distinct from other elements in the temporal succession, and then in a looser way the house and the yard form a different, even looser unit to which the plane flying overhead, and the sound of a chain saw nearby do not belong. Or if I look at the roof of a house, I am already imagining the other parts, and that is not what I imagine next, but it is already what it is to see a roof, to take it in as the roof of a house. This is supposed to depend on an a priori space of temporal possibilities projected by the imagination, a space not limited by but assuming object determinacy. (Temporal possibilities because we are talking about the possibility of distinguishing between a subjective succession of representations and a representation of objective succession.) I have not yet experienced those other elements; I have imaginatively projected them in the absence of their yet occurring. The same anticipation must be true for the anticipation of "any being at all"; that is in terms of any of its temporal

12. Again, it is clear from the text that objectivity as Kant understands it is ultimately not Heidegger's interest here. By *objectivity* he means the availability of beings, what he calls the possibility of transcendence.

dimensions. This is what Heidegger means by saying that the imagination forms the horizon of availability as such in advance, before the experience of the beings. In the second edition of the Deduction, Kant holds fast to the claim that any such projection must be categorical. In the example just used, we could not differentiate those different successive orders if we did not project the necessity that every event is necessarily connected with a prior event, from which it does not need to be perceived in such a succession. Heidegger's claim in his analysis of the principles in QT is that this holds only if we already assume that the meaning of any entity or event is its present at-hand empirical availability. But that again just assumes a meaning of Being (empirical knowability of perduring substances), and it treats that meaning on the model of an entity so conceived. In KPM, he was intrigued by the idea that Kant realized that such objective temporal ordering is not the source of any original availability but is secondary or founded, an abstraction from a wholly different (existential) experience of temporality and a nondiscursively available meaningfulness, ultimately presencing (*Anwesenheit*) or happening (*Ereignis*) within a certain world.

So, the question is not whether conceptual capacities are necessary for any experience versus whether various affordances in our experience simply engage habitual dispositions that have no apperceptively conceptual dimension. That is a falsely exclusive disjunction. The issue is rather the *mode* of conceptual actualization. The chess grand master has "immediately" "in mind" a sense of areas of threats, dangers, degrees of possibilities and probabilities, all because of the years he has spent playing and reading chess books. But those moves are determinate, and concepts are in play.

It might be useful to stress here, prior to any discussion of Heidegger's existential interpretation of imagination, his claim that any isolated view of mere perceptual intentionality is not original with him; the position he assigns to Kant is not an outlier in philosophy generally. Consider some examples. First, Sellars (1967): "To know the language of perception is to be in a position to let one's thoughts be guided by the world in a way that contrasts with free association, with day-dreaming, and, more interestingly, with the coherent imaginings of the story teller" (273). (He means by the latter phrase that such "letting," because it is not a rule-governed, active discrimination, is not open to arbitrariness, is not fictional.)

Or Strawson (1982), in discussing the role of imagination in experience (the vehicle of the sensory actualization of our conceptual capacities), notes the necessity for some role for other actual or possible perceptions in our coming to take a present perception as a perception of a distinct object and that must be the result of the imagination. Describing this "peculiarly intimate relation" (88) of such imagined perceptions to a present perception, he notes that he is not claiming that an actual occurrence of the memory or imagination of such perceptions occurs as a dated event, and he falls back to saying, "Still, in a way, we can say in such a case that the past perceptions are alive in the present perception" (87). Or, "It seems, then, not too much to say that the actual occurrent perception of an enduring object as an object of a certain kind, or as a particular object of that kind is, as it were, soaked with or animated by, or infused with—the metaphors are *à choix*— the thought of other past or possible perceptions of the same object" (89). Such a thought would be an imagined projection. And he goes on to talk about Wittgenstein on aspectual seeing and similar images as when Wittgenstein talks of the "echo of the thought in sight." Or when visual experience can be said to be suddenly "irradiated by a concept" as opposed to cases where it is "more or less steadily soaked with the concept" (93).

The point of all these metaphors is, of course, to find as many ways as possible to suggest some modality of spontaneous activity in intuiting other than assertoric judging or acts of conceptual sorting, or deliberate rule-following. We can claim that we cannot be successfully onto objects without the imaginative actualization of a sortal discriminatory power, even while insisting that the actualization of that power in the sensory presence of the object is quite different from its actualization in judgmental sorting. The different way is the way the imagination functions. Once this door is opened, we can see our way further into a philosophical anthropology and many other dimensions of imaginative activity, existential dimensions, involved in such projecting.

And we should keep in mind throughout that for Heidegger, this emphasis on the imagination in the first edition is a kind of stalking horse for his own claim that a laying of the foundation for a genuine metaphysics must be a "*Daseinsanalytic*," one in which the horizon-forming work of the imagination is not a determination of conceptual intelligibility but our comportment with a world everywhere always already "irradiated" with meaning, significance.

We get a sense of where he is headed in this passage:

> The totality of what is intuited in pure intuition does not have the unity which characterizes the universality of a concept. The unity of the totality of intuition, therefore, also cannot spring forth from the "synthesis of the understanding." It is a unity which is caught sight of in advance in the image-giving imagining [*im Bild-gebenden Einbilden*]. The "syn" of the totality of space and time belongs to a faculty of formative intuition. The pure synopsis, if it constitutes the essence of pure intuition, is only possible in the transcendental power of imagination, and that is all the more

so as this [transcendental power of imagination] is in general the origin of all that is "synthetic." (KPM, 198)

And Heidegger realizes how puzzling this will sound to a Kantian. "But the claim that thinking, which must indeed be sharply distinguished from all intuition, should have its origin in the transcendental power of imagination appears to be impossible, even if importance can no longer be attached to the order of precedence of sensibility and understanding" (KPM, 103).

As we shall see in more detail in the next section, this emphasis on the imagination is embedded in the general claim about the finitude of pure reason and so ultimately the claim that the exercise of pure reason is not the appropriate vehicle for genuine first philosophy. This even shows up in the moral philosophy in passages where Heidegger recalls the importance of the moral feeling of respect, a feeling we are subject to but that we depend on for any action-effective moral self-awareness.

> The preceding interpretation of the feeling of respect shows not only the extent to which it constitutes practical reason, but at the same time it makes it clear that the concept of feeling in the sense of an empirically intended faculty of the soul has disappeared, and into its place has stepped a transcendental, basic structure of the transcendence of the moral self. The expression "feeling" must come to be understood in this ontologico-metaphysical sense if we are to exhaust what Kant means by the characterization of respect as "moral feeling" and as "feeling of my existence." No further steps are now required in order to see that this essential structure of respect in itself allows the original constitution of the transcendental power of imagination to emerge. (KPM, 111)

(Much more on this issue below.) And it is here that Heidegger begins his claim that Kant, in the period between the two editions, "shrank back" from the implications of his own claim about the imagination and respect, aware that conceiving of the human person in terms of this finitude would require a wholesale reinterpretation of the self-determining character of pure reason.[13] "In the radicalism of his questions, Kant brought the 'possibility' of metaphysics to this abyss. He saw the unknown. He had to

---

13. The direction in which Heidegger wants his interpretation of the role of the imagination in Kant to lead us is clear from this passage in the Nietzsche lectures: "The poetizing essence of reason [*dichtende Wesen der Vernunft*] was not first discovered by Nietzsche but only emphasized by him in some particularly blunt respects, and not always adequately. Kant first explicitly perceived and thought through the poetizing character of reason in his doctrine of the transcendental imagination" (N, III 95–96, translation altered).

shrink back. It was not just that the transcendental power of imagination frightened him, but rather that in between [the two editions] pure reason as reason drew him increasingly under its spell" (KPM, 118). In particular, Kant is supposed to have shrunk back from the implications of his own schematism. If the categories can play a role only in the projection of a horizon of "really possible" objects as modes of time consciousness, then they are dependent on how time is possible, rather than vice versa. And Heidegger, claiming he is following Kant, considers true or existential temporality (as opposed to mere clock time, the time of measurement) a form of "self-affection." And in a general sense, he is certainly on solid interpretive ground, although what Kant means by a passage like the following is hardly pellucid. "Now that which, as representation, can be antecedent to every act of thinking anything, is intuition; and if it contains nothing but relations, it is the form of intuition. Since this form represents nothing except insofar as something is posited in the mind, it can be nothing other than the way the mind, through its own activity (namely, this positing of its representation), consequently comes to be affected through itself, i.e., according to an inner sense of its form" (B, 67). He means that one cannot say of a Dasein, a human person, that this sort of being is simply "in time," in some supposed "flow" of temporal moments. It can, of course, for various purposes, be considered that way, as if Dasein were a table or plant, but that aspect is derivative from how Dasein orients *itself* in time, and in that sense "affects itself." Kant means something like that attentiveness to what we noted above, the difference between a mere succession of representations and an objective succession of representations, something we do not simply perceive but must posit the manifold as subject to this distinction (which means positing "its own" manifold, and so itself), and Kant considers this always in the service of possible objectivity. Heidegger means, again in a way that involves the imagination, that we never experience time simply "passing," but our temporal awareness always (again) involves the issue of meaning. A stretch of time is too short for a job, too long, just right, wasted, sufficient, "dead," "stalled," as in boredom, or as a long, single moment in any intense involvement and so forth.

None of this, of course, is in Kant, and Heidegger does not belabor the issue in terms of his own claims about existential temporality in BT, but the notion of time is presented as kind of self-determining and so self-affecting, since time is a pure intuition, where that means not a pure intuited but a pure intuiting (cf. "the way the mind through its own activity"). This is not an empirical event, and so there is not a self that "affects" itself as already present to itself as a substance-like self, a subject. The self-affecting, despite the appearance linguistically of this dyadic structure, is the "activation" of itself as self, an essentially or fundamentally temporal self, we know from Division Two of BT. A self is the way it stretches itself along in time in the various modalities available to it. "As pure self-affection, time is not an acting affection that strikes a self which is at hand. Instead, as pure it forms the essence of something like self-activating. However, if it belongs to the essence of the finite subject to be able to be activated as a self, then time as pure self-affection forms the essential structure of subjectivity" (KPM, 132). So, "Rather, as the ground for the possibility of selfhood, time already lies within pure apperception, and so it first makes the mind into a mind" (KPM, 135).

So Heidegger considers himself to have, as it were, laid the ground for his major interpretive claim (and not coincidentally for his own project), what we referred to above as his attempt to displace any appeal to a transcendental subject or "pure thinker" with what he would call a *Daseinsanalytic*, but which he here, wanting no doubt to appeal to Kant's own instincts, suggests would be an anthropology to replace it, if the possibility of pure or a nonempirical anthropology were available to Kant. (Actually, the result of Heidegger's analysis would be grossly misconstrued if one were to take the implications of his claims about finitude to mean that the availability of beings-in-the-world must be considered empirically. The implications of his analysis are that the strict distinction between a priori and a posteriori is far too crude to understand the most important dimensions of Kant's first edition.) Hence his conclusions: "But if the task of the laying of the ground for metaphysics allows for a more original retrieval, then by means of this the essential connectedness of the problem of ground-laying and the question which led from it concerning the finitude in human beings must come to light more clearly and more precisely" (KPM, 154). Not surprisingly, we now reach the Heideggerian pivot to his own formulation. "This development has to show the extent to which the problem of the finitude in human beings and the investigations it prescribes necessarily belong to the mastering of the Question of Being. Stated basically: the essential connection between Being as such (not the being) and the finitude in human beings must be brought to light" (KPM, 155). As he has emphasized in all the texts we have looked at, this does not mean that we now can march forward and "answer" the question, or that a simplistic answer—like "the meaning of Being is time"—gets us anywhere. "Moreover, man is a being in the midst of beings in such a way that for man the being which he is himself and the being which he is not are always already manifest. We call this mode of the Being of human beings existence. Existence is only possible on the grounds of the understanding of Being" (KPM, 159).

In sum, the claim is that Kant was close to realizing that the finitude of human reason would call for an even more radical transformation of philosophy than the Copernican Revolution. This realization is the "abyss" he shrank back from. "But if the task of the laying of the ground for metaphysics allows for a more original retrieval, then by means of this the essential connectedness of the problem of ground-laying and the question which led from it concerning the finitude in human beings must come to light more clearly and more precisely" (KPM, 154).

5
Finitude in Kant's Moral Theory

Heidegger's treatment of Kant's moral theory, traces of which we saw in KPM's references to respect but which is given clearest expression in BP, is in a different register altogether than the account of the first *Critique*. We should take a few steps back in our run-up to it.

According to Heidegger, the world, a historical world, sets a horizon of possible meaningfulness—fundamentally the meaning of Being as such—and Dasein's inheritance of, understanding of, and orientation from such a horizon does not require any self-conscious discursive orientation, but is a matter of simply being involved in the interrelated nexus of practical significances that amounts to the various tasks and projects of the world. Being-in in this sense is thus a matter of concern, care, *Sorge*, commitment, an orientation from the way things matter to Dasein as the condition for their showing up in their familiarity. Meaningfulness, and thereby availability, is a modality of mattering. And things only matter for Dasein, as uniquely a thrown being-in-the-world.

The result of this analysis had been that this primordial meaningfulness of entities should be understood as (although not exclusively as) the ready-to-hand, *Zuhandenheit*, affordances, and not the present-at-hand, at-handedness simply present before us, the *vorhanden*, primarily stable substances enduring through time understood as a sequence of nows, what Heidegger generally calls standing presence, *ständige Anwesenheit*. By contrast with empirical intelligibility, our understanding of the ready-to-hand is a matter of attunement and appropriate comportment, something like skillful involvement. This fundamental level of significance has been obscured by the metaphysical tradition beginning with Plato and Aristotle. This is because of the mistaken assumption that our original familiarity with the beings in a world is illusory and truth is a struggle towards cognitive intelligibility in such a world of appearances (still an imperfect and incomplete intelligibility but of a philosophically correctable kind), and this can be traced to a commitment to the priority of what Heidegger calls "logic," or the centrality of judgment as the main vehicle of intelligibility in our access to beings.

Most importantly for present purposes, the priority of the *ständige Anwesenheit* assumption cannot be assumed in the question of our own being, how our own being is a meaningful issue, at stake for us. At the heart of Heidegger's analysis in BT is the claim that the authentic meaning of Dasein's being can also crudely but accurately be summarized: anxious being-towards-death.[1]

Every projection of what matters to us into the future involves a being, Dasein, with no inherent teleology or universal or even available ground (an answer to the question of why what fundamentally matters in the world does or ought to matter). What originally matters is inextricable from our thrownness into a certain historical world, so what comes to matter is a question of contingency, what we plan out concerning what matters is subject to the massive contingency of our lack of control not only over our own "ground" but over our fate or our ever-possible death. So, the only possible constancy to a life (and so the only way Dasein as some sort of whole is available to itself) is a background resolve, an always underlying readiness for anxiety and an unwillingness to accept in such an attunement whenever called on the tranquilizing normalcy of the everyday, inauthentic world of Das Man.

Now, in this chapter, we are raising the problem of metaphysics, the basic question, the problem of the meaning of Being and the right way to address it (mostly the wrong way to address it). But we should note what a singular picture this is of the way we should understand what for Heidegger makes a human life a distinct form of life, all in comparison with Kant. The issue of finitude as crucial emerges again and in a clearer way than with the appeal to pure imagination in KPM. Aside from the fact that, while our species certainly has a unique species form, this species form has no bearing on the *significance* of life just by being the species form it is. Heidegger's basic picture focuses on Dasein's unique awareness of our own mortality, and so the question of whether one lives with a resolute readiness for anxiety, or a flight from such awareness by the tranquilizing notions like "everyone

---

1. Of course, this formulation is very compressed. Dasein is also—uniquely—a being-in-the-world, its mode of comportment is care; it is an ecstatic temporal being. But the meaning of Dasein's being as it is experienced by Dasein is, if authentically a confrontation with its own being, this anxious being-towards-death.

must die; we can't do anything about it, so why worry about it?" or "what a morbid way to look at life."

This is also a dramatically isolating or individualizing approach. A background standing attunement to the constant impendingness of one's own death is intensely private and unsharable, and with such a notion at the center it makes almost all of ordinary life escapist and even cowardly. There seems to be behind it some dark view that the only possible human dignity is a refusal of self-deceit in the face of the ungraspability of one's death.

If we ask this question of Kant in the register in which Heidegger asks it, then it would hardly be correct to suggest that for Kant, "primordially," what it is to be a human, to exist in a distinctly human way, is to be a self-conscious knower. In that Heideggerian register, for Kant the distinctive human experience is a kind of awe at the ability of human beings to sacrifice everything of their own, of their own good, even the good, well-being, or life of their loved ones, for the sake of something like a profound respect for the equally infinite worth of every other human being as an equally free being and so an end in itself. However, Kant also notes that we are finite sensual beings, deeply impelled by self-love, so human life requires a constant struggle between righteousness and self-love—a somewhat dreary Protestant picture of meaningfulness, but the experience of such infinite worth is Kant's touchstone; the struggle, the pain, ennobles the righteousness. Against this, nothing at all counts as of comparable value. But it is also Kant's version of profound human finitude. Kant is under no illusion about the fact that our little "island" of factual knowledge of nature (A, 235/B, 294), the pinnacle of which is Newtonian mechanics, is of no deep significance for human life. This is a radical rejection of so many conceptions of philosophy, from the Socratic-Platonic notion of philosophy as a way of life to the notion of philosophy as therapeutic in the Wittgensteinian sense. Human significance and worth are based wholly on a rational faith in our moral vocation. That is what primordially matters. We don't "know" that we have such a capacity, but its availability to us is a matter of its practical undeniability.

Heidegger understands this feature of Kant, that the true sense of significance in being human does not for Kant reside in being a knowing subject. In BP, he introduces his discussion of Kant's account of the moral subject this way:

> Perhaps the question about the subject as *hupokeimenon* is falsely posed in this form; nevertheless, it must be acknowledged equally that the being of the subject does not consist merely in self-knowing—not to mention that the mode of being of this self-knowing remains undetermined—

but rather that the being of the Dasein is at the same time determined by its being in some sense—employing the expression with suitable caution—extant and in fact in such a way that it has not brought itself into existence by its own power. (BP, 153)

It is this aspect of finitude in any account of the human subject's powers, especially in what appears to be the center of Kant's interest—pure reason being practical—that engages Heidegger. This appropriation of what Heidegger finds so valuable in Kant cannot go very far because Kant is still wedded to a metaphysical view of any of the modalities of subjectivity he investigates. "It is not just that the mode of being of the whole Being—the unity of *personalitas psychologica, transcendentalis,* and *moralis* as which the human being after all in fact exists—remains ontologically undetermined; the question of the being of the Dasein as such is simply not raised. The subject remains with the indifferent characterization of being an extant entity. And defining the subject as self-consciousness states nothing about the mode of being of the ego" (BP, 153). For Kant, a moral subject is still a rational *substance,* even if our commitment to its existence is practical. In fact, apart from the substance issue, it has seemed to many that Kant thinks of the human moral subject far too exclusively as a rational subject alone and not as a human subject. Humans are rational beings, but so potentially are many other possible beings without our distinctive sensible nature. Can what ultimately matters to us have nothing to do with being an embodied, thrown, mortal human animal, and not just a rational subject? As we shall see, Heidegger is most interested in places where Kant certainly does seem to acknowledge this.

In general, what Heidegger wants to know is: "It is this moral self-consciousness that really characterizes the person in regard to what that personality is. How does Kant elucidate moral self-consciousness?" (BP, 132). Kant's answer is our inescapable awareness of the moral law, called in the *Critique of Practical Reason* the "fact of reason."[2] Most commentators are content at this point to assume that Kant thinks that any rational being is aware, just by being rational, of the requirements of that rationality, in this case pure practical rationality, formulated philosophically as the categorical imperative. Since we are talking about practical awareness, rationally determining what ought to be done, it is assumed that for Kant there is no separate issue of the motivational requirements for doing what moral law requires. What is required is dutiful compliance, and to be aware of the moral law *is* to be and to feel obligated, and we know we can always do

2. See Heidegger's account of how he understands this fact in EF, §28, 197–204.

what ought to be done, no matter how catastrophically painful. We may not want to, but moral awareness is practical awareness of what must be done. There may be all sorts of empirical motivations for doing whatever we are lawfully commanded to do in any context, but *being* lawfully commanded is itself reason/motive enough to be able to do what we are commanded to do. Kant's "proof" for this claim is the simple thought experiment: imagining someone in some dire situation where doing the right thing is extremely costly, even deadly, to one's self-love, but everyone can acknowledge that it can always be done and always ought to be done. No extra motivational help is needed. By analogy, we can't see and understand a proof in geometry and then wonder whether we ought to be committed to the truth of the conclusion. To understand the proof *is* to be committed to it. In ordinary life we are aware of this constraint on our action without being aware of it in its philosophical form, but it is enough that we are aware that we are duty bound for us to be able not to make ourselves an exception from what our actions would require as a universal rule for anyone else. The principle on which we act would be rationally incoherent, like the impossibility of believing contradictory propositions. That would not be a belief.

But Heidegger claims that this is not Kant's position. It is not enough to acknowledge our finitude in this context by noting the inevitability of moral struggle. If there is moral struggle at all, that is already an indication that the moral law is not practically motivating *just* by being acknowledged. That would be what Kant calls a "holy will." This is a pretty close analogue to his conclusion that the unity of the understanding and intuition requires that the nature of the understanding itself cannot be formulated in terms of the logic of judgment alone (that it requires the prior function of pure imagination). In the practical philosophy, the analogue is that pure reason's being practical must be conceived in the light of our being also sensibly motivated beings, and that will involve a qualification on the supposed purity of practical reason. The bearing of pure reason on our sensible inclinations cannot be understood as a mere imposition on an independently conceived sensible nature. (There is also an analogue to Hegel's early critique of Kant—that this picture of imposition means the law is experienced as wholly positive, an alien authority, as alien as a divine command theory of morality, the mere imposition of a law "from without." It is Hegel's way of raising the necessary question of what our moral vocation means to us, beyond merely "being commanded.")

We should already know from everything we have seen thus far that Heidegger would not accept that this mode of being—being primordially a rational subject—is primary; it is rather an abstraction from an ordinary mode of disclosure, here a self-disclosure. Pointing to what a purely practical rational being would do would not explain what such an awareness *would mean to a person*, in what sense it would matter. And he thinks Kant realizes this too. "According to Kant there pertains to sensibility in the broader sense not only the faculty of sensation but also the faculty he commonly designates as the feeling of pleasure and unpleasure, or delight in the agreeable, or the reverse. Pleasure in the widest sense is not only desire for something and pleasure in something but always also, as we may say, enjoyment; this is a way in which the human being, turning with pleasure toward something, experiences himself as enjoying—he is joyous" (BP, 132). Given this, Heidegger notes, "Conceived in formally universal terms, feeling expresses for Kant a peculiar mode of revelation of the ego. In having a feeling for something there is always present at the same time a self-feeling, and in this self-feeling a mode of becoming revealed to oneself. The manner in which I become manifest to myself in feeling is determined in part by that for which I have a feeling in this feeling."

Of course, there is such a feeling in Kant, a moral feeling that Kant calls *Achtung*, translated as respect—that is, both respect for the moral law and also thereby the source of self-respect for myself as a subject of such a law. In feeling obligated to the moral law, I feel on the one hand a kind of self-abasement, in that I always know that my self-love often inclines me not to do what duty requires and that is a shameful reminder of the power of egoism in human life, but also, on the other hand, precisely in such a self-debasement, and in resisting self-love in respect for the law, I feel a self-elevation, a pride in not succumbing, in being more than my sensual nature would incline me to do. That is self-respect.

The interpretive question has always been the role of such respect in the motivation to do what the law requires. And this is complicated and potentially paradoxical. I must experience and be *motivated by the law alone* in order to have this feeling (perhaps just a "helping" but not a necessary feeling), but feeling the obligatory force of the law is not quite the same as being motivated *as the sensible creature I am* to do what it requires. (Again, if we were absolutely rational beings, being aware of the law would be immediately motivating. But we are not holy wills, wills for which there is no gap between awareness of the moral law and enacting what it requires. This is an analogue on the finitude issue of a contrast with an intuitive intellect, one that can create its objects by thinking them.) But this fits Heidegger's project. Even if imperfectly, Kant realized that our access to the moral dimension of our being is through a kind of attunement, here a feeling that reveals what would otherwise not be revealed, our stake in the moral law, the meaning of being that sort of being. As in so many other cases in Kant, what look like two steps, acknowledgment of our duty, then producing a consequent feeling of respect, is actually one moment. There cannot be the former first step without the latter second. *Feeling* obligated *is* feeling respect. (A summary account of Heidegger's point would be that the whole issue of respect looks different when the framework is not the question of practical causality but the meaning of our moral vocation.)

We don't obey the moral law and repress our self-love in order to feel respect, but we cannot understand the motivating power of the moral law within a continuous life, over time, and within that totality, at any given moment of hearing the call of duty, without respect as an essential component. We have to understand something about the meaning of our moral situation and why it matters to us to be subject to moral reflection. Experiencing the call of duty as continuously painful, as if we were just assigned arbitrarily the fate of being beings who must live these torn apart, self-opposed lives, is an absurd situation. Respect is what gives the way morality fits into a life as a whole its meaning. This is why Heidegger applauds Kant so enthusiastically. "For him the moral feeling is respect, *Achtung*. In this feeling of respect the moral self-consciousness, *personalitas moralis*, man's true personality, must reveal itself. . . . Kant's interpretation of the phenomenon of respect is probably the most brilliant phenomenological analysis of the phenomenon of morality that we have from him" (BP, 133). He does not mean to say, as he does not mean to say in his general discussion of attunements like anxiety or boredom or aesthetic unconcealment, that this is what some now call an affect caused by the experience of moral obedience. It is a way of being originally oriented to the law, reveals ourselves to ourselves, and so has a kind of ontological function tied to the whole question of the meaning of our being. In the case of Kant, our dignity, or infinite worthiness, is thereby revealed. (Not that Heidegger agrees that this worthiness is the full result of such a self-orientation; he is interested in the general role of finitude, here "feeling," in our ontological self-relation. In any full assessment of Kant, he would very likely deny that the fundamental meaning of our being could possibly originate from the concept of a rational being, capable of pure practical rationality. That is a dogmatic, fantastical, and arbitrary isolation and elevation of a human capacity.)

That is, as he puts it:

This feeling of respect for the law is produced by reason itself; it is not a feeling pathologically induced by sensibility. Kant says that it does not serve for judging actions; moral feeling does not present itself after the event, following upon the ethical deed, as the manner in which I assume an attitude toward the already accomplished action. Instead, respect for the law, as a motive, first really constitutes the possibility of the action.

It is the way in which the law first becomes accessible to me as law. This means at the same time that this feeling of respect for the law also does not serve, as Kant puts it, for substantiating the law; the law is not what it is because I have respect for it, but just the reverse: my having a feeling of respect for the law and with it this specific mode of revelation of the law is the only way in which the moral law as such is able to approach me. (BP, 135)

There is more ambiguity about this in Kant than Heidegger lets on. Heidegger's interpretation of Kantian respect, at least prima facie, would ultimately not seem to be consistent with the notion of autonomy so important to Kant. (We are not "in charge" of what we feel and when in the light of whatever. That is precisely Heidegger's point, but it is at some distance from Kant on autonomy, who clearly suspects any *constitutive* role for feeling is a possible threat to such autonomy.) And Heidegger does not think Kant can make any of the metaphysically significant distinctions he wants to make between a phenomenal or psychological subject and a moral or a transcendental subject because he treats them all as substances underlying thought, action, and empirical sensations. There is no progress beyond a repetition of the metaphysical tradition in the senses we have already looked at. But his treatment of Kant on moral experience as a self-disclosure is one of his most insightful and provocative "creative interpretations" in his account of all the figures in the metaphysical tradition.

6

The Thing

In *The Question Concerning the Thing*, Heidegger is out to contrast two ontologies of things, one of which he claims is Kant's. In this 1962 book (based originally on 1935–1936 seminar, GA, 41), he is much more critical than in the 1929 KPM, now aligning Kant with the standard metaphysical tradition and assuming that Kant has abandoned his respect for finitude and his strong emphasis on the imagination. (Heidegger notes that this treatment of Kant will "make up for what was lacking in *Kant and the Problem of Metaphysics*" [QT, 87]. He says this even though he repeats approvingly his claim that Kant's demonstration that pure thinking alone has no access to beings, that it is dependent on intuition, is the death knell of traditional rationalist metaphysics [QT 96–103].) In QT, any thing, any being, is understood to be what merely lies before us, at hand, a substance bearing properties, perduring through time, a standing presence. "We showed that the answer to the question 'What is a thing?' runs: a thing is the bearer of properties, and the truth corresponding to this [conception of the thing] has its seat in the assertion, the proposition, a combination of subject and predicate. This answer, we said, is entirely natural; so, too, its justification [*Begründung*]. And so, we now ask only this: what does 'natural' mean here?" (QT, 5).

In this reading, Kant takes himself to be giving the metaphysical foundations for such a concept (insofar as anything can be known), and his result is a familiar and highly influential part of that tradition, especially for the neo-Kantianism so dominant in Heidegger's education and so important for later positivism and scientific realism.[1] He will go on to argue that this

---

1. See Heidegger's account of the history of post-Kantianism and the importance of neo-Kantianism in §14 of QT.

conception, despite a far greater and more sophisticated realization of the underlying speculative metaphysics necessary to do it justice, and despite a criticism of any conception of being in the service of what Hegel calls the understanding, is also Hegel's, and so it is a conception that can be said to culminate most self-consciously in German Idealism at its end.

The other conception of the thing or any being is what he calls primordial, authentic, originary, and closest to us—what is directly available in our ordinary comportments, a being always already irradiated, to use Wittgenstein's word, with meaning. In making this contrast, Heidegger allows us to confront again the issue that has been with us from the start: not so much what he means by *closest* but why he thinks it is (i) primordial, of deeper ontological significance, where (ii) *deeper* means that any empiricist view is dependent on such primordiality, is an abstraction from it, as well as (iii) the claim that ignoring this dependence has undesirable implications. In making this case, he also confronts what is the most interesting and paradoxical of his claims: that what remains closest to us has somehow become furthest from us, on the verge of being forever unavailable, forgotten. We have somehow come to misunderstand and distort what is and always remains most familiar to us, and we need an explanation of what this amounts to and why it has happened. In the historical world into which we have been thrown, a meaning of Being is assumed and inherited, and this means not merely a concept or a theory about Being. What we inherit is a world where the unreflective basic and orienting meaning amounts to an assumption about what matters (and therewith what doesn't matter or matter very much), that what is cared about, what in that world has "prevailed" (*gewaltet*), is manipulability, beings understood as manipulable stuff, available for satisfying human self-interests. We should recall (one last time) a fuller version of what was already quoted in chapter 2: "We board the tram, talk to other people, call the dog, look up at the stars, all in the same way— humans, vehicles, human beings, animals, heavenly bodies, everything in the same uniformity of what is present at hand. These are characteristics of our everyday Dasein that philosophy has hitherto neglected, because this all too self-evident phenomenon is what is most powerful in our Dasein, and because that which is most powerful is therefore the deadly enemy of philosophy" (FCM, 25).

This is now not just a contrast between an abstracted and so secondary ("founded") objectivist view versus what shows up in ordinary experience as familiar. It is a claim that the former is now experienced as the latter; some screen of theoretical sedimentation in our ordinary expectations has distorted everything, and what the world is like for us now in its original availability is not what it is actually like for us. We have even come to experience ourselves in this way, as things of a sort.[2] "What then is a thing? Answer: a thing is the extant bearer of many extant and changeable properties. This answer is so 'natural' that it also dominates scientific thinking, and not only 'theoretical' thinking but *also all intercourse with things, their calculation and evaluation*" (QT, 22, my emphasis). We do not recognize our own openness to meaningful being. This is not like ignorance or a mistake, something that could be corrected by coming to know something we do not or by enlightening those who do not even know and who would deny that they are ignorant. There is a kind of self-evasion even in dealing with, comporting with, objects that makes them predictable and secure, manipulable all out of a kind of thoughtless, laziness, and instrumentalizing scientism. The transformation of Dasein that Heidegger's new metaphysics seeks is not a path to knowledge but a way of reminding ourselves about—or, as he often says, of "awakening"—what we have actively forgotten.

Accordingly,

> Under certain conditions, if, for example, we undertake the effort to think through the inner situation of the contemporary natural sciences, both nonbiological and the biological, and if we also think through the relationship of machine technology to our Dasein, then the following becomes clear: knowing and questioning have here reached limits, which show that a primordial relation to things is really lacking, that [an authentic relation to things] is only simulated by the progress of discovery and technical success. We sense that what zoology and botany investigate in animals and plants and how they go about it may very well be correct. But are they still animals and plants? Are they not well-made machines in advance, of which one subsequently even concedes that they are "more cunning than we are"? (QT, 27)

He then spins out the consequences. Life, if it is considered a distinct phenomenon at all, is treated as an epiphenomenon, a consequence of purely "material being" (QT, 34).[3] As in all such cases, Heidegger does not mean that life is by contrast an immaterial being or some animistic force but that the scientific treatment of life as a biochemical phenomenon has come to be what living beings around us are unreflectively taken to mean to us. Mention is made again of the fact that "the essence of the thing [is] determined

2. It should be stressed again that Heidegger does not deny that we can also consider ourselves "rational animals," but the phenomenological claim is that this is not primary in our experience; our being is not at stake for us as rational animals but as "the basis of a nullity."

3. For a contrast between Heidegger and Hegel on the issue of life, see Pippin 2022.

on the basis of the essence of the propositions" (31). This is a point he again connects with his general history of Being. "This name for the determination of being is no arbitrary designation, rather: in this naming of the determination of being as modes of assertedness lies a unique interpretation of being. That the determinations of being are called 'categories' ever since in Western thought is the sharpest expression of what we emphasized earlier: that the structure of things hangs together with the structure of the assertion" (QT, 43).

Language, history, the work of art are all understood in terms of this ontology, which has now assumed the role of a pre-ontological orientation, distorting our self-understanding, our own experience of ourselves. He even suggests that the reason poetry is now so poorly taught (a claim he simply assumes) is because poetry teachers cannot distinguish between the distinct mode of being of a poem and a thing. By contrast, poetry and the other arts (including now film) can remind us of what we have forgotten by calling it to mind in a distinct way, an imaginative way—what Heidegger calls "awakening" what we have forgotten.

In the course of this account, which quickly turns to Kant as the primary modern expositor of this notion of the thing, he invokes examples that can easily be misunderstood as a crude defense of premodern science *as science*, which is not what he means. For example, Newton's first law states that if a body is at rest or moving at a constant speed in a straight line, it will remain at rest or keep moving in a straight line at constant speed unless it is acted upon by a force: the law of inertia. Heidegger claims, "Prior to the seventeenth century, this law was not at all self-evident. Throughout the previous 1,500 years, it was not only unknown, but nature and beings as such were experienced in such a way that this law would have been meaningless" (QT, 54). (Note it says "were experienced in such a way," not "were theorized in such a way," although that is also true, but as oriented from that experience.) He then contrasts this notion with Aristotle's, since he thinks Aristotle is giving expression to how objects are available in the "natural" world of immediate familiarity. Objects have, given the kind of objects they are, a natural place in the world. Snakes do not belong in the Arctic, trees don't grow in the desert, elephants don't belong in circuses, carpenter's tools do not belong in a kitchen, and so forth. Likewise, things, given their natural place, also have a natural motion. "How a body moves itself, i.e., how it relates itself to place and to which place it relates itself—all this has its ground in the body itself" (QT, 57).

These notions of place and motion, as well as distinctions like that between heavenly and earthly bodies and motions, are all reinterpreted in the light of the modern notion of the thing, and while such things are never available as such places and motions, they have nevertheless become what we take ourselves to encounter. "Location is no longer the place where the body belongs in accord with its inner nature, but only a position that itself occurs for the moment in relation to other arbitrary positions" (QT, 59). A distinction between natural and unnatural motion is lost; the distinction between animal motion, self-moving motion, and all other motion is lost. And the concept of nature itself changes drastically. "Nature is no longer the inner principle from which the motion of the body follows; nature is rather the way of the manifoldness of changing relative positions of bodies, their manner of presence in space and time, which are themselves only domains of possible positional ordering and ordering determination, having nothing distinctive in themselves" (QT, 60).

Heidegger ties such mathematical formalism to the will, a resolve to treat nature in a way, not to discover the meaning of nature for Dasein. By the time we are on the verge of Kant, the die has been cast and the most sophisticated defense of the notion as primary is produced by Kant. Heidegger might have quoted Kant on this score. In explaining what it means for reason to "conform" to nature, he explains it by saying, "Here reason does not beg but commands, though without being able to determine the bounds of this unity" (A, 653/B, 681). Heidegger also does not mention it to make his point, but he could have pointed to Descartes's *Second Meditation* as one place here that die is cast. We are encouraged there to imagine a piece of wax and to ask what its substance consists in. Assume it has a certain shape and imagine it near a fire melting, assuming all sorts of shapes, and note how obviously it is still the same piece of wax, leading to the only possible conclusion: that what it is to be that object or by inference any object is essentially extension in space, *res extensa*. It's the same "wax" after all. But there is no such possible inference. The example is uniquely tied to wax and other such substances. Imagine the thought experiment with a pumpkin. Smash it, burn it, liquefy the remains, and ask whether it is the same pumpkin. The answer is obviously no. Descartes has simply resolved to treat beings as suitable objects for the new science; he has hardly recovered in such an experiment what the beings mean for us in our actual encounters with them. And it goes without saying that he could have mentioned the famous passage from Descartes's *Discourse on Method*.

> For these notions made me see that it is possible to arrive at knowledge that would be very useful in life and that, in place of that speculative philosophy taught in the schools, it is possible to find a practical philosophy, by means of which, knowing the force and the actions of fire, water, air, the stars, the heavens, and all the other bodies that surround us, just as

distinctly as we know the various skills of our craftsmen, we might be able, in the same way, to use them for all the purposes for which they are appropriate, and thus render ourselves, as it were, masters and possessors of nature. This is desirable not only for the invention of an infinity of devices that would enable one to enjoy trouble-free the fruits of the earth and all the goods found there.[4]

This is the beginning of a consideration that emerges for Heidegger fully in the 1950s and '60s especially. Science is treated as another practical project—a "productionist" metaphysics,[5] where the meaning of Being is tied not so much to the structure of judgment but to whatever understanding fits the resolve to manipulate and master nature for the sake of human self-interest, narrowly conceived. Eventually in Heidegger's rhetoric, this is all in the service of a predatory subjectivity without limits, a successful absolute forgetfulness of the life-world within which we live, and our finitude, dependence.[6] And the main culprit in his story is clear enough. "To determine the transformed basic stance within our relation to beings is the task of an entire generation. But this requires that we discern more precisely and with clearer eyes what holds us captive and makes us unfree in the experience and determination of things. It is modern science, insofar as it has come to be in accord with certain elements of a universal form of thinking" (QT, 33).

It is in this context that he wants us to understand the significance of Kant's account of nature. He has ample reason, at least with respect to Kant's theory of knowledge. He reminds us that Kant wrote in the preface to *The Metaphysical Foundations of Natural Science*: "I assert, however, that in any special doctrine of nature there can be only as much proper science as there is mathematics therein" (2002, 185)

Heidegger's subsequent discussions of Kant's Principles is a close reading of Kant's text, in the light of these prior claims about the role of mathematics, the logical prejudice, and the damage this does to our sense of any "intuitively given nature," which he posits "in opposition" to the mathematical formalism (QT, 64). And even though the original Thing seminar was in 1935–1936, supposedly after Heidegger's *Kehre*, and in his post-phenomenological phase, he still reverts to the familiar claims of BT.

4. Descartes 1998, 35. Heidegger's discussion of Descartes in QT concentrates on the "I" as *subjectum*, its will to ground itself, and the mathematical (67–73).

5. He does, however, trace the origins of such productionism back to Plato on the Good and Aristotle on *techne*, both of which seem to me distorted and arbitrary interpretations.

6. This "life world" reference to Husserl is not accidental here. A great deal of what Heidegger is saying is indebted to Husserl's *The Crisis of the European Sciences*.

The following question arises: what is more in being [*Was ist seiender*], that rough-hewn chair with the tobacco pipe that shows up in van Gogh's painting, or the waves of light that correspond to the colors employed therein, or the states of sensation that we have "in us" in the contemplation of the image? Sensations play a role each time, but each time in a different sense. The color of the thing, for example, is something other than the stimulus given in the eye, which we never grasp immediately. The color of the thing belongs to the thing [itself]. Nor does it give itself as the cause of a state in us. The thing's color itself, yellow, for example, is only this yellow as belonging to the cornfield. The color and its shining are determined each time by the original unity of the colored thing itself and by the kind of thing it is. This is not first composed out of sensations. (QT, 144)

All of this raises a question we have encountered several times before. In the case of Kant, he also has a moral theory, which certainly involves a theory of moral experience, and an aesthetic theory, an account of our experience of the beautiful, and a theory of teleology with an anti-reductionist account of how living beings are available to us. So, is Heidegger's emphasis on the first *Critique* misleading? Not given his focus on the ontological issue. It may be that we find it practically unavoidable, where that also means morally obligatory, to comport ourselves towards other rational beings as if they were not things but "persons," and it may be that Kant would consider taking others only as the beings studied by medical science and biochemistry in the limited and so not "absolute" context of what can be authoritatively known about such beings, and not what they are in themselves. But this leaves the results of any alternate comportment merely subjective, with a subjective need of reason. The claim that "for all we know" we might be immaterial and immortal beings, and we may at least hope that we are (we are allowed to think that we are), has no effective status when opposed by claims that we are entitled to treat each other only in the light of what we do *know* about each other, not what we need to think. Given the connection between the scientific view and the almost unimaginable power and undeniable benefits of modern technology and the prestige of the sciences in universities, in this lack of "real" or equal standing of the alternatives, it has proven to be inevitable that our self-understanding would have to change to accommodate the approach of scientific naturalism, and that was and remains the intention of the project. A look at how modern economics understands rational agents, or how psychiatry does, or the research paradigms in the social sciences and now even in the humanities make that clear. "I don't care what being means to people, however immediate and powerful such 'folk ontology' might be. Who cares how it seems? I want to know what reality is, and I want us to adjust our behavior in the light of such knowledge" is a battle cry that has proven, as Heidegger said it would, irresistible. And Heidegger is right; it is a false disjunction. There is no distinction between what it means to us to be and what it is "really" to be. Scientific naturalism has been a practical project since Bacon. The idea has always been to transform the world in Heidegger's sense of world, the horizon of meaning, and if we accept the distinction, we are not negotiating a peace in which each, the interpretive and the objectivist, exist in their own domains. That was Kant's influential idea, so important in the founding of the modern research university by von Humboldt, and it lost credibility some time ago, especially recently when financial pressure has created a powerful reorientation in universities towards even more vocationalism. Heidegger's idea for a recovery, a new beginning in philosophy (which he accuses of complicity with this "standing presence" project since its beginning) rests on the claim that such claims of scientific objectivity can be shown to be based on a distortion of a primordial level of meaningfulness, that, for all of the sciences' quite justifiable truth claims about beings (in the sense of correctness), it is also an interpretation of ourselves and the world's meaningfulness, a distorted and willfully imposed interpretation for the sake of ends having nothing to do with genuine thoughtfulness about ourselves.

The culmination of that complicity by rationalist philosophy is said to take place in the philosophy of Hegel. This is so even though Hegel himself argues that the traditional category theories and accounts of judgment are inadequate for philosophy's inquiry into being and who uses those claims to attack the supremacy of the "understanding," the vehicle of scientific understanding, who criticizes the correspondence theory of truth for philosophy, who agrees that Kant's philosophy is subjectivistic, who understands philosophy itself as a reflection on its own history, and whose *Phenomenology* is full of what seem to be examples of nondiscursive intelligibility. So how can Heidegger call Hegel "the culmination" and thereby the "end" of traditional philosophy?

SECTION THREE
Heidegger's Hegel

7

Hegel, Idealism, and Finitude

THE IDEALISM PROBLEM

Heidegger's interest in Hegel is prepared for and accompanied by his growing attention to Kant and the entire German Idealist tradition. He lectured on German Idealism in 1929, the same year as his remarkable book on Kant, *Kant and the Problem of Metaphysics*, appeared. He lectured on Hegel's *Phenomenology* in 1930/1931, on Kant's transcendental principles (this would become the basis of his book *The Question Concerning the Thing*) in 1935/1936, on Schelling's *On the Essence of Human Freedom* in 1936, and on *The Metaphysics of German Idealism* in 1941. He continued to publish on the Idealists in the later phases of his career as well, as in his acute formulations of his differences with Hegel in *Identity and Difference* in 1957 and his evaluation of the importance of "overcoming Hegel," and Hegel's idealism, became more and more prominent.[1]

And this means always that Hegel must be overcome by radicalizing the way in which the problem is put; and at the same time, he must be "appropriated." This is the sentiment expressed in the series of quotations with which we began in the first chapter, that German Idealism and especially the

---

1. Heidegger also taught a course in 1925/1926, "Fortgeschrittene: Phänomenologische Übungen (Hegel, Logik, I. Buch)." Seminar 1925–26 WS. But there is apparently insufficient material from lecture or student notes for a volume of the GA to be published. There are eighty-two pages of student notes from Helene Weiss, a student of Heidegger's from 1920–1934, when she was forced to emigrate. That material is in the Special Collections of Stanford University, M0631, Box 3, Folder 7. Gonzalez 2021 has given us a very helpful summary of the main points made and quotes extensively from the Weiss notes, which I cite in a couple of places the way he does, as W, page number. My thanks to Daniel Fidel Ferrer for information about this seminar, as well as to Alfred Denker.

thought of Hegel represent the culmination of all philosophy and must be overcome for philosophy to have a future. *Fulfillment* is another translation for *Vollendung*, and it could mean that the basic problems posed by Greek philosophy were "solved" by Hegel, such that there is no longer philosophical work to do. But it could also mean that the distortions and obscurities inherent in the metaphysical tradition were taken on and thought through by Hegel to a point where it became clear (not to him, but retrospectively) that the whole tradition had "culminated" in a dead end, and this in a way that might suggest the necessity for and the possible direction of a new beginning. Heidegger, of course, means the latter "dead end" view, as is obvious from his claim about "perishing," the translation of "going to the ground" (*geht . . . zugrunde*). ("Where history is genuine, it does not perish merely by ending and expiring like an animal; it perishes only historically" [IM, 202]. We must understand "that Hegel himself has come to an end with philosophy because he moves in the circle of philosophical problems" [BP, 282].) Heidegger means that Hegel had made the clearest of anyone the inevitable commitment by Western philosophy (Platonism) to the metaphysics of presence, its full implications in the unavoidable ambition for a self-authorizing completion, had thereby shown what must always remain unthought in that tradition, and so inaugurated a new form of subjectivism.

Heidegger's claims about Hegel will be our main focus, but as noted, the general position he wants to oppose, to free us from, is idealism as he understands it, culminating in speculative idealism, and we should begin by saying something more about the idealism that Heidegger is interested in, the general importance he gives it, and, as a matter of context, the anti-idealism tradition Heidegger himself brings to a kind of culmination.

We should recall that idealism in this tradition (for Heidegger and, in my view, in itself) should not be understood as a claim about the mind-dependence of the world or about mind-imposed structure in experience or as a so-called objective idealism (a claim about the nonmaterial nature of the real, in favor of its ideal or immaterial nature), but first and foremost as an objection to empiricism, the claim that all knowledge is or must be based on empirical experience. By contrast, idealism in Kant, Fichte, and Hegel is a claim about the capacity of pure (empirically unaided) reason to determine that all that is knowable is knowable, and how it is knowable. Since this amounts to a claim about the normative authority of knowledge claims, and since it is pure reason alone that demonstrates such normative authority, this must mean that human reason is to be understood to be self-authorizing, a tribunal unto itself. As Heidegger notes in KPM, the idealist move results in a paradoxical self-reflection: "a philosophizing laying the ground for philosophy" (26). (Heidegger is echoing the Kantian claim that in pure critique, we are dealing with "what reason brings forth entirely from out of itself" [CPR, xx].) In the Hegelian version that will ultimately be the main focus in the following, this determination of the knowable is a determination of *all that there is* in its knowability and so is a metaphysics. The determination of the knowable is not for Hegel the determination of a limitation, as if a limitation just to the knowable-for-us. Or, in Hegel's famous and controversial phrase, this determination, this self-determination by reason of its own requirements, is "absolute," and so a determination of The Absolute, of all that is in its finally articulated knowability; and that "leaves nothing out." Reason's self-imposed requirements define and delimit all that there is and can be. In other words, idealism in this sense invokes the deepest principle of Western rationalism, the principle Heidegger is so interested in illuminating: "to be is to be rationally intelligible"; there can be nothing *alogos*, or unintelligible.[2] The most famous way of putting it looms large in Heidegger's account: there is an "identity of thinking and being." (Heidegger rightly notes that this cannot be a claim in philosophy; it is the very condition of philosophy, and therein lies the beginning of the problem with the tradition.) If we put this in Heideggerian terms, remembering that the central issue for Heidegger is always "the meaning of Being," then the claim will be that the immediate, familiar availability of beings is a consequence of our experiencing them as conceptually knowable. This in turn has assumed that what matters most, the source of our care, is such knowability. Given that, the world as it matters to us is available *because* of our conceptual and explanatory capacities. This is the founding principle of Greek metaphysics, an expression of what we purportedly originally care about, thought through to its culmination in Hegel, and it will be the heart of Heidegger's critique of the metaphysical tradition.

He formulates the issue this way in FCM:

> The question concerning the essence of world is a fundamental question of metaphysics. The problem of world as a fundamental problem of metaphysics finds itself led back to logic. Logic is therefore the proper basis of metaphysics. The connection here is so insistently obvious that we would be amazed if it had not insistently forced itself upon the attention of philosophy from time immemorial. And indeed, as we have briefly shown with respect to the problem of world, this connection

2. *Rationally* or *discursively* intelligible is the important claim, that being is to be understood as a potential object of cognition. Heidegger obviously thinks beings are intelligible in the sense that his whole project involves considering the meaning of being in terms of its availability to Dasein. The heart of the dispute with the Idealist tradition is the possibility of the nondiscursive availability of meaningfulness as "significance," *Bedeutsamkeit*.

provides the basis and path for the whole of Western metaphysics and its questions, insofar as it is logic that prescribes the examination of all problems with respect to the *logos*; and its truth as problems of metaphysics. (FCM, 289)

Kant and Hegel both agree that there is pure thinking, philosophical knowledge not derived from experience, and that the proper subject of pure thinking is thinking itself, or logic. This is obviously not a system of truth-preserving inferences but a theory of the concepts necessary for any thinking to have content (what Kant called transcendental logic), to be onto objects as they are such that judgments having such form can be true or false. For Kant, such categories provided the necessary conditions for the possibility of sense experience, and this made possible a "metaphysics of experience." For Hegel, concepts necessary for contentful thinking determined what could be in general, and so these concepts are not limited to what could be sensibly experienced.

Heidegger makes just as clear his objections to this presupposition about the priority of logic for metaphysics, for the meaning of being. "In spite of this, we must pose the question of whether this connection between logic and metaphysics, which has utterly ossified into self-evidence for us, is justified; whether there is, or must be, a more originary problematic; and whether or not precisely the usual way of asking metaphysical questions orients itself toward logic in the broadest sense precisely because insight into the peculiar character of the problem of world has hitherto been obstructed" (FCM, 289). For our future discussion of the issue announced in the notion of a culmination, we might also note how important the role is that the idealists and Hegel play for him in this scheme. "This phenomenon of the logos is not only familiar in philosophy in general, and especially in logic, but logos in the broadest sense as reason, as ratio, is the dimension from within which the problematic of being comes to be developed. That is why for Hegel—the last great metaphysician in Western metaphysics— metaphysics coincides with logic as the science of reason" (FCM, 290).

We have been pursuing the metaphysics and finitude issue throughout, but there is also an issue very much in the spirit of Heidegger (and Wittgenstein, as Cooper 1997 points out), and it can be put this way: what could it mean that what it is to be is to be knowable? We don't have an answer available to someone like Aquinas, where the world is a product of a divine mind, suffused with that divine intelligence, and made available for us by means of the capacities we are given. That mere possibility is not of the sort that allows a grounding or explanation (which would be included within the domain of the knowables). It stands as a mystery of sorts but one never entertained by Hegel. Wonder is not the origin of the need to philosophize for Hegel but what he calls *Zerrissenheit*, the torn-apartness of the modern world.

Now, to return to an issue we have seen several times before, Heidegger obviously realizes that one prominent understanding of idealism has to do with the question of whether the external world exists, or whether it can be known in itself—questions that assume our primary access in experience is to the contents of consciousness, understood as "in me," or that this world is "structured" by a form-imposing mind. But in §43a of BT, when he notes that "in principle," idealism, when properly understood, has an "advantage" over subjective idealism, he begins to make clear his own understanding of idealism and its connection to what we have been saying. "If what the term 'idealism' says, amounts to the understanding that Being can never be explained by entities but is already that which is 'transcendental' for every entity, then idealism affords the only correct possibility for a philosophical problematic. If so, Aristotle was no less an idealist than Kant" (BT, 251).[3]

Obviously, this all rests everything of significance on the idealist determination of the *necessary* requirements of intelligibility, what Hegel called a logic, and why we should think that such a determination sets out what Kant in another context called the "really," not merely logically, possible. If there is no way to defend such a claim to necessity, then there is no idealism in this German sense. The position obviously does not hold that there is nothing unknown but that there is nothing in principle unknowable, and that the logic of the form of the knowable can be fully determined.[4] Whatever is still unknown must play by the rules of the knowable. This, then, would clearly amount to a claim about the conceptual structure or logic of *what there is*. Formulated differently, to be is to be determinate, just what something is, delimitable from what it is not. The idealist claim is that pure thinking can specify the possibility of the determinability of anything at all. In so doing, idealism is a metaphysics. For Heidegger, this all indicates an errancy, a distortion from the start, since, for one thing, thought's focus is on "the beings," or what is required for a being to be the being it is. It leaves unanswered, "unthought," the meaningfulness of Being itself, *how it is* that

3. For an extended defense of this claim, especially with respect to Aristotle (and the differences between Hegel and Aristotle even so), see Pippin 2019. See also BP, 167: "Viewed with minute exactitude, the anxiety that prevails today in the face of idealism is an anxiety in the face of philosophy." And the discussion in Raffoul 1998, 52.

4. If it were not fully determinable, then the determinations would be hostage to something empirical or historical, and so not a matter of pure thinking. Brandom 2019 has developed a reading of conceptual determination in Hegel that argues for such an "open" form of thought's self-determination, or for such a subjection.

any being can be or can be available for thought at all. (What is errant for Heidegger is the idealist indifference to finitude, and he thinks Kant has appreciated this far more than the later idealists. However, even for Heidegger's Kant, such finitude is not a matter of some restriction on what could be known but is out of our reach [the standard view of Kant's results], and the spirit of Kantian idealism remains for him a kind of realism as well.) Heidegger's interpretation of Kant's Highest Principle of Synthetic Judgments resonates with Hegel's denial of any gap between subject and object that needs to be overcome. "What makes an experiencing possible at the same time makes possible the experienceable, or rather experiencing [an experienceable] [*Erfahrbare bzw. Erfahrene*] as such. This means: transcendence makes the being in itself accessible to a finite creature" (KPM, 84).[5]

In the background of this position is a claim Hegel makes and defends in his PhG. This claim begins immediately in the work's introduction. It is a criticism of any separation between epistemology and metaphysics. It amounts to an attempt to show that any isolation of the question of whether the subject's putative cognitive powers are actually adequate for the task of cognition, knowledge of reality as it is in itself, ignores the fact that any such conception of the powers of knowing presupposes a conception of the proper knowables. If we ignore that connection and take ourselves to be focusing on our cognitive powers alone, we inevitably end up with skepticism, since there is no way from "outside" the attempt at knowing to measure the exercise of these powers against what really is. (The "view from nowhere" is nowhere, nowhere any finite being could ascend to.) "We'll never know"; we'll just have whatever the exercise of those still merely putative powers results in. If we note the presupposition, we end up begging our own question. So, if we attempt to determine if the exercise of the most advanced scientific methodologies of the day provide us with genuine knowledge of reality and the only genuine knowledge there can be, we either conclude that the answer is positive because all that there is is what can be measured by such methodologies, or we will regard the question as unanswerable, and we will likely seek some way to mitigate those skeptical conclusions by an "operationalist" or pragmatist or positivist position. Interestingly, Heidegger does not so much disagree with what Hegel is claiming (its assumption is one of the reasons he can locate Kant's enterprise

5. Cf. McManus 2012: "We cannot distinguish 'what the person is doing' from 'what is happening to the objects involved' in a way that will yield two separate elements that might fit—or not fit—one another, because 'what the person is doing' is itself a matter of 'what is happening to the object involved' . . . to understand what hammering is is to understand hammers and to understand what hammers are is to understand hammering" (139).

within metaphysics) as that he disagrees with the dogmatic assumption that the meaningfulness of Being in its availability is originally its knowability.

As noted, many of the most influential figures in European philosophy in this period (roughly 1807 until the present) considered Hegel and something like this Idealism (the self-sufficiency and autonomy of pure thinking or, one might say, the autonomy of philosophy itself) as their chief opponent, and they often explicitly did so in the way Heidegger did—by identifying Hegel as the epitome or culmination of all Western philosophy. In part, this also had something to do with a kind of frustration that Hegel, especially in his *Phenomenology of Spirit*, his *Philosophy of Objective Spirit*, and his *Realphilosophie* lectures, had on the one hand seemed to turn philosophy away from purely ideal theory and to what he himself insisted on: *Wirklichkeit*, historical actuality. But on the other hand, he seemed to take back with one hand what he had given with the other, insisting not only that philosophy is bound to its own time, comprehends its own time in thought, but also claiming a developing rational core and structure to these epochs, ultimately available only to pure philosophy or pure thinking. He seemed to be saying that major historical change, widespread social practices, and institutions all were subject to a supreme invocation of the principle of sufficient reason. This did not merely mean that their existence could be empirically explained, but that there was a reason for them being as they were or for the direction of actions—progressively better and better reasons when compared with what had gone before. In the understandable reactions to such frustration, the dispute in one way or another concerns an attack on that idealist claim for the autonomy and self-sufficiency and "self-authorizing" character of rational reflection (a feature common to Kant, Fichte, and Hegel) as a foundation for all such accounts, a necessary presupposition for any account of actuality. What seemed especially outlandish to his critics was Hegel's claims for the absolute status of the results, which was attacked in favor of various versions of the finitude or limitation of any such reflection.

Now, some of these "finitist" critiques often draw large implications from what I believe to be a distorted interpretation of Hegel. However, the proposal here is not that all of modern Continental philosophy or that Heidegger's critiques of the entire metaphysical tradition rests on a mistaken interpretation of Hegel. Many other issues were certainly in play, and the figure I have focused on as the most effective challenger to Hegel's version, Heidegger, has, with some glaring exceptions, a sophisticated, deep, highly accurate, and insightful reading of what Hegel was trying to do in his main text, *The Science of Logic*. I will explain what I mean by this later in this chapter. But the contestation between idealism and anti-idealism, understood as that between a claim for the self-sufficiency of reason and a contrary claim for its putative radical finitude, is of major philosophical importance in itself. There is a way of genuinely understanding Hegel such that this long critical reaction certainly has some real grip on a real problem in Hegel. In other words, while it is true that the received Hegel interpretation is largely inaccurate,[6] pointing this out hardly settles the issues. The central general challenge to Idealism is still a powerful one. The basic claim in this long tradition about the insufficiency of Idealism, or "pure thinking," or even philosophy itself (as in Heidegger's notion of a culmination), is important enough to warrant sustained interrogation. Eventually, I want to say that Hegel's most important potential contributions to this discussion have been both misunderstood and undervalued, even by Heidegger, for all the depth and power of his interpretation. The central claim is that when the ambitions of what Hegel calls "pure thinking" (which are admittedly considerable) are properly identified, the major criticisms embodied in the finitist argument form that I want to identify do not hold. The case is different in Heidegger's treatment. Let me proceed to a ridiculously brief summation of the idealist ambition.[7]

The central idealist claim began with Kant's *Critique of Pure Reason* and his assumption that reason was capable of determining what it was entitled to claim and capable of also restricting itself if it could not provide such authority. This almost immediately generated the concern that such an enterprise would not only end in a destructive skepticism but in an all destructive "nihilism" (F. H. Jacobi's original coinage), leaving nothing of moral substance or objective status standing. But a deeper and more longstanding issue arose in the thought of Hegel, especially in his attempt in his major theoretical work, *The Science of Logic*, a book that has not, until very recently, enjoyed much of a reception in either anglophone or European philosophy. That issue looks like this.

Hegel's claim in that book has three components. The first is the claim that a priori knowledge of the world, the ordinary spatio-temporal world, is possible; this means knowledge about that world but achieved independently of empirical experience. The second component is where all the

---

6. I am certainly aware of what might well seem to be the arrogance of such a claim, but in this context, all I can do is invoke the case for such a claim made in work from Pippin 1989 to Pippin 2018. While Heidegger might appear to have interpreted Hegel in quite a traditional way, theologically, his understanding of theology is distinctive enough that it is consistent with the core of his reading of Hegel: that, for Hegel, metaphysics is logic, a "science of pure thinking," and that a completely self-reflective logic, the Absolute, has been achieved.

7. A full defense of the interpretation of Hegel's *Logic* sketched here may be found in Pippin 2019.

interpretive controversies begin. It is the claim that this a priori knowledge, while in some sense to be specified, is ultimately about the world,
consists in thinking's or reason's *knowledge of itself*; thinking's determination of thinking or, as Hegel designates, a "science of pure thinking." This is
what distinguishes classical rationalism from idealism, as Hegel (and Kant)
understood it. The former holds that reason has access to its proper objects
outside itself; the latter that the object of pure thinking is itself. But there is
clearly a question to be answered: *how* could the first two components—a
priori knowledge of being, and pure thinking's object being itself, possibly
be jointly true? One long-dominant interpretation of Hegel on this point,
the third component, and the putative resolution of this tension holds that
these two claims can be both assertable only if what there "really" is, the
"really real world," what is accessible only to pure reason alone, is itself
thought, in "thinking moments"—something like the Absolute's or God's
thinking itself, an inherent, evolving noetic structure unfolding in time
from the human perspective, but in itself a *nunc stans*, Spinoza-like absolute. Pure thought thinking itself is the manifestation of the *noesis noeseos*,
God thinking himself, or it is the divine-like apprehension of the noetic reality that underlies experienced appearances. I cannot do so here, but I have
argued for some time that this interpretation does not fit the text. So, an
alternative interpretation is necessary, and I will discuss that in a moment.

But apart from the interpretation issue, the most important critiques
of idealism in this sense all hold that any such project is doomed from the
start, that there is not and cannot be such a self-sufficient "pure thinking."
I noted before that such a broad counter claim is often summarized as a
doctrine of "radical finitude." This is an apt title since Hegel insists that, to
use an Aristotelian formulation, "thinking thinking thinking"[8] is not the
thinking of any object, and when he wants to summarize such an unusual
reflective self-relation, he notes the "infinity" of thinking's relation to itself.
Pure thinking's object is itself but not as an object or event; rather, its object is the thinking also interrogating thinking—a circle, not a dyadic relation. Hence the provocative notion of "infinity," without beginning or end.
The anti-idealist criticism holds that thinking must always be understood
as grounded on, or dependent on, or an epiphenomenon of, some sort of
non-thinking ground, or materiality or contingency or the unconscious instinct or drive of the thinker, or, as in Heidegger's very different claim, an
always already implicitly orienting understanding of the meaningfulness of
Being. Hegel's comment on the matter in SL is a perfect indication of their
differences. "The claim that the finite is an idealization defines idealism. The

---

8. This is the apt formulation of Kosman 2013.

idealism of philosophy consists in nothing else than in the recognition that the finite is not truly an existent. Every philosophy is essentially idealism or at least has idealism for its principle, and the question then is only how far this principle is carried out" (SL, 21.142).

In the most decisive case in the tradition for Heidegger, the dependence in question is what Kant emphasized, the dependence of thinking on sensible intuition, of pure thinking on pure intuition. (The significance of this for Heidegger is also existential: "man is at the same time not master of the being which he himself is" [KPM, 160].) Schelling's early formulation is also apt. The distinction between thinking and what is other than thinking, between subject and object, cannot itself either be a subjective or an objective distinction. If it were either, there would actually be no distinction. So what there really is can be characterized neither as absolute subject nor absolute object, but—and here the difficulties begin—somehow "'the' neither subject nor object." Hegel's prioritization of the Concept—in his terms, the identification of the Absolute as the Concept—is said to be a prioritization of absolute subjectivity and so to require a relation to what is other than thought, nature, as pure domination. It would be hard to overstate the influence of such an argument form (the details vary a great deal, of course, but this form of skepticism remains) from Schelling to Heidegger and Adorno.[9]

In Hegel's treatment, the topic of pure thinking is presented as having nothing to do with the existing human thinker, the subject, consciousness, the mind. Rather, the topic raises as a problem the possibility of the intelligibility of even whatever is being touted as pre-conscious source or hidden origin, the intelligibility of what is assumed in any such determinate identification as a knowledge claim, even of "the neither subject nor object." That is either something available for some kind of apprehension or it is not. If it is, it must be subject to some regime of intelligibility for this determinacy

9. For the most part, Heidegger wants to say that what German Idealism leaves unthought is the problem of the meaningfulness of Being, but he has a number of ways of making that point. As we have seen, some of the most striking and accessible stem from his use of Kant and the primacy of imagination claim Heidegger attributes to the first edition of the *Critique*. Consider: "All reinterpretation [*Umdeutung*] of the pure power of imagination as a function of pure thinking -a re-interpretation which 'German Idealism' even accentuated subsequent to the second edition of the *Critique of Pure Reason*—misunderstands its specific essence" (KPM, 138). See also KPM, 171: "And yet, in the second edition of the *Critique of Pure Reason*, did Kant not give mastery back to the understanding? And is it not a consequence of this that with Hegel metaphysics became 'Logic' more radically than ever before? . . . What has the outcome of the Kantian effort been if Hegel explains metaphysics as logic thusly: 'Logic is consequently to be grasped as the system of pure reason, as the realm of pure thought. This realm is truth, as it is without a veil, in and for itself'. . . . Can there be more compelling proof for how little the metaphysics which belongs to human nature, and hence how little 'human nature' itself, is self-evident?"

to be accounted for. This is what Heidegger denies when he insists that the meaning of Being, Being as such, is not "a" being and not subject to the requirements of determinacy. Insisting it begs the question. (This is not to mention that Dasein's access to the meaning of its own being is not access to anything determinate. What it is to be Dasein is, precisely, not to be a determinate being.) So, Hegel's project is thought's determination of what thought must be, its moments (*Denkbestimmungen*) in order to be a possible truth-bearer, a result that for Hegel immediately involves what could be the object of any truth claim. (Kant distinguished general and transcendental logic this way. General logic determines the rules necessary for thinking to be coherent thinking at all; transcendental logic "introduces" possible content, considers thinking as having content other than thinking.) In the face of this, if someone simply persists in asking "but *where* is all this thinking and explaining happening?" all one can reply is "wherever there is thinking." This is not to say that there is not always a thinker or subject of thought; it is to say that thought that can be truth-bearing is constituted by what is necessary for truth-bearing, by any being of whatever sort capable of objective (possible true or false) judgment.[10] Any such determination of a source or ground or subject-object must still, according to the case for the possible explication of absolute intelligibility, make sense within a general regime of sense-making, or nothing has been claimed by the putative claim for an Unground, or non-ground; an empty place in logical space would have just been suggested. Any such criticism, insofar as it is a thinking, a judging, a claim to know, is always already a manifestation of a dependence on pure thinking and its conditions, and such "moments" of pure thinking are to delimit (but not limit) the normative domain of intelligibility (what can *rightly* be distinguished from what, or rightly posited as "ground," for example) and not any process or series of events that goes on in supposed independence of the empirical world. Pure thinking, as Hegel understands it, is neither dependent on nor independent from the empirical, or from materiality or the brain or the "indifference point" or whatever new "absolute" comes into fashion. His position would be better understood by rough analogy with Frege or Wittgenstein of the *Tractatus* or the early Husserl on

10. There is a similar sentiment in Kant: "Pure reason, as a faculty which is merely intelligible, is not subject to the form of time, or, consequently, to the conditions of the succession of time" (A, 551/B, 579). This must mean that the subject is in no ordinary sense a substance. But given the dependence of thinking on the pure forms of intuition (essentially on time), this cannot be the whole story either, as Heidegger is at pains to point out in KPM. Thinking is not to be understood as an attribute of a mental substance, a thing, but how we should understand the subject will require a great deal of attention. Consider Heidegger's summary: "Rather this 'from-out-of-itself-toward . . . and back-to-itself' first constitutes the mental character of the mind as a finite self" (KPM, 134).

logic as metaphysics. That anti-Hegelian question already manifests (for the Hegelian) a misunderstanding of the question of pure thinking itself. This is not to deny that any reference to thinking presumes a thinker, indeed a living, purposive, finite, embodied rational thinker. (Hegel addresses that issue in his *Philosophy of Subjective Spirit* and elsewhere.) It is, rather, to argue for the autonomy of the question of "any thinking at all," whatever the existential status of the thinker. (While, as we have seen, Heidegger does not claim that pure thinking is an epiphenomenon of something else, something material, he will want to argue that the status of the subject in Kant and post-Kantian thought is seriously under-theorized and remains obscure. Pinning down the meaning of any being as the knowable is not and cannot be a topic in *Logic*. The basic question is begged, and we must return to the question of original, meaningful availability.) That is, it is to insist on the priority and autonomy of logic, and that means for him its complete self-determination of its own moments. Hegel's enterprise in *Logic* takes as its topic the categories or "thought determinations" (*Denkbestimmungen*) necessary for thought to have determinate objective content, an enterprise that at the same time specifies the determinations inherent in the possible determinacy of being itself. It is true that it would seem that Hegel is subject to his own criticism, that pure thinking must already assume a determination of what pure thinking amounts to, but Hegel's innovation here, partly derived from Fichte, is that pure thinking comes to self-consciousness about itself *by thinking*, in the sense that one understands what one believes in believing it, understands what one is doing in doing it. This is all still much too telegraphic, but it forms the core of the idealist response to anti-idealism and it will recur as an issue often in what follows.

There is a good summation of the conceptual structure of the problem this raised for Heidegger in Gadamer's study, *Hegel's Dialectic*. "Thus Heidegger's ambiguous formulation, 'the consummation of Metaphysics,' leads us finally to an ambiguity common to Hegel and Heidegger. Concisely stated, the issue here is whether or not the comprehensive mediation of every conceivable path of thought, which Hegel undertook, might not of necessity give the lie to every attempt to break out of the circle of reflection in which thought thinks itself. In the end, is even the position which Heidegger tries to establish in opposition to Hegel trapped within the sphere of the inner infinity of reflection?"[11]

Put a different way, if Hegel were making a claim about the mind's thinking nature, how we must think about the world, knowledge would be limited by its "instrument," something Hegel had been vigorously deny-

11. Gadamer 1976, 101–2.

ing since the introduction to *Phenomenology*. In knowing itself, what pure thought knows is the possible intelligibility, the knowability, of anything that is. But the intelligibility of anything is just what it is to be that thing, to be determinately "this-such" (*tode ti*), the answer to the "what is it" (*ti esti*) question definitive of metaphysics since Aristotle. To be is to be intelligibly, determinately, "what it is." So, in knowing itself, thought knows, of all things, *what it is* to be anything. As for Aristotle, the task of metaphysics is not to say of any particular thing what it is. It is to determine what must be true of *anything at all* (what in scholasticism were called the *transcendentalia*), such that what it is in particular *can* be determined by the special sciences. Of course, *Physics* and the *De Anima* are also philosophical sciences for Aristotle, and therein lies the beginning of a problem for both Hegel and Heidegger. One of the ways Heidegger characterizes traditional metaphysics is that it does indeed try to determine a priori what it is to be some kind of being or other. In traditional language it confuses the tasks of a *Metaphysica Generalis* and a *Metaphysica Specialis*. In his terms, it assumes there can be a priori ontic knowledge, knowledge of the beings or a region of beings, or knowledge of Being itself as if it were a knowledge of beings. This, according to Heidegger, is what Kant was trying to avoid by insisting that ontology give way to a Transcendental Analytic. Kant was only insisting that our original openness to Being, which Heidegger characterizes as "letting-things-stand-against" us, is of a completely different order of knowing (pre-ontological) than appreciated by traditional metaphysics, and in the proper register of finitude, Kant means to recuperate ontology as *Metaphysica Generalis*. He cites A, 845/B, 873 and the discussion in Kant's *Über die Fortschritte der Metaphysik* (KPM, 88). (This setup by Kant, followed by Heidegger, will pose a misleading problem for Hegel later. Kant and Heidegger agree that at the most basic level, thought is finite because thought, understanding, knowledge, cannot create its own objects; it depends on a comportment towards what is other than the subject. With things set up that way, it looks like Hegel's claim for the infinity of thought is a claim that thought *does* create its own objects. That is not at all his position, but it remains a common interpretation of Hegel on metaphysics. The other Kantian claim of massive importance to his critique of idealism is his argument that he has shown, or rather Kant has shown and he has exfoliated the point, that pure thinking can arrive nowhere, certainly not at the determination of the "horizon" of all possible objectivity, without being everywhere not only intertwined with but dependent on sensibility, especially with the "sensible" faculty of the imagination. This is true of pure thinking as well and so requires an explanation of pure intuition/sensibility. All of this is supposed to dislodge "Ratio and Logos" from their central role in the history of metaphysics, or to deny "the primacy of logic," something most evident in the culmination of that tradition in Hegel [KPM, 117].)

The analogy with such things as Frege's and Husserl's critique of psychologism in a theory of pure thinking goes only so far, not only because of Hegel's account of how pure thinking determines the necessary moments of the intelligibility of anything at all, already a distinctive and unprecedented position that obviously would have to be explained and defended, but also because it involves a further argument about the bearing of such results on the intelligibility of the natural world and human practices. This feature of Hegel's position, referred to earlier as an understandable frustration (textually the relation between his *Logic* and the *Philosophies of Nature* and *Spirit*) touches on another major dimension of the anti-idealist critique, one most associated with Schelling, Kierkegaard, and the Heidegger of BT. It is that thought, paradigmatically Hegel's pure thinking (or even philosophy itself, as traditionally understood), cannot contribute to any understanding of, cannot in effect even reach the most vital, concrete issues faced in a human life—existential issues, especially the meaning of one's own death.[12] This is all another implication of the finitude of thought and, it is argued, more and more radical ways of addressing, illuminating, and understanding in some way such issues are needed. Hegel certainly cannot contribute to this, so goes the criticism,[13] if Hegel is understood as he seems to require: interrogating the role of reason, some normative order, in the changing sociopolitical, religious, and artistic practices of an age. Since *Geist* (Hegelian Dasein in some sense) is self-positing, a "product of itself," according to Hegel, the development of this self-positing depends on a collective self-understanding, which in turn requires a continuing attempt by *Geist* to justify itself to itself, which Hegel regards as progressively more satisfactory. In this sense the self-understanding at issue must be "rational." Since any such justification must be incomplete and must as well depend on assumptions about justification and meaning that Dasein cannot reflectively redeem and must always already assume, Heidegger has no faith in such an insistence. Of course, this all depends on the proper understanding of what Hegel means by such an

12. Schelling makes this point but in a way that indicates his confusion about a priori knowledge: "Logic does not lay claim to anything actual. It wants to be merely a subjective activity of thought" (PR, 76). This begs the whole question against Kant and Hegel, and Aristotle as well for that matter.

13. The criticism can sound like a capacity limitation, that there is something just outside our grasp that we could obtain were our capacity not limited, but it could also be put as a limitation that descends from the object of any thought because that object itself is unthinkable, either because infinite (e.g., God) or because finite, of a sort that allows no discursive articulation and so in that sense no intelligible account (e.g., the meaning of Being in Heidegger's critique). This will be an issue for the next chapter.

appeal to reason in such practices, and my claim is that once the proper form of the structure of rationality or account-giving and justification in *Logic* is understood, its bearing on the issues Hegel himself brilliantly brought it to bear on—ethical life, art, religion—can be properly understood. The bearing of Heidegger's critique can then be properly assessed. (For Adorno and Heidegger, Hegel's claim about the absolute delimitation of rationality and so practical justifiability is not a mere philosophical mistake, but an act of hybristic self-assertion typical of Western thought, and one that has had and continues to have catastrophic real-world consequences.)

Some quotations from Hegel are relevant here to get our final bearings on the position Heidegger will try to "free us from" or "overcome."

Thus *logic* coincides with *metaphysics*, with the science of *things* grasped in *thoughts*, which used to be taken to express the *essentialities of the things*.

(Die *Logik* fällt daher mit der *Metaphysik* zusammen, der Wissenschaft der *Dinge* in *Gedanken* gefaßt, welche dafür galten, die *Wesenheiten der Dinge* auszudrücken.) (EL, §24)

We should note the change in emphasis insisted on by Hegel. The new metaphysics, logic, concerns things as grasped, *gefaßt*, in thought, whereas the old metaphysics was a thing-metaphysics, used to think of its subject matter as onto the "essence of things."

And,

The objective logic thus takes the place rather of the former metaphysics which was supposed to be the scientific edifice of the world as constructed by thoughts alone. (SL, 21.48)

Again, a logic alone takes the place of the former metaphysics, *tritt damit viehmehr an die Stelle der vormaligen Metaphysik*, which thought of its object as the scientific edifice of the world.

And finally,

The older metaphysics had in this respect a higher concept of thinking than now passes as the accepted opinion. For it presupposed as its principle that only what is known of things and in things by thought is really true [*wahrhaft Wahre*] in them, that is, what is known in them not in their immediacy but as first elevated to the form of thinking, as things of thought. This metaphysics thus held that thinking and the determination of thinking are not something alien to the subject matters, but are rather their essence, or that the things and the thinking of them agree in and for themselves (also our language expresses a kinship between them); that thinking in its immanent determinations, and the true nature of things, are one and the same content. (SL, 21.29)

I can't imagine a more definitive confirmation of the "logic as metaphysics" interpretation.

So, does any of this put us in a better position to confront the understandable skepticism from the "finitude of thought" objectors? As context for appreciating Heidegger's distinctive contribution to the debate, consider some of the most immediate, pressing objections. One is an objection we need to consider, before all of this can even get started, from the Kantian camp, a second from Schelling's point of view, and a third from Heidegger's.

KANTIAN OBJECTIONS

Some points of contrast can help sharpen the focus on Hegel's position. Although Hegel's approach descends from Kant's distinction between general and transcendental logic, any follower of Kant would object that any proposed identification of thought and being like that asserted in the last quotation, simply ignores, rather than answers, the question that marked the "critical turn" for Kant in his famous February 21, 1772, letter to Marcus Herz. This is the letter in which he claimed to have discovered the "key to the whole secret of metaphysics," a question he had simply neglected to ask in his 1770 dissertation. "What is the ground of the relation of that in us which we call 'representation' to an object?" And, "The axioms of pure reason concerning these objects—how do they agree with those objects, since the agreement has not been reached with the aid of experience?" (KA, 10:130–131). Isn't Hegel, when all is said and done, a regression to uncritical thinking, dogmatism, rather than some sort of progress beyond Kant and his supposedly objectionable subjective, "mind-imposed unity," noumenal ignorance Idealism?

It is absolutely correct to note that Hegel does not answer such a question as much as reject it as confused and resting on its own dogmatic presuppositions. Part of that rejection is supported by what he thinks he accomplished in the Jena *Phenomenology*. But it is also internal to the stance of *Logic*, and it will be important to remember when we come to Heidegger's concerns with Hegel. First, such an objectionable presupposition is obvious when Kant had noted that pure concepts are that "*in us*" which purport to be concepts of the real, "though they must have their *origin in the nature of the soul*, they are neither caused by the object, nor do they bring the object itself into being," all creating the objectivity problem, the gap between thought and being that must be closed somehow.[14] Now Kant and Hegel certainly share the so-called discursivity thesis (which Heidegger does not). Thinking for both is exclusively a spontaneous or productive power, in no sense a perceptual or passive, receptive capacity. It would be hard to exaggerate the magnitude of this common assumption. More than anything else, it sounds the death knell of traditional rationalism, and it plays the crucial role at the decisive beginning of the *Logic*, where Hegel demonstrates that the thought of mere "being" can be no actual thought at all, its indeterminacy renders it a mere "nothing" without some predicative determination other than the mere thought, being. (For Heidegger, of course, this massively begs the deepest question at issue.) Kant reasoned that since the mind is open or receptive to the world only sensibly, and since thinking cannot create the objects it thinks, then thinking cannot provide itself with any content, can only be provided with content from without, through sensible experience. This would normally lead straight to empiricism and probably an empirical skepticism too, but Kant believed he had discovered that there must be pure forms of sensible intuition, and this provided him a way, he thought, in the Deduction, to "connect" the pure forms of thinking with such pure forms of intuition and thus to get in view, as it were, a priori all possible objects of experience and argue for the validity of the categories for such objects. This, of course, had the effect of restricting those results for only possible objects of sensible experience, thus initiating the Hegelian complaints about his subjective idealism. (As we saw in chap. 4, Heidegger is not interested in the empirical or subjective idealist implications of Kant's position. What interests him is Kant's demonstration that pure thinking is not adequate to Being, and so we must settle for adequacy to our *sensory openness to Being*. Kant is a major, if ultimately timid, thinker of finitude.)

Hegel had two main objections to this position. First, Kant was hasty in arguing from the discursivity thesis to the claim that thought can provide itself with no content. Kant himself had demonstrated that that was not so, since, in the metaphysical deduction, he had himself shown that pure thinking could "give itself" not objects but its own content, its own necessary logical moments, the categorial features without which object-directed judging could not be judging. So, we return to the Hegelian claim mentioned earlier: that pure thinking's proper object is itself. Hegel has no hesitation in saying several times that thought in the *Logic* provides itself its own content or produces its content (conceptual content). Of course,

14. See Heidegger's discussion of this point in BT, 248, on "in me."

for Hegel and for many after him, Kant did not even attempt to show how this derivation was accomplished. He claimed misleadingly that he simply followed Aristotle's list, supposedly something everyone had agreed on for centuries. Moreover, Kant had realized that such forms of thought alone already provided a "clue," a "guiding thread" for the categories; he had already seen, if hesitantly, a direct link between the forms of thought and the forms of being.

Moreover, second, Kant had also already realized that the pure forms of thought were not features of the human thinker, were not in that sense psychologically subjective, but necessary for *any* discursive thinker, which means any non-divine thinker. But since these forms of judgment are the forms of any possible truth-bearer, and since truth is either truth or not, it makes no sense to say that these forms delimit something like "what is merely true for discursive thinkers." There is no such thing as "truth for X," even if there is "what seems true to X." The "subjectivizing" elements in Kant are, though, species-specific, the pure forms of intuition. And if we reject that doctrine, as Hegel does, we can return to a position like Aristotle's, where we can study being by studying the forms of predication. Or, in Aryeh Kosman's phrase, "predication is nothing but the logical or discursive face of being."[15] (Exactly! Heidegger would say. *That* is the errancy that seals the doomed fate of Western metaphysics, the priority of "logic.")

So, Hegel thinks that Kant had neglected his own achievements in the Metaphysical Deduction and in "fear of the object" needlessly subjectivized his results. It is Kant who is uncritical and dogmatic, not Hegel.

SCHELLING'S PROBLEM

Another historical source of inspiration for Heidegger's anti-idealism is Schelling. Since Heidegger shares much of Schelling's skepticism about idealism, some sense of the direction of that skepticism should be sketched since it bears on his approach to Hegel. Schelling's differences with what would become Hegel's position on logic as metaphysics are already apparent by implication in his early work: his 1797 *Ideas Concerning a Philosophy of Nature*, his 1800 *System of Transcendental Idealism*, the lectures he gave in 1802–1803, *The Philosophy of Art*, and his 1809 *Of Human Freedom*. His explicit later objections are clearest in his *Lectures on Modern Philosophy*, delivered in Munich from 1827 to the late 1830s. He reprises many of these objections in his 1841 *Philosophy of Revelation* in an interesting way that includes a story about his own relation to Kant and Fichte. The issues are all

15. Kosman 2013, 127.

large and unwieldly. They concern a basic conflict between a claim about what is always already presupposed and so forever unavailable for discursive articulation by us, versus a claim about the Absolute as always a result from which a ground can be retrospectively reconstructed and developed. (As Heidegger reminds us, for Hegel, "The beginning is the result" [ID, 53].) But the specific claims are well known. There is first the issue of ground, some sort of ultimate source that would account for the difference between, and yet also the identity between, subjects—self-conscious thinkers and free agents—and objects, material but also living, productive nature and bodily movements in space. (This is the *Urgrund* that Schelling would call the *Ungrund*, the "neither-nor" "indifference point" mentioned earlier.) The difference in their positions implies that Hegel's position, said in the language of the period, that the Absolute is the Concept does not resolve but simply avoids this issue. (The *Logic* cannot be an object to itself; absolute reflection is not possible.) Second, a related issue is an objection to Hegel's philosophy of nature, that Hegel prioritizes the concept to nature, treating nature only in terms of its conceptual intelligibility, whereas the concept, understood as a thought-determination of spontaneous pure thinking, must be understood to emerge from and already depend on nature. And in the later lectures, the problem is existence. Schelling's charge is that Hegel's program never is able to exit the realm of the merely conceptually possible. Hegelian philosophy can deal endlessly with *what* some possibility must be to be the possibility it is, but this has nothing to do with what there is, with the facticity *that*, as Schelling puts it, something exists. Hegel's results are locked up in the merely conceptually possible (in what Schelling calls "negative philosophy").[16]

Each of these objections is worthy of an independent study. But the outline of Hegel's response involves the suggestion that an ineffable *Ungrund*, unavailable for determinate thought because always presupposed, does not amount to a philosophical position. The language of the charge is well known from the preface of *Phenomenology*, where Hegel, clearly referring to Schelling (who certainly noticed) claims that this is all an attempt to pass off "its absolute as the night in which, as one says, all cows are black," which he calls "an utterly vacuous naiveté in cognition" (PhG, 12). One in-

---

16. He does not deny that, in his terms, Hegel wants to have a positive philosophy. See PR, 70–91.

Heidegger's debt to Schelling is obvious from his 1925 letter to Jaspers: "Hegel from the very beginning failed to grasp life, existence, process, and the like in a categorial way [*kategorial*]. That is, he failed to see that the inherited categories of a thing- and world-logic are insufficient—and that one must question more radically not only with regard to becoming and movement, occurring and *history* [*Geschehen und Geschichte*]—but with regard to being itself" (*Briefwechsel*, 59). Cited by Gonzalez 2021, 8.

determinacy claimed as source is indistinguishable from any other possible candidate. If it is differentiable, a determinate position, then such a source has some sort of conceptual determinacy and falls within the moments of the Concept. That which in principle falls outside the thinkable designates nothing at all. Such an *Ungrund* is an *Unsinn.* (To be sure, Schelling has a lot to say about the role of art in somehow manifesting this unmanifestable *Grund,* but I do not believe it affects the basic determinacy point. The ineffable remains ineffable.) Heidegger will restate this criticism and claim that it begs all the crucial questions.

But there is a deeper and more important point behind Schelling's concern. If there *are* both subjects and objects, and they have incompatible properties, how is it possible that pure thinking's self-determination could help us understand how that could be? Unless we are metaphysical dualists, and Hegel certainly isn't, isn't it obvious that we need some account of substance that could explain how self-conscious thinking and self-determining agency could emerge out of a material world otherwise devoid of these capacities? If so, this would seem to lead us into Schelling's language of a material nature's "self-negating" of its own unselfconscious living materiality, something that might be easier to understand if we also follow Schelling into a notion of the Absolute that manifests itself as both a living material nature with the capacity for such self-negation, and the results of that self-negation, but which can be identified as neither.

Hegel treats this way of looking at the problem as a complex of category mistakes and, on this issue, so does Heidegger. The question of the evolutionary conditions for the emergence of consciousness and language use is an empirical question, an "ontic matter," as Heidegger would put it, just as is the question of what capacities the brain must have for there to be consciousness and language use. Again, the proper question is philosophical or, in Hegel's terms, logical. In *Encyclopedia,* the "transition" from nature to spirit is not a question of substance. At some point, and it doesn't matter (for philosophy) at what point or how, natural organisms reach a level of complexity and organization such that they begin to become occupied with themselves and eventually to engage each other and to understand themselves in ways no longer appropriately explicable within the boundaries of explanations proper to nature considered apart from such capacities. Hegel's language about this is everywhere practical, not substantive. It is not that Hegel is denying that self-consciousness and intentional agency are facts. He is claiming that no fact about the organic properties of such beings accounts for *what it is* to be self-conscious or agents, and there is no need for the positing of nonmaterial entities or capacities. Those are categories of achievement—indeed, collective achievement—and the question of what is achieved is an autonomous philosophical question. Of course, spirit remains embodied and so subject to mixed explanations, in which its natural properties bear on its activities as spirit. (This is what Hegel calls *Anthropology* in *Encyclopedia*.) But fundamentally, spirit is said to be its own "self-liberation from Nature," and spirit "is a product of itself" (*Produkt seiner selbst*), and its actuality (*Wirklichkeit*) is that it "has made itself into what it is" (*dass er sich zu dem gemacht hat was er ist*) (PSS, 1:6–7). Consider this passage from the *Lectures on Fine Art*. "Art by means of its representations, while remaining within the sensuous sphere, liberates man at the same time from the power of sensuousness. Of course we may often hear favorite phraseology about man's duty to remain in immediate unity with nature; but such unity, in its abstraction, is purely and simply rudeness and ferocity, and by dissolving this unity for man, art lifts him with gentle hands out of and above imprisonment in nature" (A I, 49).

It doesn't matter that there are *also* natural-scientific explanations for what happens in the body and brain when all this occurs, or when we make or enjoy art. The question that has emerged—the only emergence that is relevant—is whether the norm, art, has been rightly and fully realized, or whether the justifications agents offer each other and themselves can in fact be defended, whether the structure of ethical life is consistent with the potential of such a self-liberating being. There is no need to appeal to a vitalist, self-dirempting nature to account for any of this, and there is no need to make a great deal about this being all "second nature," since these capacities are all developments of, educated results of, what are wholly natural capacities. This is so for Hegel because the dynamic in question is historical, not biological, even though it clearly has numerous specific natural-organic conditions and involves no commitment to anything non-natural. Correspondingly, the question of the possibility of freedom is not for Hegel a question about the possibility of how a spontaneous causal agency exists in a material world. His theory is a self-realization theory, and that asks for the right achievement in our understanding of ourselves and in our relations to others, again a historical and social question, not one that descends from any account of substance.

Likewise, Hegel does not treat the Concept as the ground of the *existence* of nature, or in any ontological sense as prior to nature. (Heidegger never makes this mistake, but many, like Schelling, try to attribute the claim to Hegel in order to refute it.) The minimal way to characterize the transition from the *Logic* to the *Philosophy of Nature* in *Encyclopedia* is that the transition entails that the conceptual structure of any interrogation of nature or spirit cannot be coherently understood as wholly empirically determined. Each aspect of *Realphilosophie* depends in some way on a nonderived con-

ceptual structure manifested in its pure form in the *Logic*. This characterization of dependence is not incorrect, but it does not yet distinguish how
Hegel thinks of that relationship in a way that will exclude the commonsense notion of an empty, subjective pure form being filled in by objective
empirical experience or imposed on an extra-logical material. This cannot
be right because in Hegel's approach any such conceptual structure already
or a priori determines any determinately intelligible empirical content.
But it does not and should not determine or derive or deduce the existent
content itself (this is clearly denied in §250 of *Philosophy of Nature*), but it
does determine the inseparable form of any such content as the intelligible
content it is. As he says in the penultimate paragraph of the *Encyclopedia
Logic*: "The method is not an external form but the soul and concept of the
content, from which it is distinguished only insofar as the moments of the
concept, even in themselves, in their [respective] determinacy, come to
appear as the totality of the concept" (EL, §243).

But in the move to *Encyclopedia Philosophies of Nature* and *of Spirit*, the
identity of form must mean that we should also attend to logical form now
understood as in some way inflected by attention to the form of what is
wholly other than pure thought in space and time, and the form of human
action in the world, including collective human action. Said another way,
Philosophy of Nature and *of Spirit* remain *philosophy*. The conceptual structure laid out in both parts aspires to a conceptual or a priori truth, even if
the results of the empirical sciences and historical actuality are everywhere
incorporated. (This is largely what Hegel means when he says frequently
that spirit seeks always to "find itself" in nature and in its own practices.
It seeks to understand them, to understand their intelligible form.) But, as
already noted, this is not because Hegel thinks of either part as a result of
a simple application of the moments of a Being and an Essence Logic to
an external indifferent matter. In these parts of the *Encyclopedia* too, the
method "is not an external form but the soul and concept of the content"
(*ist auf diese Weise nicht äußerliche Form, sondern die Seele und der Begriff
des Inhalts*).

In fact, Hegel himself makes the very point that Schelling in the later
lectures considers a damning criticism. "This idea is still logical; it is shut up
in pure thought [*in den reinen Gedanken eingeschlossen*], the science only of
the divine concept. Its systematic exposition is of course itself a realization,
but one confined within the same sphere. Because the pure idea of cognition is to this extent shut up within subjectivity, it is the impulse [*Trieb*] to
sublate it, and pure truth becomes as final result also the beginning of another sphere and science" (SL, 12.253). But this transition to a consideration

of nature is not a deduction of nature's existence, nor could it be. It is once again described in practical terms, as a felt practical insufficiency in any full comprehension of the results of the *Logic*.

HEIDEGGER'S DISTINCTION

This all only sets a very general context of anti-Idealism in favor of a "fini-tude of thought" thesis. I have been suggesting that far and away the deep-est, most thoughtful engagement with Idealist and especially Hegelian thought in post-Hegelian philosophy is Heidegger's. In fact, a good case can be made that Heidegger's distinction among all such anti-Idealism po-sitions is that his is the first genuine confrontation with Hegel in all the post-Hegelian European tradition. For our purposes, which at this point is merely to sketch the general tenor of Heidegger's approach, the discus-sion that is especially important is what was published as the second part of *Identity and Difference* (1957), originally the end of a seminar and also later a lecture, "The Onto-Theological Constitution of Metaphysics." This is because Heidegger goes immediately and directly to the heart of Hegel's enterprise and states it accurately as just what it is. Heidegger tells us that the subject matter, the *Sache*, of thinking for Hegel is "thinking as such" (*Denken als solches*). And he immediately adds exactly the right qualifica-tion. "In order not to misinterpret this definition of the matter—thinking as such—in psychological or epistemological terms, we must add by way of explanation: thinking as such—in the developed fullness in which what has been thought [*in der entwickelten Fülle des Gedachtheit der Gedachten*], has been and now is thought" (ID, 42).

Thinking in the fullness of what has been thought is Heidegger's formula-tion of the Hegelian claim that logic, properly understood, is metaphysics. The thinking of pure thinking is at the same time the thinking of the world in its thinkability, *what* has been and is now being thought. He reminds us that we can only understand this from Kant's viewpoint, although not like Kant, transcendentally, but speculatively. That is, Hegel thinks of thinking as *Being*, and not as a subjective epistemological condition; or, said con-versely, Being is only possibly available in any sense in its thinkability. Hei-degger realizes that pure thinking's taking itself as object does not result in a mere theory of thinking, or the rules of thinking, or a "philosophy of pure cognition." As Heidegger says directly, for Hegel, "being is the abso-lute self-thinking of thinking" (ID, 43). The last thing Heidegger means by this is that Being is mental activity, whether human or divine. That would merely be an account of one of the beings, a subject matter of one of the special sciences and would so presuppose a logic of intelligibility. Because of his own approach, Heidegger is in a unique position to realize that the subject matter of the *Logic* is not in any sense whatsoever a being, not "the" Absolute's self-positing, not the noetic substructure of the world, not abstract objects, not the mind of the Christian God, not a substance, but, in his language, the meaning of Being, the *Sinn des Seins*. As he puts it in his distinctive language, "The Being of beings reveals itself as the ground that gives itself ground and accounts for itself. The ground, the ratio by their essential origin are the *logos*, in the sense of the gathering of beings and letting them be. They are the *hen panta*. Thus 'science,' that is, metaphysics, is in truth 'logic'" (ID, 56). And he tells us what he thinks Hegel means by logic. "We now understand the name 'logic' in the essential sense which includes also the title used by Hegel, and only thus explains it: as the name for that kind of thinking which everywhere provides and accounts for the ground of beings as such within the whole in terms of being as ground (*logos*). The fundamental character is onto-theo-logic" (ID, 59).

The "divine" at stake in what Heidegger means by theo-logic is, he constantly explains, not a being, not anyone to whom we can pray or play music to or dance for, he notes with a hint of contempt.[17] He means: because, in Hegel as the culmination of all metaphysical thinking, thinking is self-grounding and thereby serves as ground (for any being being intelligibly what it is), this thinking is also "theology" because it concerns the *causa sui*. Pure thinking is productive and self-generating.

From his interpretation of Hegel in BT on, Heidegger has emphasized that what Hegel means by "the Being of beings reveals itself as the ground that *gives itself ground* and *accounts for itself*" is that this ground-giving is what Hegel means by the Concept "giving itself its own content," and this by means of the beating heart of the dialectical process. That is, in Hegel's language, the Concept is "self-negating negativity." Thinking is discriminating, differentiating, and thus determining, and this is possible by any "moment" of pure thinking's differentiation of itself from its other, its self-negating. That self-negating means its lack of self-sufficient determinacy, and this by means of its essential relation to and differentiation from its "other" (Being from Nothing, Quantity from Quality, Essence from Appearance, Universal from Individual). It thereby returns to a mo-

17. Cf. BNI, 6222. "Weary and used up are all the great attunements as well as constancy in them. Therefore the questioning power as world-happening is completely closed off. The fact that facile superiority of faith—a superiority which is only cowardly mendacity full of borrowings in philosophy—or the semblant vivacity (whose spiritual impotence cries to heaven) of the political" (71). (Would that Heidegger had taken that last bit to heart.)

ment of stability and putative sufficiency. It negates its own negation of that original self-sufficiency and "momentarily" reestablishes it, only to require again a self-negating of this putative independence and internal self-definition.[18] Heidegger is right that this is one way of formulating Hegel's attempt to establish an internal derivation of the moments of pure thinking required for the determinacy necessary for anything to be what it is. And here Heidegger is again correct when he claims that behind this in Hegel, what can account for the source of this development, is the apperceptive character of any thinking, that any moment of thinking is a self-conscious moment and so aware of the commitment it undertakes to establish the determinacy of a conceptual moment. But Heidegger continually interprets this "presence of the I to itself" in a Cartesian way, as if it is the "I's" demand for such a "presence" (that meaning of Being that is the original sin of Western metaphysics) to itself as the telos implicit in any moment of thinking, an interpretation that construes what Hegel is doing in a formal way and that neglects the way Hegel wants to make his case on the basis of the internal self-negation of the conceptual moment.[19] To use the formulation of the PhG, "thought disturbs thoughtlessness" because of the incompatible commitment created by such incomplete thinking, not because of a subjective dissatisfaction and demand. This just sets up Heidegger's opening to claim that there is a "negation," a "not," which cannot be re-integrable into presence, something that he stresses from his treatment of being-towards-death to the insistence of the concealing inherent in and not overcomeable by any revealing.[20]

So in summation, "metaphysics responds to Being as logic, and is accordingly in its basic characteristics everywhere logic, but a logic that thinks the Being of beings, and thus logic which is determined by what differs in the difference: onto-theo-logic" (ID, 70).

As we shall shortly see, Heidegger means that metaphysics is determined by this difference (between Being and the beings) without being able to think the difference; it is and must remain unthought in metaphysical thinking. Compare what Heidegger is saying to what Hegel says and both the

18. Hence two readings of Hegel. Either this autotelic process eventually ends without finally requiring such a self-surpassing, or it ends with a full self-awareness of the nature of this self-negating negation.

19. For example, EF, 111. Heidegger does the same thing in HCE, where he discusses only the opening chapters of the PhG and these in terms of "method," as if that issue in Hegel can be understood in abstraction. The dynamic, especially the existential dynamic introduced in the PhG in chapter 4 and beyond is not attended to.

20. See the discussion by De Boer 2000, who connects this theme to Heidegger's criticism of Hegel on temporality, 255–265.

accuracy of his characterization and the limitations of his charge of subjectivism will be immediately clear. "The logical is to be sought in a system of thought-determinations in which the antithesis between subjective and objective (in its usual meaning) disappears. This meaning of thinking and of its determinations is more precisely expressed by the ancients when they say that *nous* governs the world, or by our own saying that there is reason in the world, by which we mean that reason is the soul of the world, inhabits it, and is immanent in it as its own innermost nature, its universal" (EL, §24).

So, Hegel is said to reanimate the Platonic-Aristotelian "logical" ontology that holds that to be is to be intelligible, in principle knowable. For Hegel, again as Heidegger understood him, to be is necessarily to be determinate (a this-such, discriminable from any other "such") and the requirements of determinacy were also the requirements for anything to count as a being. Anything putatively indeterminate—an object, an event, a state of affairs, a meaning, Being—that cannot be distinguished from anything else "isn't anything."[21] That is, the basis of Hegel's claim for his logical idealism, or the identity of thinking and being, is that thinking's self-constitution of the requirements for any determinacy must already just count thereby as the only possible meaning of any being *being the being it is*—its delimitability from other beings. This is supposed to be shown in the *Logic* beginning with its opening claim that the mere thinking of "being" is not a thought at all. The indeterminacy of mere being, its indistinguishability from what is not being, makes it indistinguishable from "nothing." Therewith follows the spontaneous self-constitution by pure thinking of what *would* satisfy the determinacy conditions without which nothing could be a determinate anything. The beginning of wisdom for the early Heidegger is that, on the contrary, there *was* clearly a being not at all comprehensible as, not at all being, "determinate": the being Heidegger called "Dasein" precisely to indicate that it was not a determinate this-such. Dasein is openness to the meaning of Being itself, "being there" at the site of any manifestation of such meaning.[22] There could be no logos in the Hegelian sense to a being, Dasein, that was what it took itself to be, a being whose mode of being is *to-be*, existence, a self-interpreting being, especially not one whose mode of being was to be constantly faced with its own non-being, the possibility of the random, arbitrary end of its being in death. Such a being could never be simply "what it is."[23] But this was only the beginning of the larger claim most associated

21. See BP, 170 for an excellent summary.

22. See Carman (forthcoming) on "Existential Anti-Rationalism" for a compelling picture of Heidegger's position.

23. Any claim that, nevertheless, *that* sort of being is just *that*, determinacy enough, is a mere debater's point. Dasein's mode of being is not-being, ungrounded, the "basis of a

with Heidegger: that the meaning of being itself would be forever hidden, even forgotten, if Hegel's views about the "infinity" of pure thinking, there being nothing "outside" the conceptually determinable, were accepted. Being would be rendered a determinate object like any other, a position that would assume and not account for the meaning of Being itself. It would presume an understanding of the meaning of Being in an "ontic" way, as a being, which again would presuppose rather than address the meaning of being as such. Further down the road in the Hegelian development, as we shall see, the same is true of "life."

This is Heidegger's problem with "metaphysical thinking." He notes approvingly that Hegel's approach is developmental, not deductive, and that this developing thought-thinking thinking is intertwined with the history of thought, with the history of philosophy. (Herein one of the deepest affinities between Hegel and Heidegger: that dealing with figures in the history of philosophy is not preparatory to philosophy or exemplary for philosophy but is the highest form of philosophy itself. As Heidegger put it in his essay on "Anaximander's Saying" (1946): "The only Western thinker who has thoughtfully experienced the history of thought is Hegel" [AS, 243].) In his engagement with this thinking, Hegel tries to think rightly what really has been thought in the developing positions, and Hegel's attempt is an *Aufhebung*, a preserving and raising up of all that has been rightly but partly thought into a whole.[24] Heidegger accepts this intertwining with the history of thought but says his approach is to think what is *unthought*, remains hidden in the history of thinking as *logos*. Hegel's self-determining thinking always misses something essential to its possibility, and Heidegger's lifelong task was to help us identify what is always missing and why. Accordingly, his engagement is not an elevation, not progressive, but a "step back," a *Schritt zurück*. While Hegel thinks the ultimate identity of thinking and being, Heidegger's basic thought is difference, *Differenz*. Thinking's determination of absolute intelligibility actually "recedes" before the true subject matter of thought, Being. Something remains "unasked"—the difference between Being and beings.

Even so, even given this claim about the exfoliation of what is "unthought" in the history of pure thinking, of metaphysics, it is important that Heidegger thinks the unthought (by which he basically means the true

---

nullity." That Dasein's *determinate* being, what sets it off as what it is, *is such indeterminacy*, is nonsense.

24. Hegel's own relatively rare discussions of this term explicitly stress only the canceling and preserving dimensions, but in his use of the term he clearly believes that in such canceling and preservation some sort of elevated self-consciousness has been achieved, as in the "advance" he thinks is achieved by the Roman Empire, or Christianity, or the Reformation.

appreciation of the ontological difference, the priority of the question of Being) *in pure thinking*. In this sense, his topic is the same as Hegel's: pure thinking's reflection on its own possibility. "The term denoting this character by which being precedes beings is the expression a priori, apriority, being earlier. As a priori, being is earlier than beings. The meaning of this a priori, the sense of the earlier and its possibility, has never been cleared up" (BP, 20). And, "the a priori character of being and of all the structures of being accordingly calls for a specific kind of approach and way of apprehending being—a priori cognition" (ibid.).[25]

So, in conclusion, if Heidegger has rightly characterized the nature of Hegel's project in the *Logic*, and I think he has, what is it in the "logic as metaphysics" project that remains unasked, unthought? If we take our bearings only from BT, then we can put the point in Schelling's way: we would say that the mark of thinking's finitude is the "unreachability" of human existence itself, that such concrete existence can never be rendered fully intelligible or even determinate. It remains ineffable, not available.

Not only is existence an unfinishable temporal (or temporalizing) project, and so never something that can be taken in as an object of thought, one of its most distinctive characteristics is its very *unintelligibility* to itself. It finds itself uncanny, not at home anywhere, the anxious, null basis of a nullity, something it cannot help but flee in a tranquilizing ("falling") everydayness. But once Heidegger has fully shifted attention to the problem of metaphysics, another issue looms much larger: the absolute difference between Being and beings, our inevitable confusing of the question "what is it to be?" with "what is it to be this or that being?" But what does the thought and the criticism (if that is the right word to characterize what Heidegger has noted) mean in Hegel's terms?

The first thing one can say is that Heidegger is generally right about the *Logic*. Hegel does insist that the question of Being necessarily always amounts to a question about what it is to be this or that being. That is the result of the first moment of the *Being Logic*, and it is that moment where the

25. This a priori cognition is, at this period in Heidegger's thought, phenomenology, but this already a distinctly Heideggerian phenomenology. It is characterized this way: "Being does not become accessible like a being. We do not simply find it in front of us. As is to be shown, it must always be brought to view in a free projection. This projecting of the antecedently given being upon its being and the structures of its being we call phenomenological construction" (BP, 21–22). He aligns himself with Hegel again when he elaborates on this projection: "Because destruction belongs to construction, philosophical cognition is essentially at the same time, in a certain sense, historical cognition. 'History of philosophy,' as it is called, belongs to the concept of philosophy as science, to the concept of phenomenological investigation" (BP, 23).

deepest "confrontation" (*Auseinandersetzung*) with Heidegger must take place.[26] In this, as in so much else, Hegel follows Aristotle. Being is said in many ways, but there is some primacy to being as *tode ti*, a this-such, determinate being. I noted that this does not mean that it is the job of the *Logic* to determine what it is to be any particular determinate being, but to determine what anything at all must be to determine what any determinate being is. But this last formulation does not seem to reach the question Heidegger is interested in since it is still directed to the beings, *Seiende*. As Heidegger realizes, the closest formulation in Hegel for the "Being of beings" question is simply pure thinking, determinate intelligibility. But that topic, which Heidegger wants to treat as Being's own manifestation, its unconcealing or happening and so, as what any pure thinking as judging must presuppose, is not a topic or moment for pure thinking.

And while Heidegger agrees that there is nothing empirical about the theory of pure thinking at the center of German Idealism, he does note that such a theory never went deep enough. Again, he gets Hegel right when he notes, "In Hegel this determination of the subject as *hupokeimenon* undergoes sublation into the interpretation of the subject as self-consciousness-as self-conceiving, as concept or notion [*Begriff*]. For him the essential nature of substance lies in its being the concept of its own self" (BP, 153). But, he goes on to say,

> It must be acknowledged equally that the being of the subject does not consist merely in self-knowing—not to mention that the mode of being of this self-knowing remains undetermined—but rather that the being of the Dasein is at the same time determined by its being in some sense— employing the expression with suitable caution—extant [*vorhanden*] and in fact in such a way that it has not brought itself into existence by its own power.... The subject remains with the indifferent characterization of being an extant entity. And defining the subject as self-consciousness states nothing about the mode of being of the ego. (BP, 153)

He means here that it is one thing to have successfully warded off possible interpretations of the subject of thought as empirical, as in psychologism,

---

26. Heidegger does not call his treatment of past philosophers an interpretation or an assessment but this *Auseinandersetzung*. This, he thinks, requires him to excavate what is "unthought" in the thought of a philosopher. Both of these features, the confrontation and the reliance on the unthought result, quite consciously, in something that does not look much like the history of ideas or the history of philosophy as it is usually practiced, or even like textual interpretation.

or as metaphysical substance, as in immaterialism or the *res cogitans,* but that just tells us what the distinct mode of being of the ego *is not,* and we still need to investigate this mode of being, a major "unthought" thought in German Idealism. Kant, Hegel, and Fichte wanted to say that the only assumption necessary for an account of pure thinking is only the "I or he or it" that thinks, but Heidegger insists that this leaves out the question of the mode of being of the subject, and he is certainly right. The notion of a "transcendental-logical" subject is merely a way to avoid the question.

This is a decisive and distorting absence because of the way Heidegger wants us to understand the task of a properly reconceived metaphysics. He puts it this way in his FCM lectures. "Metaphysics is a questioning in which we inquire into beings as a whole, and inquire in such a way that in so doing we ourselves, the questioners, are thereby also included in the question, placed into question" (FCM, 9). However, it is also true that he does not mean his version of the metaphysical question to be like the alternatives proposed by psychologism and immaterialism. Those pose the question as about Dasein's "what being," as a question of substance, a kind of thing. And Heidegger's "meaning of Being" question assumes the contrary and so calls for a new mode of interrogation. When he wants to explain how metaphysical questions are comprehensive (*Inbegriffe*), he says, "They also in each case always comprehend within themselves the comprehending human being and his or her Dasein—not as an addition, but in such a way that these concepts are not comprehensive without there being a comprehending in this second sense, and vice-versa. No concept of the whole without the comprehending of philosophizing existence" (ibid.).

Although we have reached the point where a very great deal will have to be said about Heidegger's unusual language, it is here that we do seem to reach some sort of absence in Hegel's enterprise, even if the question of whether that means that something crucial is missing or not is a separate question. If the Being of beings, the Absolute, is ultimate knowability, have we asked *in* the *Logic* what it is, what it *means,* to be knowable; not to mention, have we asked if the possibility of being's meaningful availability consists in its thinkability? Pure thinkability is not one of the determinate moments of the *Logic,* and when thought's, judgment's, characteristics become self-conscious in the Concept Logic, it is the forms of judging this or that, in their determinate possible inferential relations that is attended to. I noted before that Hegel thinks we cannot provide an independent theory of the thinkable as such. We can merely manifest thinking by pure thinking. We know what pure thinking is by thinking. Any other formulation would presuppose and so elude itself. But this means that the "science of pure thinking" does not and cannot count pure thinking itself as one of its moments. And from Heidegger's point of view, this is not adequate. What we learn in the process of trying to think anything at all determinately is the possible determinacy of any being. Thinking thinking thinking is the enacting of thinking, and the reflective self-consciousness at the end of the *Logic*, the Concept of the concept, of intelligibility itself, is a form of self-consciousness about the intelligibility *of any being*, not something like "Being as intelligibility itself." That is always unasked, unthought, presupposed, even if manifested or enacted. The Concept Logic is supposed to allow the inclusion of the *Logic* itself inside "the Concept." But that just covers what we have been through in the book, what the thinking of any being amounts to. It does not and cannot include what Heidegger seems to be after: "what it means for Being to be thinking's self-determination of thinking." That question both must be and cannot be "inside" the Concept. Put another way, logic itself, or the question "what is logic?" is not a possible moment. And we know from Heidegger's 1928 lecture course, now published as *The Metaphysical Foundations of Logic*, Heidegger thinks that question is deeply intertwined with the "meaning of Being" question. So, Heidegger is right that the question remains unasked, even unthought.

This is all not to deny that there is something also quite limited and often tendentious about Heidegger's assessment of Hegel. There are other passages where he does not charge that the question of the mode of being of the thinker has been left unthought by Hegel, but that Hegel did "think" it, and as a Cartesian, that the subject is understood as nothing more than an individual center of consciousness. Here is the charge.

> The theory according to which man is initially subject and conscious-ness, and is given to himself primarily and most indubitably as con-sciousness, basically arose from quite different intentions and perspec-tives in connection with Descartes and his attempt to lay the foundations of metaphysics. It is a theory which has come to pervade all philosophy in the modern age and was subjected by Kant to a peculiar, although not an essential, transformation. This led finally to the Hegelian attempt to absolutize the approach which takes the isolated ego-subject as its point of departure, which is why we describe this philosophy as absolute ideal-ism. (FCM, 208)[27]

While it is true that Hegel does in *Encyclopedia* (albeit in the special context of *Philosophy of Nature*, §258) say such things as that spirit is "the eternal" and that the eternal is "absolute presence," it is clear from a more

---

27. See also Pippin 1997, 375–394 for a defense of Hegel's anti-Cartesianism.

charitable reading that Hegel doesn't mean present-at-hand, or standing presence,[28] as Heidegger claims when he says,

> So how does Hegel conceive the being of beings qua spirit, or the actuality of the actual? "The spirit is eternal," the way of being of the spirit is eternity. "It will not be nor was, but it is." 'The eternal is . . . absolute presence [*absolute Gegenwart*].' This is not the presence of the momentary now which immediately flows away nor is it just lasting presence in the usual sense of what continues to endure, but it is a presence which stands by itself and through itself, in self-reflected duration, a presence of the highest constancy, which itself makes I-ness [*Ichheit*] and self-abidingness possible, nor is it just lasting presence. (EF, 110)

This assumes that the dialectical self-negation of concepts and eventual sublation results in some sort of abidingness or stability, and, as so much Hegel scholarship after the war has demonstrated, that is the last thing Hegel wants to say. It would be a betrayal of speculative science and the eternality of "*movement*" as the "soul" of the Concept.

This all also raises the question of whether Heidegger is right to draw the rather apocalyptic consequences he does from this "forgetting" or not asking this question; in a word, his word, "technology." But it also raises what might seem like an unusual question from Heidegger's point of view. Is this all actually a *problem*? It is not as if Heidegger thinks this elusive topic *should* have been itself a moment within the *Logic*. He is, in many other works, asking for other modes of interrogation, from a "fundamental ontology" form of phenomenology, to *Gelassenheit*, to *Andenken*, to the fourfold. But from Hegel's point of view, there is no reason to believe that these attempts would not generate their own form of "difference" and so elusive-

---

28. Heidegger's picture of Hegel is sometimes otherwise tendentious also. Hegel's discussion of time in that passage is the time of "arising and passing away *in nature*, and therewith of the concept of time relevant to the Concept *as externalized*, nature." What Hegel wants to say is that "Only that which is natural, in that it is finite, is subject to time; that which is true however, the Idea, spirit, is eternal." When he contrasts that temporality with the Concept he also says, "The Notion of eternity should not however be grasped negatively as the abstraction of time, and as if it existed outside time; nor should it be grasped in the sense of its coming after time, for by placing eternity in the future, one turns it into a moment of time" (PN, 231). His claim is certainly that Concept is "eternally" "absolute negation and freedom," but that sort of eternality is much more like saying his doctrine of the Concept is simply true. In just the same sense, it is not open to Heidegger to claim that his notion of *aletheia* as truth, or his notions of finitude or historicity or being-in-the-world, are "true only for a time." In the general "truth" sense, Heidegger also wants what he has to say to be "eternal." Man is not just for the moment, Dasein.

ness. And for Hegel, this would be because the only kind of interrogation of Being there could be is the interrogation of any determinate being, and the mode of being of those determinations, thought determinations, *Denkbe-stimmungen*. It might be Heideggerian enough for Hegel to invoke another formulation of the same problem, that thinkability as the meaning of being can only be shown, not said. But has it been shown in Hegel's works?

Moreover, from Hegel's point of view, there is another source of unclarity in Heidegger's basic position. At the start of BP, when he is trying very hard to distinguish his understanding of the always presupposed, implicit orientation from the meaning of Being from any "world view" (*Weltanschauung*) philosophy (his target is Jaspers), Heidegger characterizes his conception of a philosophical science quite conventionally. "Philosophy is the theoretical conceptual interpretation of being, of being's structure and its possibilities. Philosophy is ontological" (BPP, 11). Heidegger does not here discuss any of the modal questions involved in philosophical conceptuality, yet that is crucial for any "scientific" philosophy. There is clearly a borrowed Kantian structure: Being is available, manifest, and so the question is, how is this possible? Even, as Heidegger will formulate it, what makes it possible? ("Unveiledness of being first makes possible the manifestness of Being" [EG, 103].) Or in BT, "but in significance [*Bedeutsamkeit*] itself, with which Dasein is always familiar, there lurks the ontological condition which makes it possible for Dasein, as something which understands and interprets, to disclose such things as 'significances' [*Bedeutungen*]; upon these in turn is founded the Being of words and language" (BT, 121).

Fair enough, but the results, if actually "theoretical conceptual," make a claim to *necessity*. A resulting formulation of a condition that could not be otherwise. Not just this or that element makes it possibly available; that would not be scientific, would give us mere sufficient conditions. We want necessary conditions. We want: without these elements in place, this availability would not be possible; only on assumption of these elements is it possible. In Kant, necessity is tied to necessary conditions of experience. That means, necessary for a unity of consciousness, the Transcendental Unity of Apperception to be possible. In Hegel, necessity is internal to development of The Concept. Any conceptual moment or "thought determination" is necessary for anything at all to be determinate, a condition of it being at all, and only possible if determinacy is supplemented by a concept of finitude. Whether this is defensible or not, we can at least see the basis of necessity in this internal self-negation and developmental necessity. And in Heidegger? Without *what* would there be no availability, no manifestness, clearing? Perhaps Dasein as Heidegger understands it, being-there, a possible site for meaningfulness; perhaps eventually beings being an *Ereignis*, an event or happening of meaning? All of this is not to say that Heidegger wants simply to reject Hegel, to charge Hegel with the kind of irrelevance that, say, Hobbes claimed for Aristotle or the scholastics. But the logical space treated by the SL, the domain of determinate intelligibility and its conditions, becomes a regional ontology, as dependent on the unasked question of the meaning of being as all such ontologies. So, Hegel can launch and perhaps even complete "the science of pure thinking" and claim some ontological relevance for it, but he cannot claim that the Concept, that model of intelligibility and determinate being, is The Absolute.

This is not a result, something like the demarcation of a regional ontology (that which, and only that which, is a fit subject for an assertion) that either would accept; Hegel because it is unsystematic and would leave unclarified the relation between such a region and any other region (in fact the result would preclude any such question), and Heidegger because it would still be the case that such a region presupposed some availability of the meaning of Being and would leave that dependence unclarified. But it may be the most consistent result of taking on board Heidegger's concerns. We shall return to the issue in the concluding chapter.

8

Hegel

The Culmination

Hegel alone seemingly succeeded in leaping over this shadow—but only in such a way that he eliminated the shadow (i.e., the finitude of the human being) and leapt into the sun itself. Hegel leapt over the shadow, but he did not thereby surpass the shadow. (QT, 105)

LOGIC AND PURE THINKING

Heidegger's interpretation and critique of Hegel's *Science of Logic* in his *Identity and Difference* was partly an attempt to explain why he thinks that project, which for many readers remains one of the most baffling and unusual texts in philosophy, actually successfully represents the core of the rationalist enterprise in philosophy and shows us its culmination. He means both that it is the most consistent and so successful realization of that "core"—a science of pure thinking that is a science of being—and by being that reveals what has always been "unthought," what cannot be thought within that tradition, the meaning of Being, the most important issue in metaphysics and forever unavailable to any form of discursive rationality. One of the main issues was the idea of the finitude of pure thinking—or, in Hegel's case, the denial of finitude for pure thinking (the beginning of the *Logic* is supposed to be presuppositionless). As emphasized before, throughout his various treatments Heidegger clearly does not mean by such an appeal to finitude and so to the limitations of pure thinking to open any doors to an empirical-psychological or neurological or historical materialist interpretation of that finitude. That is not the dependence and finitude he wants to illuminate. Heidegger clearly agrees with what Hegel would say: that even *that* sort of appeal must fall *within* Hegel's attempted account of the conceptual moments of possible determinacy, cannot coherently be conceived *"outside"* it. (Materialism is a philosophical not an empirical claim; it is another moment of *logos*.) And they are all also simply further examples of the thoughtless assumption that the meaning of being is standing presence. This is the same claim Kant made about the pure concepts of understanding and the pure forms of intuition. They are not subject to empirical disconfirmation, and our main contrast with Hegel was Heidegger's Kant interpretation. Besides exploring the dimensions of any claim to articulate the role of pure thinking in the possible availability of beings, we did this in order to begin to discuss the issue always raised when he discusses German Idealism, finitude, and the priority of logic. Having seen the details of that interpretation, we can now raise further questions about Heidegger's critique of Hegel.

First, we should note that traditionally the essential activity in rendering anything intelligible (any being, *Seiende*, in Heidegger's terminology) is predication. Recall that phrase by Kosman already cited, that for Aristotle (and, I have claimed, for Hegel), "predication is the face of being," a perfect opening for Heidegger because it is precisely what Heidegger means by the too central role of logic, the science of predication, in Western metaphysics, what we have been characterizing, following Dahlstrom, as his claim that there exists a "logical prejudice" in that tradition.

But in Hegel's case, the philosophical attempt to render such "rendering intelligible" intelligible is *not* discursive predication. Another way of putting this is to say that it—speculative philosophy—does not have objects, beings, or the possible availability of beings for its object but itself, and thinking as such is not an object except in some mere grammatical sense. This is not an altogether unusual type of claim in philosophy. "The world is all that is the case" is not one of the things that happens to be the case in the world; the transcendental "I" in Kant is the form of experience, not an object available in experience. There are lots of variations, and Heidegger's worldhood of the world is another example. But if pure thinking is not predicative determination but "the moments of the self-moving Concept," what is that reflective activity?

Second, Hegel strongly distinguishes judgment, *Urteil*, from proposition, *Satz*. He says a lot of things about this, but he seems to mean that a *Satz* is (paradigmatically, at least) an empirical proposition or a law in mathematical physics that is experimentally answerable to the world, whereas judgments in the proper sense are answerable only to themselves. One way Hegel puts this is to say that we do not try to show in speculation that a pure concept agrees with an object, and we do not follow Kant in saying that objects must conform to concept but that "the concept agrees with itself." This means that in the *Logic*, in pure thinking, The Concept, all possible discursive bivalent thinkability, must be shown to agree with itself, with all that is required for the thinkable to be thinkable, and when completed, attains the status of Absolute Idea. In this sense, it is propositions, *Sätze*, that are truth bearers; conceptual self-determinations in the way Hegel has defined them are not, because what they establish can have no contraries. They articulate what is necessary for a proposition, the content of an assertion, *to be* a truth bearer, which articulation is not true by agreeing with what we (somehow) already know a truth bearer must be in order to be a truth bearer (except again in a formal sense).[1] What conditions must be satisfied is precisely the question. This is true, as are other philosophical claims, like value claims, also not empirically answerable but formulable in what have the appearance of bivalent judgments, which are judgments in Hegel's special sense. His clearest examples are evaluation or essence judgments. "This plant is curative" is a judgment, whereas "this plant has these biochemical markers" is not. "This is a good house," "This is a bad polis" are not for him of the same logical kind as "this is a yellow house" or "this polis existed two thousand years ago," all for the reasons just stated. This can get pretty confusing because it is all pre-Frege and idiosyncratic to Hegel. (As far as I know, no one else makes this sort of differentiation between judgment and proposition, certainly not after Hegel.)

The implications of this bear on what counts as pure thinking's success in articulating itself. It is not by directly arguing against any possible contraries and not by answerability to the world but by some sort of case for indispensability and so internal necessity. In the interpretation I have defended (2018), this is what the ontological realist interpretations of Hegel— viz., Concepts as abstract objects—do not get right, that the *Logic* does not begin with Being but with the attempt—Hegel says "the resolve"—*to think being*. That doesn't make Being a concept or a thought any more than trying to determine what a number or a possibility is is all about and only about the concept or the thought of a number or possibility. A concept is a concept, not a possibility or a number. But one can ask what must be thought

1. Cf. from the SL:

The *identity* of the idea with itself is one with the *process*; the thought that liberates actuality from the seeming of purposeless mutability and transfigures it into *idea* must not represent this truth of actuality as dead repose, as a mere *picture*, numb, without impulse and movement, as a genius [*Genius (sic)*] or number, or as an abstract thought; the idea, because of the freedom which the concept has attained in it, also has the *most stubborn opposition* within it; its repose consists in the assurance and the certainty with which it eternally generates that opposition and eternally overcomes it, and in it rejoins itself. (12.177)

in order for the thought to capture what must be the case for an object to count as a number, without that attempt being about thinking, *not* numbers. Likewise, the possible thinking of being, and so "what it could be to be," are in that speculative identity Hegel wants to tout.[2] So the demonstration must involve what must be assumed, what is indispensable, in anything at all being intelligible, a.k.a. being possibly whatever it is.[3] So a science of logic must be a reflection of what thinking must be for any discursive thinking about objects (and not pure thinking) to be a truth bearer, which Kant and Hegel understand as: what must be true of anything at all (which topic is not a topic about an object) for discursive determinacy (in the logical mode: assertions being possibly true or false) to be possible.

However, this means that the conception of the task of pure thinking, the relation between pure thinking and thinking that is not pure thinking, is (for Heidegger) still saddled with the orienting assumption that intelligibility (or thinkability) *is* a matter of discursive, bivalent determinacy-determining judgings, and that means that Being or any of the beings is "measured by," understood in terms of, such an assumed starting point, from Plato and Aristotle to Hegel. This gets the whole issue of the meaning of Being off on the wrong track.

Heidegger, however, does not consider those passages where Hegel is quite clear that the standard judgmental form is inappropriate for speculative thinking or first philosophy. Speculative concepts are so interrelated that there is no stable, isolatable judgmental form in which any moment, any "thought-determination" (*Denkbestimmung*) or moment in the Concept's development, can be individually expressed except elliptically. If there is a speculative judgment, it consists of the *whole* of the SL. Moreover, it may be that when Hegel calls the SL "the realm of shadows, the world of simple essentialities, freed of all sensuous concretion" (21.43), he confirms Heidegger's claims about the exclusion of any element of finitude from the *Logic*, but he ignores the strange claim that these essentialities should be considered "shadows." (More on these metaphors below, but the obvious question is: what are the originals that these shadows are reflections of?)

2. I here assume that case made for this interpretation in Pippin 2019, that this is not a mere "category theory" in Hegel, once one assumes that the possibility of any being being what it is is determinacy, it being discriminable from what it is not. (A heap of junk exists, but it is not anything, not an entity.)

3. It might seem possible to call all of this a "conceptual scheme idealism," if one agrees with Davidson that there is only one conceptual scheme, that nothing is intelligible and so available "outside" such a scheme. But putting it that way invites a kind of "impositionist" idealism (scheme-content distinction) and also invites claims about "alternate conceptual schemes." This is exactly the move Herder made, and we are still living with the implications of that move.

To come to the contrast with Kant, Heidegger wants to say that what he claims to discover in Kant, the unity of pure thinking and intuition, bears on the issue of finitude (is the issue), which Hegel did not acknowledge. But (i) Kant almost saw that in his first edition claims about the role of the imagination in that unity, but (ii) "shrank back" and reasserted the dominant role of the understanding in the second edition, a textual claim we do not need to pursue again.[4] (Whether or not Kant was on the verge of breaking free of the metaphysical tradition, he nevertheless did not, and that is Heidegger's final verdict.) What he ultimately means when we get to Hegel is that when Hegel begins by asking what the thinking of anything at all, any being, must involve, his beginning is not presuppositionless. He has already assumed in the *Logic*'s very first move (given the link to the sole model of intelligibility for nonpure thinking) that the meaning of beings, what primordially confronts us in our exchange with the world, is our interest in, our "care" about, discursive determinability. But that is an unwarranted and misleading assumption on Hegel's part, as well as limiting the notion of meaningfulness to determinate conceptual content. (Hegel does have an account of what Heidegger would consider *Bedeutsamkeit*, and we will come to that issue soon.) As we have seen, that Hegelian notion of the availability of the meaning of determinate being is irrelevant for Dasein's meaning. Dasein's distinctive mode of being cannot be captured in any discursive account of its determinacy. Lots of implications follow here that are among Heidegger's most controversial. Such an originally orienting meaning is not itself subject to a science of logic; it is historically given, a historical world that is contingent, into which we are thrown, which cannot be grounded or itself rendered intelligible, but "disclosed" in a way that also obscures such a dark inheritance. There is no transcendence into a "wordless" domain of pure objectivity, the True, and it is certainly the case that Hegel does seem to claim that. In one version of Hegel's claim, we have reached that standpoint by means of the *Phenomenology of Spirit*, the "ladder to the Absolute." As always, it is important to stress that there is no indication in Heidegger that he thinks there cannot be methodological procedures that allow one to make objective claims, truth claims, that can be resolved. His objection is to the claim that the ontological assumption underlying what such a methodological procedure allows—standing presence, the present at hand—discloses the original meaningfulness, significance, of Being. If that were true, then any being, aesthetic object, human being, language,

---

4. Again, Hegel's criticism is different. His claim is that the postulation of pure forms of intuition as distinct but inseparable elements of experience is dogmatic and ultimately merely psychological.

life, must all be treated, at bottom, the same ontological way. Regardless of the various ways Hegel formulates the claim, Hegel does think that pure thinking can be so self-grounded and so "absolute." That is systematicity. This is all also consistent with Heidegger's view that philosophy does not make claims or progress or discover or prove anything. It seeks to reveal to us what in some sense or other we already know. But Heidegger wants to show (to "awaken" us to the point) that we do not already know that being is discursive determinability; in fact, what is most familiar to us, what we do and must begin by assuming, is the being of the *zuhanden*, affordances, the ready to hand. That is not a point integrable into the *Science of Logic*.[5] And neither is what is involved in Heidegger's claim for the priority of "disclosure" rather than assertion in any first philosophy, autonomous pure thinking. And as we have been noting throughout, no doubt the first Hegelian response to this claim is "so what?" Why ask the SL a question irrelevant to its purpose? And again, the claim is that the *Logic does* assume an answer to the meaning of Being question: that this is dogmatic and that its unasked status renders the claim for any sort of absolute, even for an absolute status to discursive determinability, question-begging.

It is also true that Heidegger is right that the SL is the fundamental text in Hegel. Hegel does say in several of his nonlogical works that everything he will say ultimately depends on the *Science of Logic*. But Heidegger and many Hegel scholars pay no attention to the strange limitation Hegel suggests, that Hegel calls these essentialities "shadows." Here is what Hegel says:

> The system of logic is the realm of shadows, the world of simple essentialities, freed of all sensuous concretion. To study this science, to dwell and to labor in this realm of shadows, is the absolute culture and discipline of consciousness. Its task is one which is remote from the intuitions and the goals of the senses. . . . But above all, thought thereby gains self-subsistence and independence. It will make itself at home in abstractions and in the ways of working with concepts without sensuous substrata, will develop an unconscious power to assimilate in rational form the otherwise dispersed manifold of cognitions and sciences, the power to grasp and hold them in their essentiality remote from feelings and from the world of merely fancied representation. (SL, 21.42–43).[6]

5. Hegel discusses the notion of a tool in a general discussion of purposive rationality, folding it into an account of the means in a practical syllogism—in other words, as a moment in purposive rationality. See SL, 12.166–67.

6. Yet another metaphor in the *Philosophy of Nature*, when Hegel points out that the richness and vitality of nature become, "in the quietude of thought," rather like a "dull northern fog" (PN, §246Z).

In the *Encyclopedia*, he expresses this limitation (a.k.a. finitude) in another way. "The method is not an external form but the soul and concept of the content, from which it is distinguished only insofar as the moments of the concept, even in themselves, in their [respective] determinacy, come to appear as the totality of the concept" (EL, §243).[7] The limitation is embedded in the "come to appear as the totality of the concept" (*als die Totalität des Begriffs zu erscheinen*). The same indication of the misleading implications of the isolation of the SL surfaces several times, as in the "*eingeschlossen*" here: "This idea is still logical; it is shut up in pure thought [*in den reinen Gedanken eingeschlossen*], the science only of the divine concept. Its systematic exposition is of course itself a realization, but one confined within the same sphere. Because the pure idea of cognition is to this extent shut up within subjectivity, it is the impulse [*Trieb*] to sublate it, and pure truth becomes as final result also the beginning of another sphere and science" (12.253).[8]

In the quotation used as an epigram above, Heidegger is continuing a claim he made about Kant and all great philosophers, that his revolution in philosophy casts a long shadow into the future, but Kant could not see what his revolution required and so could not jump over his own shadow into that post-Kantian future. No philosopher can. Here he says that Hegel thought he could jump over any future development, that anything in the future discourse of philosophy, anything conceptually essential, has been anticipated and systematically incorporated, given that the Absolute has been fully articulated. In effect, he thought he could "jump into the sun," the source or ground of shadows, or the meaning of beings. But he did not succeed, could not jump into the sun. (Heidegger is no doubt trading on Socrates, and the claim that the sun cannot be looked at; it is known only by what it illuminates.) But this is not what Hegel means by calling the *Logic* the realm of shadows. What he does mean is a concession to finitude that Heidegger does not see. I said above that Heidegger has a certain point in claiming that, regardless of all the unique characteristics Hegel assigns to

7. In this context, however, Hegel wants to effect a transition between the logic and the philosophies of nature of spirit; the latter are not independent but externalizations and internalizations of the Absolute Idea. Schelling has an interesting point to make about this:

> Putting logic first, in order to prove the existence of the absolute, is rather wondrous, as one has the Absolute as a result twice. The second time—at the end of the system—at the end of the logic already as resulting existence. (PR, 75)

8. See also SL, 12.180. Heidegger will himself appeal to this issue as arising in the PhG as well, in his 1931–1932 HPG, 197. "Im Grunde aber geht es um die Überführung des Wissens in die absolute Gestelltheit des Wissenden auf sich selbst, um eine Erwirkung *der in sich aufgeschlossenen Wirklichkeit des Geistes*" (my emphasis).

a *Science of Logic,* he is still oriented towards the possible thinkability of individual substances, Aristotle's *tode ti,* the answer to the primary metaphysical question, *ti to on.* What is a being? But Hegel's speculative identity claim, which Heidegger is so enthusiastic about (the completion of what Parmenides began, with the systematic incorporation of what Parmenides could not: reflective subjectivity), is wrongly characterized by the traditional notion of individual determinacy. The relation of dependence goes the other way around too. Such determinacy must be rethought in the light of the theory of interanimated pure concepts. (This is roughly the same logical point we saw in the implications of the inseparability of thought and intuition in our discussion of Kant.) For the purposes of what Hegel calls "the understanding" (*Verstand*), the paradigm of which is scientific rationality, such determinacy can be limited to what is necessary for a stable content for a proposition, but that is an abstraction from the interrelated conditions all necessary for such determinacy, the provenance of reason (*Vernunft*). This abstraction, the understanding's, does not lead to anything like "the meaning of Being." Hegel has many of the same objections to the understanding—"forgetting" its provisional and merely useful status—as Heidegger does.

Hegel also means to refer to the role of the *Logic* in his *Encyclopedia,* which is the true system. If Heidegger means to criticize the "Hegelian culmination" as a failure, while it is true that that *Logic* is the heart of that system, as with any organic treatment, the heart cannot be understood if the function it occupies within a body and so its place in a living body is ignored. (This is the strongest point that Schelling makes against Hegel in PR.) A heart isolated and studied as a mere individual object is not a heart. The metaphors can threaten to pile on each other clumsily here, but it is essential to see that by "shadows," Hegel means to point to the *insufficiency* of the *Logic*—even as a metaphysics—if considered as a stand-alone part, when considered as a speculative science. It is an abstraction, a necessary one, but its isolation from the system it animates, while necessary, can produce only conceptual shadows of the Absolute. We must see it "alive" in the development of the sciences of nature and in the historical development of human *Geist* before it can be fully understood. It is the same with Aristotle, Hegel's guide in so much. "What really is" is the being-at-work (*energeia*) of the individuated species form in a particular, a *tode ti.* The universal species form is indispensable in *knowing,* but isolated it is a "shadow" in the same sense.

The implications of this holism in Hegel—which Heidegger might have noticed as "the unity of concept and intuition" in Hegel—are too complex to follow out here, but one implication stands out immediately and should have resonated with Heidegger on *Ereignis.* Since Hegel's *Philosophy of*

Nature clearly incorporates unanticipatable historical developments in the natural sciences, and since the *Philosophy of Spirit* refers to many distinctly modern elements of civil society and the state, then the reciprocal relation between the *Logic* and the *Encyclopedia* cannot be "closed." Further developments in either normative domain must affect what could count as the logical moment they depend on. To be sure, this point does not mean that logical or conceptual reflections are "driven" by empirical discovery and historical novelty.[9] Every such change must be understood as an amplification and further substantialization of what in the *Logic* are mere shadows. Any such amplification and deepening must always occur "shadowed" by the necessities of the Logic's requirements for intelligibility. This does, however, mean, at least given this qualification, that the Hegelian a priori for the philosophies of nature and spirit must be a historical a priori, what is conceptually indispensable and so not empirically disconfirmable but at a moment of development in the investigation of nature and the developments of civil society. Nothing of any prior moment must be discarded but sublated in the Hegelian way, where "the Hegelian way" means as required by the *Logic*.

Does any of this mean that Heidegger's critique misses the mark? Not decisively, I would suggest. No matter how unusual Hegel's position on both conceptual and real determinacy turns out to be, the driving impetus in his account is to account for the knowability of Being and to account for Being itself in terms of its knowability. If Heidegger is right that such an assumption dogmatically assumes such a meaning of Being and that this is important, that something of the greatest importance in philosophy and not only in philosophy is thereby missed and or distorted, then, however unusual and unprecedented is the "logic" Hegel advances in his case for knowability, he is still an example of the logical prejudice. The same would have to be said if Hegel's system is interpreted in a historically "open" and not "closed" way, as commentators sometimes try to suggest. That has little to do with being thrown into a historical world of meaning, marking our finitude in a way Hegel would reject in the name of the possibility of transcendence (or continual transcendence) that Heidegger is challenging.[10] There is no way into or out of Hegel without the Absolute, The Concept, the *Science of Logic*. And Heidegger is right. There is no Absolute. There cannot be an Absolute. And this is not a peculiarity of Hegel. Scientific materialism, elimina-

9. Although, given the shadows problem we are discussing, it is understandable that Brandom (2019) in his Hegel interpretation adopts this view. For a critique, see Pippin 2015.

10. Heidegger has his own notion of transcendence, but it is not Hegel's. Despite his fatalism, Heidegger still maintains that we can own up to our destiny and "seize control" of it, not merely be subject to it.

tive materialism, Kantian moralism, dualism, divine command theories of morality—all are claims about an Absolute, and Heidegger means to show us why, especially in its historical consequences, the search for such an absolute is both fruitless and blinding.

All of this depends on whether Heidegger has some compelling alternative account of such meaningfulness (determinate knowability as opposed to what?) and also whether he can show that the neglect of this alternative has the consequence he insists it has throughout the 1930s and '40s—most dramatically, nihilism. But we are not done with the things he wants to say about Hegel's culmination.

ABSOLUTE SUBJECTIVITY

Recall the passage by Hegel quoted in the discussion above: "Because the pure idea of cognition is to this extent shut up within subjectivity, it is the impulse [*Trieb*] to sublate it, and pure truth becomes as final result also the beginning of another sphere and science" (SL, 12.253).[11]

He is explaining the idea of a transition from the *Logic* to the rest of the *Encyclopedia,* and given Hegel's own critique of the "subjective idealism" of Kant and Fichte, it seems odd for him to qualify his own results in the *Logic* with that description about the results being "shut up in" subjectivity.[12] That book, after all, concludes with "The *Absolute* Idea," which is said to be the unity of the Idea of the Good and the Idea of the True, of the practical and theoretical idea. In one sense, Hegel is merely conceding the obvious, that thinking is always thinking by some subject, even though it should not be considered because of that a psychological event. There is no thinking going on without a subject who thinks. No aspect of the question of Being or about what makes any being the being it is is a question except as one addressed to thinking. Any being is available only as thought, and the identity of thinking and being does not mean that the beings in the world are "thought-determinations" in the nonspeculative sense of identity. In order to understand beings, we must think about them, but since Hegel rejects Kant's reliance on species-specific pure forms of intuition, this should not

11. Schelling makes a witty but unfair remark about this idea in PR. "When Hegel says that the Idea, in its infinite freedom, decides to empty itself, etc. . . . this could be a timid expression for the Idea positing itself as Becoming-Other. . . . In any case, here the doubt sets in: Did Hegel understand the Idea as existing in actuality? Obviously a mere concept cannot make a decision" (80). It is unfair because Schelling knows how the teleology of the concept in its movement, both internally and outside of itself, is supposed to work. (Even though he has different objections to that as well [84].)

12. This is far and away among commentators on the *Logic* the most overlooked peculiarity in Hegel's own account of his SL. See Pippin 2019, 319–322.

count as a limitation. It is not merely what "we" think but what any thinker must think for there to be objects of judgment. We are supposed to have arrived at "absolute subjectivity," not human subjectivity. So, his account of what the conclusion of the *Logic* should have shown is this: "Accordingly, in this result cognition is restored and united with the practical idea; the previously discovered reality is at the same time determined as the realized absolute purpose, no longer an object of investigation, a merely objective world without the subjectivity of the concept, but as an objective world whose inner ground and actual subsistence [*wirkliches Bestehen*] is rather the concept. This is the absolute idea" (12.235).

In what appears something like another concession, or some sort of indication of the finitude of pure thinking, he notes in the concluding passage of the *Logic*, "but what is posited by this first resolve of the pure idea to determine itself as external idea is only the mediation out of which the concept, as free concrete existence that from externality has come to itself, raises itself up, completes this self-liberation *in the science of spirit*, and in the science of logic finds the highest concept of itself, the pure concept conceptually comprehending itself" (12.253). He means to say that the real completion of the *Logic* occurs after the *Philosophy of Nature* and at the conclusion of the *Philosophy of Spirit*; only at that point does the pure concept finally comprehend itself.

But the other curious thing about the former passage is the reference to an impulse, *Trieb*. This is consistent with his claim in the last paragraph of the book that the "transition" to the philosophies of nature and spirit is in fact not a logical transition, certainly not like those that occur in the book. He gives the example of the transition from subjective purpose to Life, which is a logical transition like others in the book. We may have come to the conclusion that the objective world is a "really possible" world only "because of" the concept, its inner ground and the source of its "actual subsistence." But that seems to be *practically* unsatisfying; it is only if, as he says, the Absolute Idea "frees" and "releases" itself into "exteriority" so that it can finally comprehend itself. This is supposed to be because the Absolute Idea serves as a final cause in a dual sense: the teleological completion of nonlogical concepts in the Idea, and the teleological completion of the Idea in the *Realphilosophie*.

Apart from this vague indication of a practical dissatisfaction and his locating the source of this dissatisfaction in being "shut up in" subjectivity, *even if* "*Absolute* Subjectivity," it is this status that provokes this practical dissatisfaction, the implications of which cannot be pursued here.[13] We

13. See the discussion in chapter 9 in Pippin 2019.

need this general summary to prepare for Heidegger's remarks about Hegel in his 1958 essay "Hegel and the Greeks." The main point of the essay is yet again to explain what it means to claim that the entire history of philosophy culminates in Hegel, and the decisive issue this time is the meaning of subjectivity. This claim follows Hegel's lead, for whom the decisive event in that history is the emergence of the philosophical theme of subjectivity in modernity, above all in Descartes. (Heidegger quotes Hegel's remark in his *Lectures on the History of Philosophy* that, after philosophy's long journey on stormy seas, with Descartes for the first time we can finally shout "land-ho," we can hope that our wandering will soon be over [HG, 325].) This sighting of the centrality of the question of subjectivity originally meant a worry that the mind's access was only to its own subjective states, representations in a theater of the mind, creating the problems of external-world and other-minds skepticism. But Heidegger accepts the basic Kantian narrative of how this misunderstands the problem of subjectivity, is uncritical because the very possibility of the "I think X" has not been established, and when that problem is raised in that way, the status of the problem of subjectivity changes. (The "I think" necessary for even my representations to be mine, to be thought, is not the "I" whose contents are mental events.)

> However, this subject is first taken hold of in the right way—namely, in the Kantian sense, transcendentally and completely, i.e., in the sense of speculative idealism—when the whole structure and movement of the subjectivity of the subject unfolds and is taken up into absolute self-knowing. In knowing itself as this knowing that conditions all objectivity, the subject is, as this knowing, the absolute itself. True being is the thinking that thinks itself absolutely. For Hegel, being and thinking are the same, specifically in the sense that everything is taken back into thinking and is determined according to what Hegel simply calls "thought." (HG, 325)

This formulation can sound too Kantian or transcendental with words like "conditions" and "taken back into," but we have already seen that Heidegger realizes that Hegel does not separate thinking and intuiting, such that thought imposes itself on the material of sensation, and so takes in something alien to thought. His comments reflect Hegel's own concession, for want of a better word, that at the end of the *Logic*, despite the speculative identity of thinking and being, we find ourselves "shut up within subjectivity," even though it is now absolute subjectivity, or pure thinking, the thinking by which Being is available at all. He seems to mean that regardless of the identity we still find ourselves on the subjective side of that identity.

The *Logic* establishes that the meaning of being is The Concept, or absolute intelligibility, and thereby a determination of all that being could possibly be. This completes the beginning of Western rationalism in Plato's identification of the meaning of Being as "idea," and Aristotle's hylomorphic emendation, and the realization since Descartes that thinking's possible relation to being was a problem that, if not properly resolved, would leave us a radical skepticism. Hence, Heidegger's main claim:

> But the statement concerning the completion of philosophy does not mean that philosophy is at an end in the sense of a cessation and breaking off. Rather the completion first provides the possibility of diverse transformations down to the simplest forms: brutal inversion and vehement opposition. Marx and Kierkegaard are the greatest of Hegelians. They are this against their will. The completion of philosophy is neither its end, nor does it consist in the isolated system of speculative idealism. The completion is only as the whole course of the history of philosophy, in whose course the beginning remains as essential as the completion: Hegel and the Greeks. (HG 326)[14]

But Heidegger then begins to raise his basic question to Hegel on the issue of truth. Heidegger wants to deny that *the* truth, or "the True," the meaning of Being, could culminate in absolute subjectivity's self-satisfaction or self-certainty. The movement of the *Logic*, the demonstration of conceptual interanimation, is a kind of radicalization of Kant on the spontaneity of thinking, leading Hegel to insist that pure spontaneous thinking can provide itself its own content just by thinking and reflecting. This is the equivalent of the idea that philosophy (classically conceived, or pre-Kant) is self-sufficient, autonomous, not originally or fundamentally a reflection on empirical discoveries, ethical intuitions, ordinary language, the development of mathematics or current social conditions. So, all philosophy, whether acknowledged or not, is reason's reflection on itself, and that is why Hegel

14. See also: "Therefore am I in the habit of saying that Hegel is the most radical Greek there ever was. With the means that were pre-formed in Greek ontology as if in a seed, the means that lay at the roots of Greek ontology, Hegel grasped something (roughly speaking: spirit, history) that in this form was never experienced by the Greeks. This is only asserted here. Proof of this thesis is naturally very difficult" (W, 8). And, Hegel "is in agreement with Aristotle *in the principle of the idea of being.* Or, formulated in a different way: everything that Hegel takes up and sublates (from the intervening history, Descartes, Kant) remains within Greek ontology" (ibid.). Heidegger admits, though, that Hegel was onto something, or thought he was onto something, absent from Greek ontology: the historical character of being. But he will charge that this is an illusion, that Hegel does not in fact grasp the historical in its ontological character (W, 16).

counts as its culmination. But Heidegger raises his familiar objection. In this context, he wants to note that the modern notion of subjectivity ignores rather than incorporates a crucial aspect of the Greek beginning: truth as *aletheia*, uncovering. So, what Hegel culminates is a kind of continuous forgetfulness. In this text, Heidegger uses another of his words for disclosure, this time *Entbergung*, an unconcealing or literally "un-hiding."

> If Hegel allows the fundamental position of his system to culminate in the absolute idea, in the complete self-appearing of spirit, this provokes the question as to whether disclosure must not also be in play even in this shining, i.e., in the phenomenology of spirit and therefore in absolute self-knowing and its certainty. And at once we are faced with the further question as to whether disclosure has its site in spirit as the absolute subject, or whether disclosure itself is the site and points to the site wherein something like representing subject can first "be" what it is. (HG, 332)

Heidegger is actually making a simple point that we have seen before, and by now I think we can say, or I want to say, it is a good one. Hegel's case for the logic as metaphysics claim, for the identity of being and thinking, is his version (his because of the incorporation of the modern notion of subjectivity) of the assumption that Being is intelligibility or thinkability, or, most importantly, its knowability. This is how Heidegger, correctly in my view, interprets Hegel's claim from the preface to the PhG that everything depends on understanding "the True not only as Substance but as Subject." That is, substance must itself be conceived as conceptual intelligibility, knowability; "*nous* rules the world." The claim cannot mean that substance is "really" a thinking mind, Spirit, God. That would be simply to say that Spirit is a special kind of substance. Although this is far and away the most prevalent reading of the equivalence, a moment's reflection will show that this cannot be the right reading. Heidegger puts it all in his own terminology: "But for Hegel, subjectivity is not the I-ness [*Ichheit*] of the familiar empirical egos of individual finite persons, but rather the absolute subject [which, crucially Heidegger glosses as] the pure self-grasping of the totality of beings which in and for itself grasps the whole multiplicity of beings as such, i.e., which can grasp all otherness of beings from itself as the mediation of its self-othering" (EF, 75).

The *Logic*, we recall, begins with the "resolve" to think Being, and it is fair enough for Heidegger to interpret this as a question about the meaning of Being. And, since all thinking is inherently apperceptive, upon reflection the result of attempting to think Being itself is shown to be an unsustainable thought because indeterminate and so unthinkable, not a thought.

Heidegger therefore says, "For, when Hegel conceives being as the indeterminate immediate, he experiences it as what is posited by the determining and conceiving subject" (HG, 333). This makes it impossible for Hegel to incorporate a crucial moment in the Greek beginning of philosophy, without which, Heidegger wants to say, philosophy has not reached the most fundamental issue. "Accordingly, he is not able to release *einai*, being in the Greek sense, from the relation to the subject, and set it free into its own essence. This essence, however, is presencing, that is to say, an enduring coming forth from concealment into unconcealment. In coming to presence, disclosure is at play" (HG, 333).

In other words, Hegel draws exactly the wrong lesson from the unthinkability of Being as such, a generality that is so general it dissolves into something unavailable. But its unavailability *to discourse*, and by contrast its presencing *in* disclosure, is precisely the point. It ought to have led Hegel to question the identification of the Absolute as absolute intelligibility. In fact, Heidegger claims in his 1925/1926 seminar on the *Logic* that the problem of this beginning is the "greatest predicament [*Verlegenheit*] of Hegelian logic as a whole" (W, 24). The true Hegelian beginning is not being or its identity with nothing but becoming, *Werden*, but all that means is the expression of the already presupposed, the condition of differentiation itself. In effect the beginning is the assertion of thinking as discursive differentiation. Hegel "actually begins with becoming, and only apparently with being; he wants to fool us" (W, 31).[15] Moreover, even becoming is not becoming, temporal change from one state to what it is not, but a merely formal category. In other words, thinking is really "the first, substantive beginning" (W, 42).

In *Identity and Difference*, Heidegger even uses one of Hegel's own examples, which Hegel intended to dismiss the attempt to think such generality, or Being as such, against him. "Hegel at one point mentions the following case to characterize the generality of what is general: Someone wants to buy fruit in a store. He asks for fruit. He is offered apples and pears, he is offered peaches, cherries, grapes. But he rejects all that is offered. He absolutely wants to have fruit. What was offered to him in every instance is fruit and yet, it turns out, fruit cannot be bought" (ID, 66). For Hegel, we should conclude by the analogy that Being in itself cannot be discursively thought and must be determined initially as becoming, not that the shopper's request is a confusion that should be cleared up by pointing out the Being is not a being. (The shopper conflates the ontological difference, just like Hegel. He tries to think of "fruit" as if it were another object.) This allows Heidegger to make the main claim in his philosophy again. "But here,

15. See also Henrich 1971.

too, Being gives itself only in the light that cleared itself for Hegel's thinking. That is to say: the manner in which it, Being, gives itself, is itself determined by the way in which it clears itself. This way, however, is a historic, always epochal character which has being for us as such only when we release it into its own native past. We attain to the nearness of the historic only in that sudden moment of a recall in thinking" (ID, 67).

Heidegger fully realizes that his own position holds something like the "belonging together" of man and being. Although as his thinking develops, he pays less attention to the mode of attentiveness necessary for Being to be available to Dasein, and more and more frequently considers Dasein as simply a site, an openness, there is still no sense to the question of the meaning of Being except with reference to the being for whom things can mean at all. But he denies that the right way to think about Dasein is as a subject in the Kantian and Hegelian sense—at its most distinctive, self-conscious pure thinking. He notes, referring to what might be a *tu quoque* objection: "It has indeed often been remarked that there cannot be an unconcealment in itself, that unconcealment is after all always unconcealment 'for someone.' It is thereby unavoidably 'subjectivized'" (HG, 334).

But he responds,

Nevertheless, must the human being—which is what is being thought here—necessarily be determined as subject? Does "for human beings" already unconditionally mean: posited by human beings? We may deny both options, and must recall the fact that *aletheia*, thought in a Greek manner, certainly holds sway for human beings, but that the human being remains determined by logos. . . . The human being is the being that, in saying, lets what is presencing lie before us in its presence, apprehending what ties before. Human beings can speak only insofar as they are sayers. (Ibid.)

This emphasis on the priority of disclosure is also put another way by Heidegger: that in order to remain true to the original manifestation of the meaning of Being, we need to reconceive philosophical thinking as something other than discursive rationality. However, his main question and the critique it is based on are only weighty, fundamental in his sense, if it does not remain a kind of black box of chaotic indeterminate, unsayable revelations across historical time. What is this new sort of thinking? What would it mean in this post-culmination or post-Idealist context to *struggle* to understand the meaning of Being, to resolve obscurity about what meaning is disclosed, to avoid simply leaving us with this very general notion of dependence? Without some answer to such a question, it is Heidegger who looks like our shopper searching in vain for "fruit." We'll come to that question in the next chapter. First, there is a final element in Heidegger's treatment of Hegel. He finally turns his attention to the *Phenomenology* (or at least to its introduction), a work he generally neglects in favor of the *Logic*, in his 1942–1943 essay, "Hegel's Concept of Experience."

THE RELEASE

In Heidegger's *Introduction to Metaphysics*, originally presented as a lecture course in 1935, and then published as an essay in 1953, one of the most important sections for our purposes occurs towards the very end, a subsection called "Being and Thinking." There he repeats a familiar characterization of the philosophical understanding of the availability of Being to thinking, one that reaches a supposed culmination in German Idealism. "Thinking sets itself against Being in such a way that Being is re-presented to thinking, and consequently stands against thinking like an ob-ject. . . . Consequently, thinking is no longer just the opposing member in some new distinction but becomes the basis on which one decides about what stands against it, so much so that Being in general gets interpreted on the basis of thinking" (IM, 123).

In the light of the interpretation we have been defending, this should be understood to claim: Being is taken to be meaningfully available originally (paradigmatically in the modern epoch) as thinkability, ultimately knowability. We know why Heidegger thinks this is so problematic. He is willing to make a rapid leap from the very principle of sufficient reason, inaugurated as such by Crusius but formulated as "the most noble" principle by Leibniz to its implications for the modern world. "One must think in both a literal and a substantive sense, namely, that the unique unleashing of the demand to render reasons threatens everything of humans' being-at-home and robs them of the roots of their subsistence, the roots from out of which every great human age, every world-opening spirit, every molding of the human form has thus far grown" (POR, 30). Likewise, he will go on to say, once the very question of nature is posed by Kant as a question about the *conditions* for its possibility, it is inevitable that nature must be understood as what meets and only what meets those conditions. All of being is understood to be available only by means of conditions that Kant is certainly willing to call "subjective," and even though he thinks he can establish the objectivity of what satisfies those conditions, that objectivity is also understood in terms of necessary conditions for the possibility of human experience understood as sense experience.

In this context we have heard another, much more abstract, concern.

We have just heard again, from his essay on "Hegel and the Greeks," that Hegel represents the culmination of this distortion of Being as knowability, as measured by "logic." "Accordingly, he is not able to release [*loslassen*] *einai*, being in the Greek sense, from the relation to the subject, and set it free [*freigeben*] into its own essence. This essence, however, is presencing [*Anwesen*], that is to say, an enduring coming forth from concealment into unconcealment. In coming to presence [*An-wesen*], disclosure is at play" (HG, 333).

But how does one accomplish this releasing, setting free, disclosing as coming to presence, not merely present at hand? In Heidegger's view of Hegel's interpretation of the Greek philosophical world, which he largely shares, this did not emerge as a problem. In an early draft of "Hegel and the Greeks," he notes that "the degree of Greek consciousness is the degree of beauty" and explains Hegel's view as he understands it:

> Being has not yet found its foundation in subjectivity which knows itself, which is self-consciousness or rather "self-knowing." Being is more like pure splendor, pure appearing of what is objective. If it is true that the Greeks lived in the element of pure subjectivity, but failed to understand it as such, how did they correspond to what is objective, that is, to Beauty? From the most ancient times, the Greeks were concerned in displaying and celebrating beings. By making this remark, Hegel shows that he deeply understood the Greek universe. What Hegel saw, we can enunciate in a few words: the fundamental attitude of the Greeks facing Being is one of respectful and reserved emotion in front of the Beautiful. As we ponder about it, we are tempted to hear Hölderlin's voice who in the draft of his novel *Hyperion, or the Hermit in Greece* thinks Being as Beauty.[16]

In commenting on Hölderlin's claim that the gods have fled, Heidegger invokes this image in WP, 89 as the extinguishing from world history of "the divine radiance," the *Glanz der Gottheit*. He immediately glosses the metaphorical expression by noting that it means "there fails to appear for the world the ground that grounds it"; there is only the *Abgrund*, the abyss, a much more dramatic way of saying that the meaningfulness of Being question has been so thoroughly forgotten that it is not even available to us as a

---

16. This is a French version of the lecture, translated by Beaufret and Savage 1959, 356. A slightly different version of the lecture was published in Henrich et al. 1960, 43–57. This translation from the French version is by Taminiaux 1991, 191.

question (WP, 90).[17] We are not content with having forgotten or ignored the questions of the sources of meaningfulness in a world; we do not think there is any such question.

The gods have fled, though, and some "new thinking" (thinking that is not what he had called "logic") is necessary if Heidegger is posing a real alternative to the twenty-five hundred years of metaphysics begun by Greek "aesthetic objectivism." But before broaching that topic, we should finish our exploration of Hegel and quickly note that Hegel himself has an account of the issue Heidegger is raising ("releasing" Being), both in the PhG and the *Logic*, and the account is couched in the very terms Heidegger suggests. Hegel's claims turn on his use of *Entäußerung*, Luther's term for *kenosis*, God's emptying himself into the world, releasing himself, setting itself free in its own other. "However, spirit has shown itself to us to be neither the mere withdrawal of self-consciousness into its pure inwardness, nor the mere immersion of self-consciousness into substance and the non-being of its difference. Rather, it has shown itself to be this movement of the self which relinquishes itself of itself and immerses itself in its substance, and which likewise, as subject, has both taken the inward turn into itself from out of that substance and has made its substance into an object and a content" (PhG, 464).

And,

Therefore, in this knowing, spirit has brought to a close the movement of giving shape to itself inasmuch as that movement is burdened with the insurmountable differences of consciousness. Spirit has won the pure element of its existence, the concept. According to the freedom of its being, the content is the *self-relinquishing itself of itself*, or it is the immediate unity of self-knowing. Considered with regard to the content, the pure movement of this self-relinquishing constitutes the necessity of this content. (PhG, 465, my emphasis)[18]

It is difficult to know, simply from these passages, exactly what Hegel means, but it is possible to note that, for all the similarity to Heidegger's similar claims, there is a major difference. For Hegel had noted that "time is the concept itself that is there and is represented to consciousness as empty intuition" (PhG, 461). But he had gone on to note something that marks a

17. For a discussion of why Heidegger should associate the beautiful with the meaningfulness of existence in general and strictly for itself, see Gelvin 1979.

18. See the account by Pinkard of this issue in the introduction to his translation (PhG, xlii).

clear difference with Heidegger. "Consequently, spirit necessarily appears in time, and it appears in time *as long as it does not grasp its pure concept*, which is to say, as long as it does not erase time. Time is the pure self externally intuited by the self but not grasped by the self; it is only the intuited concept. As this concept grasps itself, it sublates its temporal form, conceptually comprehends the intuiting, and is conceptually comprehended and conceptually comprehending intuiting" (PhG, 461–462).

Hegel does not mean that Spirit will no longer exist in time but that its self-comprehending over time assumes a teleological structure, a goal that, when reached, transcends its necessary appearance in time, or its finitude, in Heideggerian terms. In other words, systematic, pure philosophy is possible, not an enterprise aiming forever at some asymptotic, ultimately unreachable goal. As we have been seeing, Heidegger denies that Dasein has any such structure or goal, and that Hegel's own language about a release into its other and especially *its return to itself* is a denial of this finitude, not its assertion. (The temporal form of the fundamental meaning of Spirit's being is for Hegel provisional; not final.) Such a denial is unwarranted and dogmatic, according to Heidegger. This means that anyone commenting on Hegel has a choice at this point; to stay within the bounds of paraphrase-as-commentary and simply note that, however implausible or even unintelligible the idea of a systematic, absolute completion of philosophy is, Hegel as a historical fact believed it had been accomplished (perhaps adding that all of Western metaphysics must presuppose the possibility of such a completion),[19] or to attempt to deny the implausibility and offer a defense of the basic claim. It does not seem to me that either approach will meet Heidegger's concerns head-on.

The same problem exists in Hegel's unusual language about the implications of his *Logic* for the *Realphilosophie*, the *Philosophy of Nature* and the *Philosophy of Spirit*. This would be another version of "releasing" Being from the "relation to the subject." He tells us that the Absolute Idea—which I am interpreting as the necessary moments in the knowability of any being, and, given the assumption that to be is to be knowable, determines what it means to be an entity at all—is not itself a substantive position. The absolute idea, he notes, "has shown itself to amount to this, namely that determinateness does not have the shape of a content, but that it is simply as form, and that accordingly the idea is the absolutely universal idea. What

---

19. This would be quite false. There is a long tradition, stretching back to Socrates, of an aporetic conception of philosophy and that, accordingly, philosophy is a way of life, not doctrinal.

is left to be considered here, therefore, is thus not a content as such, but the universal character of its form—that is, method" (12.237).

But he also tells us something about such a method that resonates directly with Heidegger. He notes (in the EL), "The method is not an external form but the soul and concept of the content, from which it is distinguished only insofar as the moments of the concept, even in themselves, in their [respective] determinacy, come to appear as the totality of the concept" (EL, §243); and claims, "Yet the absolute freedom of the idea is that it does not merely pass over into life or let life shine in itself as finite knowing, but instead, in the absolute truth of itself, resolves to release freely from itself the moment of its particularity or the first determining and otherness, the immediate idea, as its reflection itself as nature" (EL, §244).

This, of course, is not what Heidegger means by "*loslassen*" or releasing being to be, and that makes for a dramatic contrast. Hegel is talking about the *completing* of the Idea's self-comprehension in the completion of systematic philosophy, in the Philosophy of Nature and the Philosophy of Spirit, both extensions of the fundamental assumption of the theoretical enterprise.[20] Hegelian releasement is a stage in the final self-comprehension of the Absolute, its return to itself after its externalization.

EXPERIENCE

Hegel's 1807 *Phenomenology of Spirit* is supposed to be the "scientific history of consciousness." In the body of that work itself, Hegel calls the work "the path of the soul wandering through the series of ways it takes shape, as if these were stations put forward in advance to it by its own nature, so that it purifies itself into spirit by arriving at a cognition" (PhG, 52).

He famously calls the *Phenomenology* "the path of doubt," indeed "the path of despair," a "self-consummating skepticism" and thereby "the series of the figurations of consciousness which consciousness traverses on this path is the full history of the cultivation of consciousness itself into science" (PhG, 52). It is quite an idealized history, a word that in the early nineteenth century could just as easily mean systematic, a staged, not literal journey by what will become, in order for such knowledge to be able to withstand its own skepticism, a collective or like-minded subject, Geist, from the most

20. See also: "But what is posited by this first resolve of the pure idea to determine itself as external idea is only the mediation out of which the concept, as free concrete existence that from externality has come to itself, raises itself up, completes this self-liberation in the science of spirit, and in the science of logic finds the highest concept of itself, the pure concept conceptually comprehending itself" (12.253).

naive assumptions about the availability of beings to a knowing subject through stages of self-consciousness and reason. (Clearly a Kantian architectonic echo.) Only then is Spirit's drive for certainly treated in actual historical terms in the Geist chapter in a narration from the ancient Greek and Roman world though the Enlightenment, the French Revolution, and the modern moral point of view.

This means that by this unusual procedure Hegel proposes to assess the various competencies involved in distinctly human sentience, sapience, and agency and their interrelation. The account is unusual, his own version of "phenomenology," which has enough connection with the project of articulating "what it is like" for an experiencing subject for the project to be recognizable as what would be called, with many differences, phenomenology in the post-Husserlian world. But here Hegel interrogates not just what the experience, under some assumption about the content of experiences, would be like but what a subject is able to say successfully about what it takes away from such an experience or what it regards as justifying a claim emanating from it. At a minimum this involves imagining possible models of experience, primarily experience of objects and of other subjects, restricted to one or some set of competencies, or in some specific relation, and then demonstrating by a series of essentially reductio ad absurdum arguments that such an imagined experience, when imagined from the point of view of the experiencer, really could not be a possible experience because the experiencer cannot successfully say what it experiences. (And in keeping with the identity theory central to his Idealism, each problem and its overcoming in a mode of knowing sets what could be a possible knowable.) Eventually such an internal testing of models of experience becomes, in the course of Hegel's developmental account, so detailed and rich that it amounts to an examination of the possibility and viability of an actual historical form of life, a historical experience conducted under the assumption of such competencies and their interrelationship.

Heidegger in this essay (there is also a 1930–1931 lecture course, *Hegels Phänomenologie des Geistes*) concentrates on the introduction to the book and unarguably the most important concept in that chapter and in the book, experience, *Erfahrung* (an alternate title was "Science of the Experience of Consciousness"). This putative journey begins with what Hegel calls "natural consciousness"—the commonsense view that knowing is saying truly how things are, or that knowing is holding oneself answerable to objects as they are. This beginning conceives of such knowing as passive, onto objects directly by means of the direct deliverances of sensibility, what Hegel calls "sense certainty." But this assumes some answer to "what it is" to hold oneself answerable *rightly*, an implicit conception of itself that must be able to be expressed and tested such that consciousness cannot just *be* in such a state but can say what it knows. (The assumption here is our old friend, apperception; the fact that every such exercise of a competency is self-conscious; a subject takes itself to be exercising it.) It cannot be coherently stated, according to Hegel's account, and the process goes on with a similar model. It is this notion of a genuinely progressive inner self-correction that Heidegger challenges as *merely* staged, as if the ultimate notion of the Absolute, comprehensive knowability as the meaning of Being,[21] is not "present" until Spirit reaches that realization in the culmination of the journey. Here is how Heidegger formulates his basic objection to this enterprise.

> However, even if science keeps itself clear of critical considerations unsuited to it, it will still remain under the suspicion that though it indeed asserts itself absolutely as absolute knowledge, it does not prove itself to be such. It therefore offends most bitterly against the claim of certainty, the pure fulfillment of which it claims to be. Science must, therefore, be brought before the forum which alone is competent to decide how it is to be examined. This forum can only be the *parousia* of the absolute. Therefore, it is of renewed importance to clarify the absoluteness of the absolute. (HCE, 103)

By referring to *parousia*, a word associated with the claim for the indwelling, the presence of God in the world, translated by Heidegger as "being with us," Heidegger means to repeat his usual charge that Hegel does not *reach* his conception of the (logical) Absolute by, in various stages, showing the progressive failure of merely finite forms of knowing (considered with attention to their reliance on the Absolute), various empirical, mathematical, practical, and aesthetic modalities of finite knowledge, until the reality of the Absolute, this already assumed presupposition about the meaning of Being, cannot be denied and emerges as the truth in all previous partial attempts to say how beings are and to act under some understanding of one's agency. That conception of the Absolute is always already presupposed, "present" as the implicit but hidden criterion. Again, the meaning of Being has been assumed and the assumption is a distortion of what is truly "originary."

21. Cf. Heidegger in ID: "Near the end of the *Science of Logic* (Lasson edition, Vol. 11,484), Hegel says of the absolute Idea: 'Only the absolute Idea is *Being*, imperishable *Life*, *self-knowing Truth*, and it is all *Truth*.' Thus Hegel himself explicitly gives to the matter of his thinking that name which is inscribed over the whole matter of Western thinking, the name: Being" (ID, 43).

A key issue in what bothers Heidegger about this procedure and indeed the key to understanding what Hegel is trying to do is the concept of negation involved in Spirit's periodic self-negation, that "self-consuming skepticism." This sort of phenomenological negation is said by Hegel not to be indeterminate, as if all we know when we know that some model is not possible is that a possible propositional position in logical space, to use the Tractarian formulation, is empty, and what is true is located simply "elsewhere," if anywhere, indeterminately, in the infinity of such logical space. As Hegel puts it,

> The completeness of the forms of non-real consciousness will emerge through the very necessity of their progression and their interrelations. To make this comprehensible, it can be noted in general at the outset that the exposition of non-truthful consciousness in its untruth is not a merely negative movement. Such a one-sided view is what natural consciousness generally has of it; and a knowing which makes this one-sidedness into its essence is one of the shapes of incomplete consciousness which lies within the course of the path itself and which will serve itself up in that path. That is, such a one-sided view is the skepticism which sees in the result always only pure nothing and which abstracts from the fact that this nothing is determinately the nothing of that from which it results. However, only when taken as the nothing of that from which it is emerges is the nothing in fact the true result; thus it is itself a determinate nothing and it has a content. (PhG, 53)

We are familiar both with this notion of an internal self-undermining and with this sort of negation. The former is a staple of the Socratic elenchus. If Thrasymachus claims that justice is serving the interests of the stronger, Socrates, appealing only to Thrasymachus's claim, can point out that the rule exercised by a shepherd over his flock must see to the interests of the sheep or the herder's interests will not be served. So, the stronger must work for the interests of the weaker, and justice cannot be simply serving the interests of the stronger. That position has been "internally" negated, but we know much more than that this claim should have a negation sign in front of it. And the latter is just as familiar. It is common in "exclusive" disjunctive syllogisms. When we say something is not wet, we generally mean that it is not-wet; we mean it is dry. The assumption is that it is either wet or dry but cannot be both. Or, in an exclusive disjunction, because we know that $p \lor q$ is true, we know that $\sim(p \mathrel{\&} q)$ and $\sim (\sim p \mathrel{\&} \sim q)$ are also true. But therein lies Heidegger's worry. We know this, can get this determinate result because we already know, have assumed, that either p or q must be true and not both for the disjunction to be true; there is a whole assumed within which the inference is justified. (Likewise, we assume that something is either wet or it isn't). So Heidegger thinks there is an unwarranted assumption (about the Hegelian Absolute; that the meaning of Being is discursive intelligibility) at the heart of Hegel's dramatic claims, such as:

> Consciousness suffers this violence at its own hands and brings to ruin its own restricted satisfaction. Feeling this violence, anxiety about the truth might well retreat and strive to hold onto what it is in danger of losing. But it can find no peace; even if it wants to remain in an unthinking lethargy, thought spoils thoughtlessness, and its unrest disturbs that lethargy. Even if it fortifies itself with a sentimentality which assures it that it will find that everything *is good in its own way*, this assurance likewise suffers violence by the rationality that straightaway finds out that precisely because it is just "that way" and thus not good. (PhG, 54)

The simplest way to put Heidegger's objection is that consciousness becomes dissatisfied with itself because it already knows what it is looking for—viz., a way to articulate and justify what it claims to experience about the world. The journey is governed by the assumption that any moment must be a "self-knowing knowing," that any being must be discursively articulable. And this is also a claim about what spirit means to itself—what must matter to it for anything else to matter. But there is a prior question about the meaning for Spirit of what it experiences, a meaning Hegel simply assumes rather than concludes: articulable, systematic intelligibility. Because that is already assumed as the goal, it is the source of the negation, functioning like the whole in the example of disjunctive syllogisms above. Hence Heidegger's objections. "Yet what the phenomenology of spirit, conceived of in this way, appears to be is not what it is in its essence. This appearance, however, is not deceptive by chance. It is a consequence of the essence of the phenomenology of spirit; it forces itself before that essence and conceals it. The appearance, taken in itself, leads us astray. Natural representation, which has here insinuated itself into philosophy, takes phenomenal knowledge only as phenomenal; behind it a non-phenomenal, a non-appearing, knowledge keeps itself hidden" (HCE, 107).

As Heidegger points out in ID, Hegel admits this, that "the beginning is the result" (ID, 53). Thus, according to Heidegger, we are not simply watching the self-development of Spirit, and there is no real internal negation: "With its first step if not before, the presentation dismisses natural consciousness as constitutionally incapable of following the presentation.

The presentation of phenomenal knowledge is not a route which natural consciousness can take. Nor, however, is it a path that at each step gains distance from natural consciousness in order to meet up with absolute knowledge somewhere in its subsequent course. Nonetheless, the presentation is a path. Nonetheless, it moves back and forth constantly in the interstice that obtains between natural consciousness and science" (HCE, 108).

By "back and forth," Heidegger appears to mean that Hegel presents what he claims to be wholly internal to the model of consciousness under examination while also surreptitiously appealing to his notion of a criterion, science, to make the transition work. Or, there is no reason to think that a natural consciousness thinking of itself onto sensible objects by their mere sensory givenness, confronted by the problem of finding referring expressions stable enough to identify what is said to be seen, would find the failure dissatisfying enough to reject the notion of mere sensory particulars in favor of perceptual universals inhering in a stable substance, much less that this is already what the subject thinks *in* thinking of the negated position. Our natural consciousness would stubbornly insist it knows what it sees, even if it cannot say so precisely. Hegel's contrary claim is that the inherent and avoidable commitment to full logical intelligibility ("science") is both partially and ever more self-consciously revealed as an inherent, unacknowledged commitment in any claim to know or (ultimately in the journey) to act justifiably and that we are led to a full acknowledged commitment in full self-consciousness about what we had been doing. There is nothing illicit in the presence of the assumption; that is what is being demonstrated. It is simply un-self-conscious and coming to self-consciousness. But Heidegger would claim that our only warrant for assuming that such a commitment *is* un-self-consciously held must be the (already accomplished) putative journey to the realization of its unavoidability, and so in fact there is no "journey." We are just exfoliating what we already take to be the case.

This is not the way Hegel looks at the development of a concept into its implicit implications, either in his own case or in the development of a historical position into its historical implications. Consider the way he talks about the problem of finitude in Aristotle, as it is usually understood.

The finitude of knowing lies in the presupposition of a world already found before it, and in the process the knowing subject appears as a tabula rasa. This representation of things has been ascribed to Aristotle, although no one is more removed from this external way of construing knowing than Aristotle. This *knowing does not yet know [weiß] itself as the activity of the concept, something which it is only in itself, but not for itself.* Its behavior [*Verhalten*] appears to it as something passive, yet it is in fact active. (EL, §226, my emphasis)

Heidegger has, in other words, confused the fact that an implication may be implicit in a position and coming to see that and why a claim that an implication is implicit in a position is justified. We may know at the end of Hegel's journey that "the Absolute" was "already assumed, already present," but we are not entitled to any such position at the outset. It must be earned by the "pathway of doubt and despair." Hegel may not be able to do that without begging some questions, but that requires more of an engagement with his position than Heidegger offers. And Heidegger, even in his more textually sensitive 1930–1931 seminar on the *Phenomenology*, does not work to undermine Hegel's claims to find, say, that the concept of perception is implicitly committed to theoretical posits like "force" and so to explanation by laws of nature.

A second criticism is also a familiar and predictable one. Who is the "subject" of this putative experience? From the course of the development in the book, we might say: initially (and inadequately) natural consciousness, then self-consciousness (incorporating and sublating, as in all these moments, what came "before"), then the subject is "reason," then Spirit, articulated in religion and absolute knowledge. Ultimately, then, when the right degree of self-consciousness has been reached, the subject "Geist," Spirit, is finally "absolutely" self-conscious about itself and its powers. But consciousness/Spirit is also assumed to be a being. Its mode of being is Spirit, a collective subjectivity. What is such a mode of being? Heidegger suggests: "Consciousness, being-conscious, refers to a kind of being. However, this 'being'—must not remain a mere empty sound for us. It says: presencing in the mode of the gathering of what has been caught sight of. And yet, in accordance with a usage that has long been customary, the 'being'—we have just used means at the same time the beings themselves that are in this mode. The other name for beings that are in the mode of knowledge is 'subject'" (HCE, 109). In showing us the mode of being of this subject, Heidegger claims that a deep assumption of natural consciousness is never left behind in Hegel; being is still presence, the present at hand, substances enduring through alterations in properties over time. And Spirit is treated, unthinkingly, as a mode of such being, understanding itself as such a being in *thinking* itself, in treating itself as a possible object of a (speculative) judgment. The meaning of its being is not questioned.

Natural consciousness is alive in all shapes of the spirit; it lives each spiritual shape in its own way, including (and especially) that shape of absolute knowledge which occurs as absolute metaphysics and is at times visible to a few thinkers only. This metaphysics is far from having collapsed when it was confronted by the positivism of the nineteenth and twentieth centuries; on the contrary, the modern technological world in its unlimited entitlement is nothing other than natural consciousness which (in accordance with the manner of its opinion) has at last made feasible the unlimited, self-securing production of all beings through the inexorable objectification of each and every thing. (HCE, 112)

So yet again, as with Kant and German idealism generally,[22] Hegel's metaphysics inherits the basic forgetfulness of Western philosophy in general. In the language used in this essay, it does not free itself from natural consciousness, which, contrary to Hegel's usage, is just the view that the meaning of being is presence, the standing present at hand character of determinate substances in time, the beings to which consciousness is answerable in knowledge. This means that what natural consciousness finds natural is not natural in the sense of what is "closest" to us, most familiar and original in our experience. It is a distortion due to the influence of the pre-judgment, the prejudice, of the metaphysical tradition, a distortion Heidegger here ties to the predatory appropriation of the world for the subject he summarizes as "technology."

In his 1930–1931 course on the *Phenomenology*, Heidegger goes beyond the first three chapters into the chapter on self-consciousness. He realizes that consciousness has come to understand that its answerability to an external object (the standpoint of mere consciousness) requires its own determination, on its own, of what answerability itself is, that its object is non-empirical and so its own (force), that relation to an object is essentially relation to itself, and it knows this is problematic. So in the lectures, he extends his textual analysis into the self-consciousness chapter, but he doesn't get very far, concentrating on the idea of self-consciousness itself, and ignoring the famous claims of the section, that self-consciousness is desire in general, that self-consciousness finds satisfaction only in another self-consciousness, that there is a struggle to the death over recognition, and that this conflict has something to do with stoicism, skepticism, and "the unhappy consciousness." (His course ends with the initial moment of the self-consciousness chapter, the discussion of life. More specifically, it ends with a kind of advertisement for *Being and Time*.) He does offer fuller

22. As throughout, by referring to German Idealism, I mean to refer to Fichte and Schelling when they were idealists in something like the Kantian sense, prior to the so-called "later" Fichte or Schelling.

accounts of the problem of the PhG presupposing itself, weaving that critique into the issue of finitude (HPG, 52–57). His clear assumption is that any such subject will still be "thing" or "substance" like and will not diverge from the basic presuppositions Heidegger notices in the consciousness section. He notes in the lecture course that what Hegel means by *das Seiende* and *das Sein* throughout the book is "*Vorhanden*" and "*Vorhandenheit*" (HPG, 59), and he never qualifies that charge. Likewise with the emergence of the logical prejudice in his explanation of the transition from consciousness to self-consciousness, that "being is determined logically, such that logic manifests itself as egology" (*Das Sein bestimmt sich logisch, aber so, daß das Logische sich ausweist als das Egologisch*) (HPG, 182). And again, this is all said to be the culmination of the original orientation of Western metaphysics towards the Being question. That is, Hegel's position, and this decisive turn to self-consciousness as the truth of natural consciousness, is what that orientation must come to when thought through consistently.

It would take an interpretation of all the first four chapters of the PhG to challenge Heidegger's reading, but we should at least note in passing that, at least as Hegel understands his book, it cannot be considered an "egology," like Fichte's, say. (At least as Heidegger explains Fichte in his 1929 lecture course.) Rather, individual egos should not be understood as, ex ante, atomistic, self-sufficient egological origins of such commitments to a collective subject, as if *Geist* comes into being only as a result of constituting acts by ex-ante spiritless (*geistlose*) atomic individuals. They are the individuals they are only as already "formed" (*gebildet*) within and as inheriting such collectivities, a point that, at the most general level, Heidegger would agree with. The difference between Hegel's "shapes of Spirit" and Heidegger's "world" comes down to whether such shapes of spirit can become self-conscious to themselves in ways reflected in art, religion, and philosophy, and in coming to do so, reflect on and move on from deficiencies in such self-understanding. World is the background condition of logos in Heidegger, not subject to logos. This co-constituting mutual dependence is why Hegel can frequently say something that would otherwise be quite mysterious, that spirit, this social subjectivity, is "a product of itself." (Geist *is* this co-constituting relation—the product of individuals who are themselves the products of their participation in Geist. Geist has no substantial existence apart from this mutual reflection.)

SECTION FOUR
Post-Culmination

9

Poetic Thinking?

Hölderlin's thinking poetry has also stamped this realm of the poetic thinking. His poetry dwells in this place more intimately than any other poetry of his time. The place into which Hölderlin came is one where being is manifest, a manifestness which itself belongs in the destiny of being; out of this destiny, the manifestness is intended for the poet. (WP. 203)

"TRACES OF THE FUGITIVE GODS"[1]

It is commonplace in descriptions of Heidegger to hear that the later Heidegger concentrated simply "on Being" and not "on Dasein" or on any notion with a whiff of the subjective. But this would be quite puzzling. The later Heidegger's work is dominated by reflections on thinking, poetry, and language. That is, his focus remains on the meaningfulness of Being, now as embodied in language and in material works of art, not in Dasein's comportments and actions, but that still requires an inquiry into how such a meaning might be available to the one being open to such meaning, whether Heidegger calls that being Dasein or not. Perhaps the clearest passage on the issue is from his work from the early '50s, *What Is Called Thinking?* (*Was heißt Denken?*). "*No* way of thought, not even the way of metaphysical thought, begins with man's essential nature and goes on from there to Being, nor in reverse from Being and then back to man. Rather every way of thinking *takes its way* already within the totality of Being and man's nature, or else it is not thinking at all" (WT, 49–50).

Moreover, he constantly stresses the great difficulty of the uncovering

1. WP, 91.

or disclosing striven for in any understanding of the meaning of Being, going so far as to note frequently that this requires a kind of "violence" on
our part in order to "achieve" such an openness. "In truth beings are torn
from concealment. Truth is understood by the Greeks as something stolen,
something that must be torn from concealment in a confrontation in which
precisely *phusis* strives to conceal itself. Truth is innermost confrontation
of the essence of man with the whole of beings themselves. This has nothing to do with the business of proving propositions at the writing desk"
(FCM, 29).

And in IM he ties this active struggle explicitly to what he means by the
poetic, as well to other moments of disclosure, all understood as "work."
"We know from Heraclitus and Parmenides that the unconcealment of beings is not simply present at hand. Unconcealment happens only in so far
as it is *brought about by the work*: the work of the word as poetry, the work
of stone in temple and statue, the work of the word as thinking, the work of
the polis as the site of history that grounds and preserves all this" (IM, 204,
my emphasis).

The problem he poses throughout the later work, in other words, is that
we are still not thinking, not "working," and so still not receptive to what
would otherwise be available. A genuine renewal of a philosophical tradition that has gone dead must involve a new understanding of thinking—
not ratiocinative, discursive, or propositional—and therewith a new understanding of the meaning of Being, an avoidance of our inheritance of Being
as standing presence and original availability as cognitive. The obvious difficulty for Heidegger is that this is not something that by his lights we can
just resolve to do or bring about by our efforts. We can in effect "clear the
ground" for the possibility of a new "attunement" by the "destruction" of
the metaphysical tradition, but that can lead only to an attentive waiting,
a kind of descendant of "anticipatory resoluteness" in BT. An attention to
the work of poetic thinking is another kind of preparation but that emerges
as the crucial post-culmination form of philosophy after the war.[2] We have
noted several times that Heidegger's charge of forgetfulness and the consequences of this forgetfulness in a technological, spiritless, even nihilistic
world would be empty were there not some contrast with this rejection
of the prioritization of discursive intelligibility as the thinking proper to
sources of meaningfulness in an epoch. We know that such a "new thinking" must be oriented from a conception of truth as *aletheia*, or uncon-

2. See Hoy 1979 for a discussion about Heidegger's concession that his desired "step
back" behind the explicit history of philosophy may never escape "modern metaphysical-
technological" thinking, and so why "philosophy can only explore its possibilities in the
subjunctive" (63ff).

cealment, and so of thinking's task as disclosure, a disclosure consistent with our finitude and so with inevitable concealing. He tackles this question with increasing urgency from the 1950s on, and many of his formulations are among his most difficult to understand. But there are indications, in his treatment of Rilke in his BPP and WP, in his *On the Origin of the Work of Art*, in his seminars and essays on Heraclitus and Hölderlin, and of the ancient tragic poets in IM, of a strain of thought that is somewhat more accessible.[3]

The most familiar term for this new sort of thinking is "poetic," by which Heidegger means in very general terms the authentic sort of contemplative activity, expressed in a suitable language, rightly attuned to the disclosure of meaningfulness. "Admittedly, the first thing we must learn at this moment of world history is that making poems is also a matter of thinking. We will take the poem as a practice exercise in poetic reflection" (WP, 207).

And in IM he had gone very far in stressing the role of "poetry" "at this moment of history."

> The work of art is work not primarily because it is worked, made, but because it puts Being to work in a being. To put to work here means to bring into the work—a work within which as what appears, the emerging that holds sway, *phusis*, comes to seem. Through the artwork, as Being that is *das seiende Sein, everything else* that appears and that we can find around us first becomes confirmed and accessible, interpretable and understandable, as a being, or else as an unbeing. (IM, 170, my emphasis)

He also has other formulations of what might be an appropriate language and thinking for this task now, some of which evoke religious imagery (the sacred, the holy, the divine) and others that focus on the notion of release or letting-be, like *Gelassenheit*. But poetic thinking is a major strain since IM, and he also means to concentrate not just on the very general notion of such a poetic contemplation, a possibility in all the arts, but on poetry itself, and this from very early on.[4] His emphasis changes, however.

As far back as BT, Heidegger seems to consider poetry or poetic language deeply important, but at that point in terms of some sort of romantic expressivism. He briefly raises the issue in his account of communication: "In 'poetical' discourse, the communication of the existential possibilities of one's state-of-mind can become an aim in itself, and this amounts to a

---

3. Although he doesn't discuss his notion in terms of poetic thinking, Carman 2003 has offered the interesting label for ontological truth as "hermeneutic salience" (258–263).

4. "As the setting-into-work of truth, art is poetry." And "The essence of art is poetry. The essence of poetry, however, is the founding [*Stiftung*] of truth" (OWA, 47).

disclosing of existence" (BT, 205). But in his Marburg lectures on *The Basic Problems of Phenomenology* given in the same year, he has another, more ontologically significant position on the poetic. He introduces his remarks on a passage from Rilke's *Notebooks* this way in a passage we have seen before: "Poetry, creative literature, is nothing but the elementary emergence into words, the becoming-uncovered, of existence as being-in-the-world. For the others who before it were blind, the world first becomes visible by what is thus spoken" (BP, 171–172).

Poetry is now treated in the terms used for what is demanded of "thinking," the uncovering of meaningful existence as being-in-the-world. Since the possibility of this sort of disclosure requires the appropriate attunement, and since any new thinking cannot be disinterested speculation but a matter of being gripped, it is easy enough to see why he would turn to the arts and poetic language in particular as modalities of such attunement, as "awakening" such an attunement. In what we would call modernist poetry, Rilke's especially, this is an attunement to what is missing, to evoking our sense of dependence on a primordial "site" of possible meaningfulness that seems available only by its continuing elusiveness or absence or decay.

At this point, however, turning to Heidegger's voluminous work on Hölderlin and poetry would amount to beginning another book, and without that detail, the contrastive and disclosive work he expects from poetic thinking is hard to appreciate. There is only so far one can go in what amounts to promises about the resources of nineteenth- and twentieth-century German poetry. The general remarks soon become repetitious, and at that level of generality the promises about the potential weightiness and depth of thought in poetic thinking, especially as some sort of new alternative to Plato, Leibniz, Kant, and Hegel, cannot be persuasive. And often in essays on individual poets, Heidegger's attention seems focused more on the poem and the poet and on issues more typically literary and hermeneutic, and their bearing on rationalism and Idealism can be hard to make out. In his 1952 essay on the Austrian poet Georg Trakl, for example, he concentrates on such issues as how any poem should be read, how Trakl's poems make themselves questionable for any interpretation and so emphasize by their saying what remains unsaid in the poem, pointed to as unsaid, silent (concealed), and therewith its philosophical importance in our age is supposed to be clear. Or he discusses whether a poet should be interpreted as having basically one poem, and he broaches the specific theme of "apartness" or *Abgeschiedenheit*, the wandering, placeless stranger in Trakl (LP, 172), another evocation of homelessness, and so another evocation of Idealism's failure to make us at home anywhere in the modern world. In the Trakl discussion, Heidegger suggests that it is the yearning for at-home-ness *itself* that sets us on the wrong path in the first place, given that it originated in the original misdirection of metaphysics. The task instead is an attunement to our homelessness in all its dimensions and inflections that is genuine. Only poetic language can accomplish this since it constantly works against the determinacy language requires without leading us into a merely undifferentiable indeterminacy.[5] That is, even in these essays, Heidegger's purpose is never entirely, although it can be largely, textual explication. Criticism, as Heidegger clearly understands it, can be philosophical criticism (if the right texts or objects are chosen),[6] an exfoliation of the philosophic disclosure by poetic and literary language together with a rigorous attention to those formulations and the whole of which they are a part, all attended to as disclosing dimensions of meaningfulness at a time or in some cases even the possibility or impossibility of meaningful orientation in the world at all. And again, in our destitute time, art cannot be like the art of the Greek temple, radiantly manifesting the distinctiveness of the Greek world and the meaning of Being (beauty) that it inherits. Our worldly theme is absence, the *Abgrund*, and our denial of dependence on any possible source of *Bedeutsamkeit*. There are also brief, scattered remarks about René Char, Mörike, and Rimbaud in his large late collection, *Aus der Erfahrung des Denkens*, but for our purposes, his most important work on the poetic is his courses and essays on Hölderlin, his account of the tragic poets in IM, and his account of Rilke in BP. His interpretations of Hölderlin are especially important since Hölderlin for him represents the paradigmatic poet of the modern age, the one who asks most rigorously what poetry should be now in the "desolate" age "after the gods have fled."[7] "It is in the essence of poets who are truly poets at such a world-era that from out of the desolation of the time, the condition and vocation of the poet have first become poetic questions for them. That is why 'poets in a desolate time' must specifically speak the essence of poetry in their poems" (WP, 203).

A general maxim for the task of such poets is given in the essay "Why Poets?"

However, there would be and there is the single necessity: by thinking soberly in what is said in his poetry, to experience what is unsaid. This is

5. See Harries 1979. "The language of poetry has its place in-between idle talk and silence. It is a recovery of silence in the midst of idle talk" (164). Harries rightly connects this with the struggle between earth and world in OWA (166).

6. I discuss in more general terms what philosophical criticism might amount to in Pippin 2021, 3–18.

7. There is a valuable account of Heidegger's Hölderlin interpretation in Halliburton 1981, 77–112.

the course of the history of being. If we enter upon this course, it brings thinking and poetry together in a dialogue engaged with the history of being. Researchers in literary history will inevitably see the dialogue as an unscholarly violation of what they take to be the facts. Philosophers will see it as a baffled descent into mysticism [*ein Abweg der Ratlosigkeit in die Schwärmeri*]. However, destiny pursues its course untroubled by all that. (WP, 204)

Paradoxically, Heidegger makes clear in the essay that he does not mean that the task of poetry is to render the unsaid sayable; it is precisely to disclose such meaning *in* its unsayability, obviously a difficult and paradoxical notion. As he puts it in a remark on Heraclitus, "When Heraclitus speaks of fire, he is thinking above all of the illuminating power that holds sway, the showing that gives and withdraws" (VA, 3, 71).[8]

On the next page, he formulates this illuminating power of the poetic as *lichtend-bergende* and *entbergend-verbergender*, both a disclosing and concealing at the same time (Ibid., 72). The maxim about experiencing the unsaid is a prelude to his discussion of Rilke in that essay, and his account of Rilke there and in BP can give us some initial idea of the purpose of Heidegger's appeal to poetry and literature as embodying a new thinking, post-culmination. The same theme is echoed somewhat more enigmatically in "poetically man dwells . . ."

> Yet—and this is what we must now listen to and keep in mind—for Hölderlin, God, as the one who he is, is unknown and it is just as this Unknown One that he is the measure for the poet. This is also why Hölderlin is perplexed by the exciting question: how can that which by its very nature remains unknown ever become a measure? For something that man measures himself by must after all impart itself, must appear. But if it appears, it is known. The god, however, is unknown, and he is the measure nonetheless. (PLT, 220)

A good deal of Heidegger's commentary is like this, an explication of something evoked that cannot be named; something disclosed but with no determinate content, a revelation with nothing revealed (no determinate content but not mere absence); rather an evocation of absence with density of possible inflections and implications that it defies critical paraphrase.[9]

8. Halliburton's translation 1981, 119.
9. One way of thinking about what he is trying to point to is to see the issue as something like a descendant of the "authenticity" issue in BT. The temptation is to think of authenticity as some determinate state, some achievement in any being-toward-the-future or

In the Rilke passage in BP, we think that there is nothing very interesting about a young man whose encounter with architectural decay prompts a kind of disgust and revulsion about what he regards as the remnants or traces of absent human life in an exposed wall. But we also think that there would be very little point to Rilke's recording such fictional reactions simply to be recording them, and the power of the descriptions grips us in a way that a mere psychological recording would not. Our sense of "the point" of such a passage might be informed by what else we know about Malte in the novel and especially by what we know about Rilke, his relation to Rodin, his other works. But *our* attention to the poetic register contained in the passage seems very like *Malte's* encounter with what has been exposed in the wall. There is another side to the wall, and the disclosure of something like human meaningfulness, or its absence, in the sights and smells, terrifies Malte without his naming what terrifies him. We sense that same discomfort in reading and thinking about the poem and our own discomfort is not nameable—something uncanny, not nothing but not formalizable or discursively available, try as we might to circle around a "meaning." Heidegger, after all, refers to his confrontation with the metaphysical tradition as a "Destruktion," an image that raises the metaphorical question of what the "remnants" of that destruction look like, what it is like to live in the aftermath. It might very well look like something analogous to what Malte "sees" in the remaining "last" wall. And what that is can be something to which we are somehow attuned in the reading of the poem, something we have to try to express even in the light of its ultimate elusiveness. In trying to do so, we are thinking with Rilke as much as about him. I cannot believe that Heidegger chose this passage only in order to make his brief point about being-in-the-world.

It could, of course, be coincidental that Malte uses the term *the terrible*, *das Schreckliche*, that Heidegger makes so much of in his interpretation of the choral ode in *Antigone, to deinon*, the terrible or terrifying or overwhelming. But I doubt it. "Thus, the *deinon* as the overwhelming (*dike*) and the *deinon* as the violence-doing (*techne*) stand over against each other, although not as two present-at-hand things. This over-against consists, instead, in the fact that techne breaks out against dike, which for its part, as fittingness, has all techne at its disposal. The reciprocal over-against is. It is, only insofar as the uncanniest, Being-human, happens—insofar as humanity essentially unfolds as history" (IM, 171).

---

projection, "after which" everything looks different to one. But, I would suggest, it has no such status; there is no *resolution* of the issue of its achievement or failure. It is rather, if the issue is to bear on a being like Dasein, always "at issue." Indeed, *that* is what it is; always being at issue and being unresolved.

What Rilke is doing and, just as importantly, what we are doing, seems so resonant with so many of the tasks Heidegger assigns to his new poetic thinking. "Because the understanding of Being fades away, at first and for the most part, in an indefinite meaning, and nonetheless remains certain and definite in this knowledge—because consequently the understanding of Being, despite all its rank, is dark, confused, covered over and concealed—it must be illuminated, disentangled, and ripped away from concealment. That can happen only insofar as we inquire about this understanding of Being—which at first we simply treated as a fact—in order to put it into question" (IM, 87). Putting something into question is not a simple matter of raising a question. We complacently assume there is nothing to be questioned; being is just its cognitive availability. But we need to be knocked out of this complacency, and a poem or a poetic literary passage can certainly do that. And being so displaced is a mode of illumination in itself.

He is more forthcoming about the late modern situation, although linguistically much more obscure, in examining some unpublished fragments of Rilke's, and bits of his sonnets and elegies in WP. While Hölderlin's poetry is treated as elegiac, and so in its remembrance still alive to what the modern age in its forgetfulness has lost, Rilke's is treated more as a cry of despair, an attunement to absence with little or no resonance with what had been lost. He wants to show that what fills the void, the absence of meaning, is human willfulness, a self-asserting that does not realize, as Heidegger puts it, that its own willfulness is itself "willed," reflects a dependence on a degraded form of meaningfulness it cannot even acknowledge.

> To our grandparents, a "house," a "well," a familiar steeple, even their own clothes, their cloak still meant infinitely more, were infinitely more intimate—almost everything a vessel in which they found something human already there, and added to its human store. Now there are intruding, from America, empty indifferent things, sham things, dummies of life. . . . A house, as the Americans understand it, an American apple or a winestock from over there, have nothing in common with the house, the fruit, the grape into which the hope and thoughtfulness of our forefathers had entered. (WP, 111)

Here is a typical gloss of what he thinks Rilke is trying to show.

> In place of all the world-content of things that was formerly perceived and used to grant freely of itself, the object-character of technological dominion spreads itself over the earth ever more quickly, ruthlessly, and

completely. Not only does it establish all things as producible in the process of production; it also delivers the products of production by means of the market. In self-assertive production, the humanness of man and the thingness of things dissolve into the calculated market value of a market which not only spans the whole earth as a world market, but also, as the will to will, trades in the nature of Being and thus subjects all beings to the trade of a calculation that dominates most tenaciously in those areas where there is no need of numbers. (WP, 110–111)

And all of this in a deep forgetfulness: "Rilke's poem thinks of man as the being who is ventured into a willing, the being who, *without as yet experiencing it*, is willed in the will to will" (WP, 112, my emphasis). This is a jumble of new Heideggerian terms. He wants to suggest that the world disclosed in Rilke's poems is tied to nature or life as it came to mean what it did in the modern West since Leibniz, which he sums up with the notion of will, that what it means for us to be and for anything to be is understood within the horizon of possible will, all "for us" as present and mere present objects to be used. This something that introduces, given the unlimited drive for productive power, a disorienting contingency, which Heidegger refers to as giving us over to what Hofstatder translates as "ventures" (*dem Wagnis überläßt*), even saying that Being "ventures us" (*Es wagt uns, die Menschen*). A *Wagnis* is a dare, a risk, a venture in the sense of a risky adventure. The possible meaningfulness of Being, then, is said to dare us. Heidegger here and throughout is speaking from within the ruined and destitute world evoked by Rilke's poetry, and he is suggesting that when mattering, meaningfulness, is seen as what-is-willed, a daring and risky venture ensues, cut off from any authentic receptiveness to any source of mattering other than will. Here is a somewhat clearer expression of what he is trying to say.

The willing of which we speak here is the putting-through, the self-assertion, whose purpose has already posited the world as the whole of producible objects. This willing determines the nature of modern man, though at first he is not aware of its far-reaching implication, though he could not already know today by what will, as the Being of beings, this willing is willed. By such willing, modern man turns out to be the being who, in all relations to all that is, and thus in his relation to himself as well, rises up as the producer who puts through, carries out, his own self and establishes this uprising as the absolute rule. The whole objective inventory in terms of which the world appears is given over to, commended to, and thus subjected to the command of self-assertive production. (WP, 108)

(Although he would never put it this way, it would not be unfair to invoke another word to capture this situation: *capitalism.*) But Heidegger continues to explore the implications of the modern technological worldview and does not return to the issue of the particular uniqueness and fittingness of the poetic as a means of disclosure, a form of nondiscursive thinking, at least not beyond repeating that an authentic poet in these times is one whose poetry questions the status of poetry itself, a familiar characterization of modernism in the arts. Accordingly, while Heidegger does credibly suggest that poetry should be considered a form of philosophical thought, it also has to be said that he rather opens a door than shows us how to enter or what we might find when we do.

DENKEN AND *DICHTEN:* THINKING AND POETICIZING

> Thinking says what the truth of being dictates. Thinking is the ur-poetry that precedes all poesy. But it precedes, too, the poetic in art insofar as art's becoming an artwork happens within the realm of language. All poeticizing, in both this broader and narrower sense of the poetic is, at bottom, thinking. The poeticizing essence of thought preserves the sway of the truth of being. (AS, 247–248)

The claim that the arts can be understood as forms of reflective and especially contemplative thought that have standing as philosophy, or, as in the case of Heidegger, that must have that standing now, after metaphysics, provokes a common complaint: that this cannot be so because a poem or a novel does not assert anything, take any sort of stand. No work of art, least of all a Greek temple or a lyric poem, asserts anything with philosophical import, certainly not the source of any meaningfulness in an epoch. And, if it were to appear to propound some thesis, say in the mouth of a main, sympathetic, intelligent character in a novel, Lambert Sterether, say, in Henry James's *Ambassadors,* there are still no arguments advanced to defend such a claim, and the assertion is indexed to some particular character with some particular psychological background and interests, in some particular setting. If one claims that some general meaning in some phenomenon or action is disclosed by a work, something typologically important, common to human experience but that lies unnoticed until so disclosed, then the objection is that this too must ultimately be expressed propositionally and defended discursively against other possible interpretations of meaning and defended, especially as to its truth. But if one accepted this latter line of reasoning, the literary or artistic work would then be wholly dispensable, a merely decorative rhetoric for some implied assertoric judgment. If we understand artistic meaning to be potentially disclosive on its own rather than implicitly assertoric, then the proper attempt to understand what meaning is disclosed must obviously not be a matter of translation or paraphrasing, and the enterprise would be superfluous. We might as well just consider and assess the judgments themselves. This means that the role of the interpreter must be continuous with the role of the artist, that there is "a parallelism between the role of the artist and the role of the interpreter of art."[10]

Heidegger has not proposed a general theory of literary or poetic meaning. He is interested in only one aspect of any significant work of art: its ontologically disclosive function, something he thinks is particularly essential in a "post-metaphysical" age.[11] And again, by the culmination and future impossibility of metaphysics, Heidegger does not mean that all aspects of philosophical work are somehow impossible "now." He means that the only question metaphysically important—the meaning of Being—is not available in any way continuous with such projects, something that becomes fully manifest in Hegel, and because of that, the significance of such metaphysical projects changes, diminishes drastically since they are all dependent on an address to a question they ignore. Nor does it mean that what Hegel has accomplished in the *Logic* or the *Philosophy of Right* has turned out to be worthless. Hegel would not himself accept his relegation to a regional ontology, say, the region of the knowables (something like the "logic" of the present-at-hand), for reasons we have discussed, and we can still assert what Heidegger does: that the basic question of metaphysics has been almost completely forgotten, and this in a way that shows the inability of the rationalist tradition to deal with it, can respond only in quite a limited way to the question of why philosophical rationalism matters, and matters in and to its current world at all. After he believes he has established that the most significant question in metaphysics cannot be addressed within the limits of what he generally calls logic, and after he believes he has established that the illusion that it can be so addressed involves a forgetfulness with world-historical (and disastrous) implications, for the most part he wants only to show in various exemplary contexts the potentially disclosive power of great

10. Halliburton 1981, 30. See also his discussion of the general relation between literary criticism and philosophy in chapter 3 and 136 in chapter 5.
11. This is true at least in the later writings on literature. In BT, he also ascribed to poetical discourse a disclosive function central to capturing the uniquely existential dimension of Dasein (BT, 205). In BP he also calls poetry "none other than the essential way in which existence as Being-in-the-world is discovered" (BP, 171–172). So, for example, in OWA, it is even the case that "the art work lets us know what shoes are in truth" (15). In OWA, he also associates the work's ontological disclosure with the destiny of a people, even going so far as to say that a people's historical existence is art (49).

works of art, and only with respect to the question of the meaningfulness of being. Moreover, once he has defended his claim that primordial ontological truth involves *aletheia*, uncovering, and not "correctness," the objections raised above become immediately irrelevant. If he can show what he aims to show with Hölderlin and Rilke, then there is no possible question like "*should* Being be meaningful in this way?" or "*is* it true that this is 'what' Being means?" or even a discursive, propositional paraphrase of "just what such meaningfulness amounts to." This is what he means by speaking of Being's *Geschick* or destiny or fate—something we are simply subject to—in the way we have described how mattering is not subject to human will or assessment. The fate of Being is the obvious descendant within Heidegger's History of Being project of his earlier emphasis on thrownness.

This still leaves relatively open the question of what, if Heidegger is basically right, all this would mean in living out one's life, in somehow being attuned to some disclosure of some intimation of possible meaningfulness, inseparable from the unclarity and confusion (not indeterminacy) of concealment. It might seem ironic to appeal to Nietzsche here, ironic because Heidegger, in his later Nietzsche lectures, wants to show that Nietzsche failed to be the first "post-metaphysical" thinker and was still complicit with metaphysics, but this passage from *Twilight of the Idols* might well serve as the beginning of a response. For what follows from a question like "what follows if Heidegger is right?" is clearly not something like a belief in something or a new position in ontology. It might be intimated in this passage.

Learning to see—habituating the eye to repose, to patience, to letting things come to it; learning to defer judgement, to investigate and comprehend the individual in all its aspects. This is the first schooling in spirituality: not to react immediately to a stimulus, but to have the restraining, stock-taking instincts in one's control. Learning to see, as I understand it, is almost what is called in unphilosophical language strong will-power [*starken Willen*]: the essence of it is precisely not to "will," the ability to defer decision. All unspirituality, all vulgarity, is due to the incapacity to resist a stimulus—one has to react, one obeys a stimulus. In many instances, such a compulsion is already morbidity, decline, a symptom of exhaustion. . . . To stand with all doors open, to prostrate oneself submissively before every petty fact, to be ever itching to mingle with, plunge into other people and other things, in short our celebrated modern "objectivity," is bad taste, is ignoble par excellence. (TI, 64–65)[12]

12. Cf. also the Heidegger resonances of "a person is necessary, a person is a piece of the whole—there is nothing that can judge, measure, compare or condemn our being, because

A FINAL WORD

If we look for a similar sort of issue in Hegel, and descend a bit from the airy heights of metaphysics, then we can say that there is in the *Encyclopedia* system a non-theoretical, nondiscursive, and philosophically significant role for art. But that makes Heidegger's point in another way, a way Heidegger does not discuss (although Schelling does). The role of art is to make available the speculative truth of philosophy in a sensible and affective register, and that means in an incomplete and finally unsatisfactory, because not fully self-conscious, way,[13] and that way must be and can only fully be articulated in the *Logic*. Obviously, this touches on the basic issue that has arisen scores of times in the preceding: is there or is there not a form of nondiscursively available meaningfulness in human experience, and one that bears directly on philosophy in a fundamental way, given that such original familiar meaningfulness must count as bearing on the "first" question all philosophy must be oriented from—the possible availability of anything at all, the availability of being qua being? Heidegger's affirmative answer to such a question ranges from his early emphasis on the disclosive role of "attunements" to his latter emphasis on historical "uncoverings and self-concealings" in the arts. There is a partial affirmative answer to this question in Hegel, formulated in the way just cited, that fine art should count as a "sensible and affective" register of what could be called the way in which the meaning of Geist's being is available to it at a historical period in a historical community. But this is an answer with severe limitations in that, first, the notion of a merely sensible register of meaningfulness is quite limited.[14] It amounts to something like "what it *feels* like" to be Geist in conflict with itself at a time. Since such a conflict is not conceptually self-conscious to itself, its importance is merely preliminary and propadeutic; its significance is wholly parasitic on full philosophical self-consciousness for its significance. As we have been seeing, for Heidegger the order of dependence goes the other way. Any such disclosure of sources of meaningfulness, for example how and why philosophical self-consciousness could come to matter as it does, or could cease to matter as it did, is fundamental, not preliminary and propadeutic, and

---

it would mean judging, measuring, comparing and condemning the whole. . . . *But there is nothing outside the whole*" (TI, 182).

13. Heidegger certainly *does* challenge the view that an ultimate source of what matters in a life must be self-consciousness. "The satisfactions of self-consciousness" could be a question-begging smugness.

14. It is also an oddly "isolated" treatment of such a sensible register, given Hegel's general treatment of the conceptual and sensible orders of intelligibility.

only originally available nondiscursively. This all must remain "unthought" in the way Hegel characterizes art in his Encyclopedic system.[15]

And there is an even more basic, related disagreement. From Heidegger's point of view, Hegel had simply assumed that there is an unavoidable matter of fundamental meaningfulness in the very possibility of Geist or Spirit being the being it is—freedom. What matters, what *must* matter, is the realization of freedom, a state of self-consciously realized self-knowledge as a free being in "being with self in an other," ultimately in the rational structure of modern ethical life.[16] It is by wholeheartedly living out one's social role that an individual acquires an ethical status and so a meaningful existence. This is so because all of the different social roles are reconcilable rationally in an ethical whole, and so again the basis of our reconciliation with others and our existence is reason. Heidegger has noted in an extraordinarily wide number of contexts, taking up scores of philosophers and artists, that from the time of Plato and Aristotle to Kant and Hegel, the main source of any possible reconcilability with a natural and historical world is that world's availability to reason, its cognizability. This is even true of religious life, since the reconciling work of "rendering intelligible" in that context proceeds through revelation and tradition and to some extent through natural theology. So for a resolute Hegelian, the absence of such a realization—the fact that the crucial social mediations Hegel insisted on (Corporations, the Estates, the Police, the constitutional monarch) have all gone dead, must look to us like mere anachronisms—itself still *matters* even when, especially when, their realization becomes impossible. For a Hegelian has to insist that such deficiencies are all still matters of incompleteness and potential transformability (and *insist* is the right word). Datedness and irrelevance should be the result of the self-negation of any model of knowing or any practical project embodying historically unsustainable claims to rational justifiability, and this is in a way inseparable from its own transformability. Heidegger's charge is that nothing in Hegel's theoretical apparatus establishes that this dynamic of reason must be so. Without such a defense, the demonstration of some moment of self-undermining, like the Master's impasse in the Master-Bondsman dialectic, could just be that: an isolated episode. The same would be the case in his attempt to show the

---

15. This not to say that there are not, inspired by Hegel's approach, very valuable resources for understanding the issue he is concerned with: Geist's self-understanding at a time, and especially its inability to reconcile itself with itself and its world. At least, I have found that to be the case. See "Prologue: Film and Philosophy," in Pippin 2017, 1–11; "Cinematic Reflection," in Pippin 2020, 3–22, and "Philosophical Criticism," in Pippin 2021, 3–18.

16. See Pippin 2014a and 2016.

incomplete, not fully self-conscious account of the "logical" intelligibility of being, a negation that negates itself determinately. The very first moment of the *Phenomenology of Spirit* manifests this sort of problem. The idealized first subject of the PhG, Consciousness as Sense-Certainty, assumes the world is available to it simply by virtue of its sensible presence. One is immediately onto sensed objects directly just by sensing them. But any distinctly human form of apprehension must, insists Hegel, be able to say what it claims to know, otherwise it is just differentially responsive and not an instance of knowing. The absence of such saying would be untrue to its experienced nature as a human *knower* and in that sense, not being who one is, would be unfree. It puts itself unavoidably to the test by trying to say what it knows and failing. This is the first manifestation of the conatus of freedom, the realization of self-conscious self-knowledge. But whence comes the weightiness of this self-test *mattering* as much as Hegel claims, or at all? As we have seen Heidegger argue, Hegel can demonstrate this "because he has already assumed the Absolute"—in phenomenological terms *the ultimacy of this conatus*, from the beginning, and that means that metaphysics as unconditioned thinking on thinking, conceived dialectically like this, is an illusion, question-begging.[17]

This is not an issue limited to Hegel or Kant, and it is not at all a matter of whether some case made for some insufficiency and that some correcting move is determinately warranted, a good argument or not. Heidegger has framed all such issues as dependent on, and reflecting some sense of, the historical meaningfulness of Being and that means the context of his question about the reconciling powers of reason is a question about mattering. How *could* Hegel approach a question like whether a mutual recognitive status in modern ethical life matters, and if so how much, and if a lot, why? It is to Hegel's enormous credit that he realized that in the emerging modern world of market capitalism and competitive economies a critical source of meaningfulness would have to be one's ethical standing among others, the sources of self-respect in a world (or mutuality of recognition),

17. I state here the Heideggerian position, not my own view. Heidegger has to claim that what for the Hegelian, or in the Hegelian tradition, must count as the pathologies of modernity—alienation, reification, domination instead of mutuality of recognitive status, the humiliating conditions of the modern organization of labor, anomie, deracination—are all best understood as implications of the still "unthought" question, the meaning of Being, as descendants of the "metaphysical" tradition. As I have suggested, this claim is worth taking more seriously than it has been, but the way Heidegger formulates the issue seems to exclude all other options as derivative from and so complicit with that tradition. Even on strictly hermeneutical grounds, such exclusivity leaves us with an incomplete interpretation of what we need to understand—what has happened to us.

but given that global capitalism has effectively destroyed the possibility of any such standing, how could he possibly think that it just *must* be the case that such a deficiency and the system responsible for it would determinately negate and transform itself? Why would not the world of Hegelian ethical life resemble nothing so much as the decayed remnants of Malte's building, redolent of what might have been but without hope for what could be?

Bibliography

Arendt, Hannah. 1978. *The Life of the Mind*. 2 vols. New York: Harcourt Brace.

Barton, W. B., Jr. 1973. "An Introduction to Heidegger's *What Is a Thing?*" *Southern Journal of Philosophy* 11 (1): 15–25.

Beaufret, Jean, and Catherine Savage. 1959. "Hegel et les Grecs." *Cahiers du Sud* 349: 355–368.

Blattner, William. 1999. *Heidegger's Temporal Idealism*. Cambridge: Cambridge University Press.

Brandom, Robert. 2019. *A Spirit of Trust: A Reading of Hegel's "Phenomenology."* Cambridge, MA: Harvard University Press.

Carman, Taylor. 2003. *Heidegger's Analytic: Interpretation, Discourse, and Authenticity in "Being and Time."* Cambridge: Cambridge University Press.

———. 2015. "Heidegger on Unconcealment and Correctness." In *The Transcendental Turn*, edited by Sebastian Gardner and Matthew Grist, 264–277. Oxford: Oxford University Press.

———. Forthcoming. "Existentialism as Anti-Rationalism." In *Markus Gabriel's New Realism*. Springer.

Carnap, R. 1931. "Uberwindung der Metaphysik durch logische Analyse der Sprache." *Erkenntnis* 2: 219–241.

Comay, Rebecca, and John McCumber. 1999. *Endings: Questions of Memory in Hegel and Heidegger*. Evanston, IL: Northwestern University Press.

Courtine, Jean-François. 1990. *Heidegger et la phénomenologie*. Paris: J. Vrin.

Crichton, Cristina. 2020. "Thought in the Service of Intuition: Heidegger's Appropriation of Kant's Synthetic A Priori in *Die Frage nach dem Ding*." *Kriterion* 146: 339–361.

Crowell, Steven. 2001. *Husserl, Heidegger and the Space of Meaning: Paths toward Transcendental Phenomenology*. Evanston, IL: Northwestern University Press.

———. 2013. *Normativity and Phenomenology in Husserl and Heidegger*. Cambridge: Cambridge University Press.

Dahlstrom, Daniel. 1991. "Heidegger's Kantian Turn: Notes on His Commentary on the *Kritik der reinen Vernunft.*" *Review of Metaphysics* 45 (2): 329–361.

———. 2001. *Heidegger's Concept of Truth.* Cambridge: Cambridge University Press.

———. 2001a. "The Scattered Logos: Metaphysics and the Logical Prejudice." In Polt and Fried 2001, 83–102.

———. 2005. "Heidegger and German Idealism." In Dreyfus and Wrathall 2005, 65–79.

———, ed. 2011. *Interpreting Heidegger: Critical Essays.* Cambridge: Cambridge University Press.

De Boer, Karin. 2000. *Thinking in the Light of Time: Heidegger's Encounter with Hegel.* Albany: State University of New York Press.

Deleuze, Gilles. 1995. "Letter to a Harsh Critic." In *Negotiations,* translated by Martin Joughin. New York: Columbia University Press.

Derrida, Jacques, and J.-L. Houdebine. 1973. "Interview: Jacques Derrida." *Diacritics* 3 (1) (spring): 33–46.

Descartes, René. 1998. *Discourse on Method and Meditations on First Philosophy.* Translated by Donald A. Cress. Indianapolis, IN: Hackett.

Dreyfus, Hubert, and Harrison Hall. 1992. *Heidegger: A Critical Reader.* Oxford: Blackwell.

Dreyfus, Hubert, and Mark Wrathall. 2005. *A Companion to Heidegger.* Oxford: Blackwell.

Foucault, Michel. 1981. "The Order of Discourse." In Young 1981, 48–78.

Friedman, Michael. 2000. *A Parting of the Ways: Carnap, Cassirer, and Heidegger.* Chicago: Open Court.

Gadamer, Hans. 1976. *Hegel's Dialectic: Five Hermeneutical Studies.* Translated by P. Christopher Smith. New Haven, CT: Yale University Press.

Gelvin, Michael. 1979. "Heidegger and Tragedy." In Spanos 1979, 215–230.

———. 1989. *A Commentary on Heidegger's "Being and Time."* DeKalb: Northern Illinois University Press.

Gethman, Karl Friedrich. 1993. "Die Wahrheitsbegriff in den Marburger Vorlesungen" and "Zum Wahrheitsbegriff." In *Dasein: Erkennen und Handeln.* Berlin: De Gruyter.

Golob, Sacha. 2014. *Heidegger on Concepts, Freedom and Normativity.* Cambridge: Cambridge University Press.

Gonzalez, Francisco. 2021. "Heidegger and Gadamer on Hegel's Greek Conception of Being and Time in an Unpublished 1925/26 Seminar." *Archiv für Geschichte der Philosophie,* 1–24.

Gordon, Peter E. 2010. *Continental Divide: Heidegger, Cassirer, Davos.* Cambridge, MA: Harvard University Press.

Graubner, Hans. 1972. *Form und Wesen. Ein Beitrag zur Deutung des Formbegriffs in Kants Kritik der reinen Vernunft.* Bonn: Bouvier.

Guignon, Charles, ed. 1993. *The Cambridge Companion to Heidegger.* Cambridge: Cambridge University Press.

———. 2001. "Being as Appearing: Retrieving the Greek Experience of Phusis." In Polt and Fried 2001, 34–56.

Haar, Michel. 1992. "Attunement and Thinking." In Dreyfus and Hall 1992, 159–172.

Hadjioannou, Christos. 2019. "Heidegger's Critique of Techno-Science as a Critique of Husserl's Reductive Method." In *Heidegger on Technology,* edited by Aaron James Wendland, Christopher Merwin, and Hadjioannou. New York: Routledge.

Halliburton, David. 1981. *Poetic Thinking: An Approach to Heidegger*. Chicago: University of Chicago Press.

Harries, Karsten. 1979. "Language and Silence: Heidegger's Dialogue with Georg Trakl." In Spanos 1979, 155–171.

Haugeland, John. 2013. *Dasein Disclosed*. Edited by J. Rouse. Cambridge, MA: Harvard University Press.

Hegel, Georg. 1956. "Rede zum Antritt des philosophisches Lehramtes an der Universität Berlin." In *Berliner Schriften 1818–1831*, edited by J. Hoffmeister. Hamburg: Felix Meiner.

Henrich, Dieter. 1971. "Anfang und Methode der Logik." In *Hegel im Kontext*, 73–94. Frankfurt: Suhrkamp.

Henrich, Dieter, Walter Schulz, and Karl-Heinz Volkman-Schluk, eds. 1960. *Die Gegenwart der Briechen in der neuren Denken. Festschift für Hans-Georg Gadamer zum 60. Geburtstag*. Tübingen: J. C. Mohr.

Houle, Karen, and Jim Vernon, eds. 2013. *Hegel and Deleuze: Together Again for the First Time*. Evanston, IL: Northwestern University Press.

Hoy, David. 1979. "The Owl and the Poet: Heidegger's Critique of Hegel." In Spanos 1979, 53–70.

Käufer, Stephan. 2011. "Heidegger's Interpretation of Kant." In Dahlstrom 2011, 174–196.

Kiesel, Theodore. 1995. *The Genesis of Heidegger's "Being and Time."* Berkeley: University of California Press.

———. 2002a. *Heidegger's Way of Thought*. Edited by Alfred Denker and Marion Heinz. New York: Continuum.

———. 2002b. "Heidegger (1907–27): The Transformation of the Categorial." In Kiesel 2002a, 84–100.

———. 2002c. "From Intuition to Understanding: On Heidegger's Transformation of Husserl's Phenomenology." In Kiesel 2002a, 174–186.

Kimhi, Irad. 2018. *Thinking and Being*. Cambridge, MA: Harvard University Press.

Kosman, Aryeh. 2013. *The Activity of Being: An Essay on Aristotle's Ontology*. Cambridge, MA: Harvard University Press.

Levinas, Emmanuel. 2003. "A Language Familiar to Us." In *Unforeseen History*, translated by Nidra Poller, 92–95. Urbana-Champaign: University of Illinois Press.

Levy, Heinrich. 1932. "Heideggers Kantinterpretation." *Logos* vol. 21.

Löwith, Karl. 1995. *Martin Heidegger: European Nihilism*. Edited by Richard Wolin. New York: Columbia University Press.

Marcuse, Herbert. 1964. *One-Dimensional Man*. Second edition. Boston: Beacon Press.

McCumber, John. 1999. "Introduction." In Comay and McCumber 1999, 1–25.

McDowell, John. 2009. "Conceptual Capacities in Perception." In *Having the World in View: Essays on Kant, Hegel, and Sellars*, 127–144. Cambridge, MA: Harvard University Press.

McManus, Denis. 2012. *Heidegger and the Measure of Truth*. Oxford: Oxford University Press.

———. 2013. "Heidegger on Skepticism, Truth, and Falsehood." In Wrathall 2013, 239–259.

Moore, A. W. 2012. *The Evolution of Modern Metaphysics: Making Sense of Things*. Cambridge: Cambridge University Press.

Okrent, Mark. 1988. *Heidegger's Pragmatism: Understanding, Being, and the Critique of Metaphysics*. Ithaca, NY: Cornell University Press.

Overgaard, Søren. 2002. "Heidegger's Concept of Truth Revisited." *SATS: The Nordic Journal of Philosophy* 3 (2): 73-90.

Pippin, Robert. 1989. *Hegel's Idealism: The Satisfactions of Self-Consciousness*. Cambridge: Cambridge University Press.

———. 1997. *Idealism as Modernism: Hegelian Variations*. Cambridge: Cambridge University Press.

———. 1999. *Modernism as a Philosophical Problem: On the Dissatisfactions of European High Culture*. Second edition (original 1991). Oxford: Blackwell.

———. 2000. "Fichte's Alleged One-Sided, Subjective, Psychological Idealism." In *The Reception of Kant's Critical Philosophy: Fichte, Schelling, and Hegel*, edited by Sally Sedgwick, 147-70. Cambridge: Cambridge University Press.

———. 2005. "Concept and Intuition: On Distinguishability and Separability." *Hegel-Studien*, Bd. 40.

———. 2007. "Necessary Conditions for the Possibility of What Isn't: Heidegger on Failed Meaning." In *Transcendental Heidegger*, edited by Steven Crowell and Jeff Malpas, 199-214. Stanford, CA: Stanford University Press.

———. 2013. "Heidegger on Nietzsche on Nihilism." In *Political Philosophy Cross-Examined: Perennial Challenges to the Philosophical Life*, 173-188. New York: Palgrave Macmillan.

———. 2013a. "Reason's Form." In *The Impact of Idealism: The Legacy of Post-Kantian German Thought*, vol. 1, edited by N. Boyle, L. Disley, and K. Ameriks, 373-94. Cambridge: Cambridge University Press.

———. 2014. *After the Beautiful: Hegel and the Philosophy of Pictorial Modernism*. Chicago: University of Chicago Press.

———. 2014a. *Hegel on Self-Consciousness: Desire and Death in "The Phenomenology of Spirit."* Princeton, NJ: Princeton University Press.

———. 2015. "Robert Brandom's Hegel." In *Interanimations: Receiving Modern German Philosophy*, 29-62. Chicago: University of Chicago Press.

———. 2016. "Selbstüberwindung, Versöhnung und Modernität bei Nietzsche und Hegel." In Robert Pippin, *Die Aktualität des Deutschen Idealismus*, 383-402. Berlin: Suhrkamp.

———. 2017. *The Philosophical Hitchcock: Vertigo and the Anxieties of Unknowingness*. Chicago: University of Chicago Press.

———. 2019. *Hegel's Realm of Shadows: Logic as Metaphysics in the "Science of Logic."* Chicago: University of Chicago Press.

———. 2020. *Filmed Thought: Cinema as Reflective Form*. Chicago: University of Chicago Press.

———. 2021. *Philosophy by Other Means: The Arts in Philosophy and Philosophy in the Arts*. Chicago: University of Chicago Press.

———. 2022. "The Phenomenology and the Logic of Life: Heidegger and Hegel." In *Nature and Naturalism in Classical German Philosophy*, edited by Luca Corti and Johannes-Georg Schülein. New York: Routledge.

Pöggeler, Otto. 1972. *Philosophie und Politik bei Heidegger*. Munich: Karl Alber.

———. 1987. *Martin Heidegger's Path of Thinking*. Translated by D. Magurshak and S. Barber. Atlantic Highlands, NJ: Humanities Press International.

Polt, Richard. 2005. "Ereignis." In Dreyfus and Wrathall 2005, 375-391.

Polt, Richard, and Gregory Fried. 2001. *A Companion to Heidegger's "Introduction to Metaphysics."* New Haven, CT: Yale University Press.

Precht, Oliver. 2020. *Heidegger: Zur Selbst- und Fremdbestimmung seiner Philosophie.* Hamburg: Felix Meiner.

Raffoul, François. 1998. *Heidegger and the Subject.* Translated by David Pettigrew and Gregory Recco. Atlantic Highlands, NJ: Humanities Press.

Regehly, Thomas. 1991. "Übersicht über die 'Heideggeriana' im Herbert Macuse-Archiv der Stadt- und Universitätsbibliothek in Frankfurt am Main." *Heidegger Studies* 7: 179–209.

Richardson, William J. 2003. *Heidegger: Through Phenomenology to Thought.* New York: Fordham University Press.

Rorty, Richard. 1989. *Contingency, Irony, Solidarity.* Cambridge: Cambridge University Press.

———. 1991. "Heidegger, Contingency, and Pragmatism." In *Essays on Heidegger and Others,* 27–49. Cambridge: Cambridge University Press.

Rouse, Joseph. 1985. "Science and the Theoretical 'Discovery' of the Present-at-Hand." In *Descriptions,* edited by Don Ihde and Hugh J. Silverman. Albany: SUNY Press.

Rosen, Stanley. 1993. *The Question of Being: A Reversal of Heidegger.* New Haven, CT: Yale University Press.

Schalow, Frank, and Alfred Denker. 2010. *Historical Dictionary of Heidegger's Philosophy.* Lanham, MD: Scarecrow.

Schear, Joseph. 2007. "Judgment and Ontology in Heidegger's Phenomenology." *The New Yearbook for Phenomenology and Phenomenological Philosophy* 7: 127–158.

Schmidt, Dennis J. 1988. *The Ubiquity of the Finite: Hegel, Heidegger, and the Entitlements of Philosophy.* Cambridge, MA: MIT Press.

Schürmann, Reiner. 1990. *Heidegger: On Being and Acting: From Principles to Anarchy.* Translated by Christine-Marie Gros and the author. Bloomington: Indiana University Press.

Sellars, W. 1967. "Some Remarks on Kant's Theory of Experience." *Journal of Philosophy* 64 (20): 633–647.

Sheehan, Thomas. 2015. *Making Sense of Heidegger: A Paradigm Shift.* London: Rowman and Littlefield.

Spanos, William V., ed. 1979. *Martin Heidegger and the Question of Literature: Towards a Postmodern Literary Hermeneutics.* Bloomington: Indiana University Press.

Strauss, Leo. 1980. *Persecution and the Art of Writing.* Chicago: University of Chicago Press.

Strawson, P. F. 1982. "Imagination and Perception." In *Kant on Pure Reason,* edited by R. Walker. Oxford: Oxford University Press.

Taminiaux, Jacques. 1991. *Heidegger and the Project of Fundamental Ontology.* Translated and edited by Michael Gendre. Albany: SUNY Press.

Thomas Aquinas. 1968. *On Being and Essence.* Translated by Armand Maurer. Toronto: Pontifical Institute of Medieval Studies.

Thomson, Iain. 2011. *Heidegger, Art, and Postmodernity.* Cambridge: Cambridge University Press.

Truwant, Simon. 2022. *Cassirer and Heidegger in Davos.* Cambridge: Cambridge University Press.

Tugendhat, Ernst. 1970. *Der Wahrheitsbegriff bei Husserl und Heidegger.* Second edition. Berlin: De Gruyter.

Weatherston, Martin. 2002. *Heidegger's Interpretation of Kant: Categories, Imagination and Temporality.* New York: Palgrave Macmillan.

Wellbery, David. 2010. "Stimmung." In *Äesthetische Grundbegriffe,* edited by Karlheinz Barck, Martin Fontius, Dieter Schlenstedt, Burkhart Steinwachs, and Friedrich Wolfzettel, 702–33. Stuttgart: J. B. Metzler.

Wellbery, David. Unpublished. "Notes on the Passage from Rilke's *Aufzeichnungen des Malte Laurids Brigge* (1910). Quoted in Martin Heidegger's 1927 *Grundprobleme der Phänomenologie.*"

White, David. 1978. *Heidegger and the Language of Poetry.* Lincoln: University of Nebraska Press.

Witherspoon, Edward. 2002. "Logic and the Inexpressible in Frege and Heidegger." *Journal of the History of Philosophy* 40 (1): 89–113.

Withy, Katherine. 2022. *Heidegger on Being Self-Concealing.* Oxford: Oxford University Press.

Woessner, Martin. 2011. *Heidegger in America.* Cambridge: Cambridge University Press.

Wrathall, M. 2005. "Unconcealment." In Dreyfus and Wrathall 2005, 337–357.

———. 2011. *Heidegger and Unconcealment: Truth, Language, and History.* Cambridge: Cambridge University Press.

———. 2013. *The Cambridge Companion to Heidegger's "Being and Time."* Cambridge: Cambridge University Press.

Young, Julian. 2001. *Heidegger's Philosophy of Art.* Cambridge: Cambridge University Press.

Young, Robert, ed. 1981. *Untying the Text: A Post-Structuralist Reader.* London: Routledge & Kegan Paul.

Index